THE ULTIMATE GUIDE TO TRACTORS

GULDNER G 30

THE ULTIMATE GUIDE TO TRACTORS

JIM GLASTONBURY

An illustrated encyclopedia with over 600 photographs

LORENZ BOOKS

This edition published in 2010 by Lorenz Books, an imprint of Anness Publishing Ltd, Hermes House, 88–89 Blackfriars Road, London SE1 8HA, UK; tel. 020 7401 2077; fax 020 7633 9499

www.lorenzbooks.com; www.annesspublishing.com

UK agent: The Manning Partnership Ltd; tel. 01225 478444; fax 01225 478440; sales@manning-partnership.co.uk
UK distributor: Book Trade Services; tel. 0116 2759086; fax 0116 2759090; uksales@booktradeservices.com; exportsales@booktradeservices.com
North American agent/distributor: National Book Network; tel. 301 459 3366; fax 301 429 5746; www.nbnbooks.com
Australian agent/distributor: Pan Macmillan Australia; tel. 1300 135 113; fax 1300 135 103; customer.service@macmillan.com.au
New Zealand agent/distributor: David Bateman Ltd; tel. (09) 415 7664; fax (09) 415 8892

For all editorial enquiries, please contact Regency House Publishing at www.regencyhousepublishing.com

ETHICAL TRADING POLICY
Because of Anness Publishing's ongoing ecological investment programme, you, as our customer, can have the pleasure and reassurance of knowing that a tree is being cultivated on your behalf to naturally replace the materials used to make the book you are holding. For further information about this scheme, go to www.annesspublishing.com/trees

PUBLISHER'S NOTE
Although the information in this book is believed to be accurate and true at the time of going to press, neither the authors nor the publisher can accept any legal responsibility or liability for any errors or omissions that may be made.

ACKNOWLEDGEMENTS
The special photography in this book is by Andrew Morland.
Thanks also to the owners and restorers who supplied us with photographs of their tractors. We are also grateful to the following manufacturers for providing photographs of their more recent models: Claas, John Deere, JCB, Massey-Ferguson, McCormick, Renault, and John Nicholls at Valtra/Valmet.

THE NEW
HUBER
MARION
OHIO

RUMELY
OILPULL
TRACTOR
LA PORTE, IND.
GUARANTEED
TO BURN SUCCESSFULLY ALL GRADES OF KERO-SENE UNDER ALL CONDITIONS, AT ALL LOADS UP TO ITS RATED BRAKE HORSE POWER.
ADVANCE-RUMELY THRESHER CO. INC.

CASE INTERNATIONAL
5140

There have been so many amazing discoveries and inventions in the history of mankind that one would be hard put to place them in order of importance. Many have revolutionized the way society works, such as the microchip, which in our own times makes the miracle of today's information superhighway possible. But a modest case could also be made for the humble farm tractor. Without it, modern farms would be unable to produce the vast amounts of food required by an overwhelmingly urban population that, with little thought concerning its origins, takes it for granted that food will appear as if by magic. For this reason alone, the tractor must qualify as a small but essential cog in the vast machine that is the modern world.

However, the tractor did not spring, fully-formed, from nowhere. It evolved. Steam power had been mechanizing farms for 100 years before the first gasoline tractors came along; but steam engines were heavy and expensive, only large farms could afford the expense, and they needed skilled men to operate them. But the four-stroke gasoline engine, invented by Nikolaus August Otto in 1885, was lighter, more compact and affordable than steam, and soon came to be regarded as a promising alternative.

John Charter and John Froelich built pioneer gas tractors in 1889 and 1892 respectively; however, they were large, cumbersome things, designed on the same scale as a steam traction engine. Indeed, early production tractors, such as the Advance-Rumely OilPull, were assumed to be straight replacements for the giants of steam. Meanwhile, as early as 1901 in England, Dan Albone had built a small lightweight gas tractor, even though production was limited and it made little impact.

It was in North America, however, where there were vast acreages of land under the plough, that tractor development was focused for the next 20 years. Moreover, America already had a strong agricultural implements industry, with well-established names like John Deere, Case, Oliver and Allis-Chalmers already much in evidence. With a few exceptions, the major U.S. tractors evolved from these ranks, building on expertise that had already been established.

But it was not until around 1910 that small tractors began to work American fields. They could be more accurately described as motor ploughs, often consisting simply of two wheels and an engine to which existing horse-drawn implements could be attached. Motor ploughs were cheap, but failed to

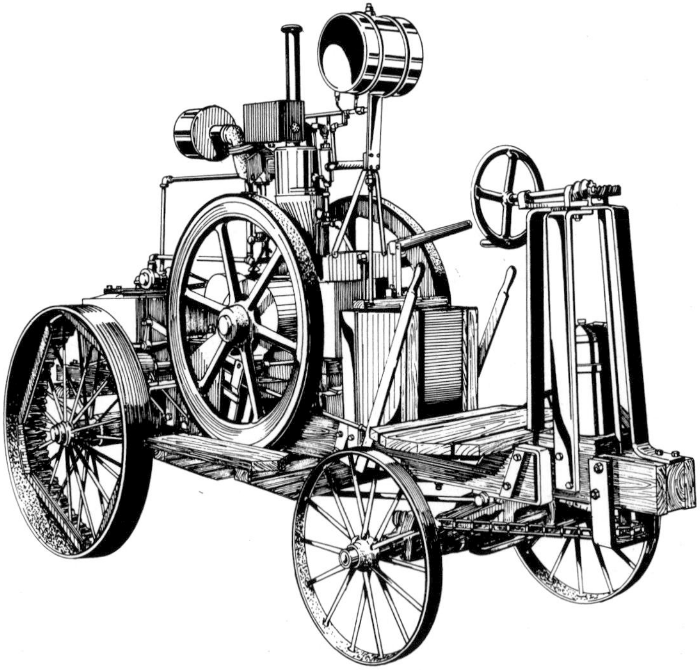

RIGHT
The 16-hp John Froelich gas tractor of 1892.

LEFT
Advance-Rumely OilPull.

BELOW
International Harvester Mogul.

benefit from the extra power of gasoline; this fell to a new breed of lightweight, full-sized four-wheel tractors that began to appear shortly afterwards. For example, there was the Wallis of 1913, which utilized the engine and transmission as stressed members; it needed no separate chassis, thus saving weight and cost. International Harvester recognized the trend and produced its little 8–16-hp Mogul in 1914 and the 10–20-hp Titan the year after. So successful were they that International Harvester dropped its larger tractors to concentrate on the smaller ones. J.I. Case and Allis-Chalmers also entered the fray at around this time.

But the greatest impact did not come from any of these names, well-established in agriculture. Henry Ford had been raised on a farm and knew from personal experience just how back-breaking it was to work the land, even using traditional horsepower. So even before his Model T brought motoring to the masses Henry was dreaming of doing the same for farmers; in other words, he envisaged a simple, cheap tractor that would be within the means of even the smallest farmer.

In 1917, after ten years of experimentation, Ford launched the Fordson Model F, though oddly it was in response to the British Government, which was desperate to increase U.K. food production at home. The F was quite simply the most significant tractor ever made, not only for its technical attributes, though with four cylinders and unit construction it was up to the minute, but also by reason of its price. Here was a full-sized tractor that would sell for less than the price of a motor plough. Henry had used his mass-production know-how to cut costs to the bone: at one point, he managed to slash the price to an incredible $230. As a result, many of the 260 rival manufacturers in competition with Ford simply couldn't compete and gave up.

Some, of course, deserved to go to the wall. The burgeoning American market was attracting any number of tricksters and charlatans, some of whom were tempting gullible investors with tractors that only existed on paper. Even those tractors that did make it to metal often failed to live up to the extravagant claims concerning their performance, which led to the University of Nebraska's famous tractor tests, begun in 1920. As a result, no tractor could be sold in the state without undergoing a set of standard

ABOVE
Ford Model T prototype.

RIGHT
John Deere Waterloo Boy.

OPPOSITE
Fordson N.

tests, which eventually set a national, even international yardstick still of value to tractor buyers today.

Despite the Fordson, stiffer tests, and a slump in tractor sales in the early 1920s, other tractor makers did manage to flourish. Take the John Deere company, for example, which had bought its way into the tractor business in 1918 by absorbing the Waterloo company. The Waterloo Boy tractor may have been outdated, but when John Deere replaced it with the Model D in 1923 it used the same horizontal twin-cylinder engine layout, which was simple and effective and delivered the slow, lugging power than many farmers wanted; it was so successful that John Deere stayed with it for the next 40 years. Moreover, the John Deere 'Johnny Popper' was an integral part of the American landscape until 1960, when the company replaced it overnight with an all-new range of four- and six-cylinder tractors.

The International Harvester Farmall also survived the Fordson era. As its name suggests, it was a tractor that could turn its hand to anything. Until then, tractors could be divided into two types: powerful, lumbering machines for powering threshers and so on, and nimble lightweights for row-crop work. Farmers wanted a tractor that could do both, and this is where the Farmall scored. With over 20hp at the belt, it was powerful enough to drive a thresher, yet its lightness and manoevrability enabled it to work row crops without damaging them. Like John Deere's twin-cylinder Popper, International had discovered a successful formula, compelling every major manufacturer to follow suit.

Cheap and simple, reliable and useful: by 1930 modern tractors were all of these things, but they had one major drawback in common. They ran on bare steel wheels with large spade lugs to pull them through the sticky clay. Even with bands bolted on to cover the lugs (itself a laborious job), they were still restricted to a fast walking pace on the road. Allis-Chalmers made the breakthrough in 1932 by offering rubber pneumatic tyres on a production tractor for the first time. They cost $150 extra, but the benefits were so overwhelming that within a few years most new tractors followed suit, which allowed higher road speeds and made the tractor more comfortable and easier to steer. Moreover, rubber actually proved more efficient than steel in the field, and another element of the modern tractor found its allotted place.

But the best was yet to come. Irishman

Fordson
Fordson

John Deere Overtime N.

Harry Ferguson, like Henry Ford, was a farmer's son, and had a talent for engineering that was close to genius and plenty of business acumen. Also like Henry Ford he knew his own mind and could be difficult to work with; in fact, of the three business agreements he was to make during the course of his career, all ended in acrimony. But along with Ford, Harry Ferguson really can be regarded as a pioneer of the modern tractor.

Ferguson sold Overtime tractors (Waterloo Boy by another name) in Ireland during the First World War, and became interested in the different ways in which implements could be attached. When using a simple tow hitch, a great deal of drag was exerted on the tractor, and if soil conditions were heavy, the tractor would easily become bogged down. This would cause it to stall or, worse still, rear over backwards, which in the days before safety cabs often led to driver fatalities. Moreover, hitching and unhitching implements, even with the latest hydraulic or motorized lifts, was still a time-consuming task.

Harry Ferguson's three-point-hitch solved all this. Its clever geometry transferred the implement's weight to the tractor's rear wheels, thus improving traction. It had draft control, which would automatically lift the implement, reducing drag until the sticky patch had been passed. The geometry also prevented the tractor from rearing up, and fully hydraulic control made hitching up quick, easy and simple. In other words, the Ferguson three-point-hitch was the single, most significant advance in tractor technology, bar none.

Ferguson even designed a tractor to go with his hitch, but his agreement with David Brown of England to build the machine did not come to fruition. Harry decided to cross the Atlantic to demonstrate his system to Henry Ford, who was so impressed he agreed then and there to build a new tractor to suit. The Ford 9N of 1939 repeated the success of the original Fordson F in that it was small and lightweight, but with the added advantage of the Ferguson hitch it was able to do the work of a far larger machine. The 9N was a huge success, but sadly the Ford/Ferguson agreement came to grief and ended in a multi-million-dollar law suit.

The Second World War called a halt to further tractor development, though there had been some advances in the late 1930s. The

Oliver 70, for example, used a relatively small six-cylinder engine where most rivals had two or four cylinders. With a high compression and using high-octane gasoline, it was impressively smooth and powerful for its size. Minneapolis-Moline's UDLX Comfortractor was less successful, but was nevertheless a pointer to the future, with its all-steel integral cab, well-equipped with heater, radio and glazed windows. Minneapolis-Moline was also the first manufacturer to add a high ratio to the transmission, which in the Comfortractor's case meant 40mph (64km/h) on the road.

During the first few years of peacetime following 1945, tractor manufacturers across the world simply concentrated on keeping up with demand. In England, the Morris car company entered the tractor business, exporting its Nuffield Universal in large numbers. In France, Germany, Italy, Hungary and Spain, single-cylinder semi-diesel tractors were the favoured format, and the trend continued into the late 1950s. Germany had been the diesel pioneer before the Second World War, but only now did America – the land of cheap gasoline, after all – start to catch up. John Deere unveiled its Model R in 1949, a dieselized version of the classic John Deere twin-cylinder engine, but larger at 416 cubic inches (6.8 litres) and producing 51 horsepower at the PTO (Power Take-Off). It

nor does the farmer...
"LIVE BY BREAD ALONE"
The OLIVER Corporation 400 West Madison Street, Chicago 6, Ill.
OLIVER
"FINEST IN FARM MACHINERY"

also set a new fuel economy record at Nebraska, and probably did more than any other machine to introduce American farmers to the advantages of diesel power; 20,000 were sold in three years. Gradually, the other American manufacturers introduced their own diesels, though gasoline (and later, LPG or liquified petroleum gas) was to remain an option right through to the early 1970s.

In fact, the 1950s was a decade of great technological advance. It seemed as though, after five years of war and another five trying to keep pace with demand, manufacturers were now able to spread their wings. The Allis-Chalmers WD45 of 1953 positively bristled with innovation. Power Shift was a means of adjusting the rear-wheel tread using engine power; two-clutch Power Control provided continuous power take-off, so that

LEFT
Advertisement for the Oliver Row Crop.

BELOW LEFT
Racing Allis-Chalmers Model Us.

RIGHT
Allis-Chalmers WD45.

BELOW RIGHT
Caterpillar Magazine.

the PTO would not stop when one declutched; there were live hydraulics, too, automatic draft control, and a new six-cylinder diesel engine.

The next giant step was in transmissions. Until then, tractors had used simple single-range gearboxes with three, four or perhaps five speeds. Not only did these have a limited number of ratios, but changing down in the field meant stopping the tractor and restarting it, the last thing one needed on sticky soil with a heavy plough in tow. International Harvester's Torque Amplifier provided the breakthrough, adding a two-speed epicyclic gearbox to the main one. This effectively doubled the ratios available (to ten in the case of the Farmall MTA); better still, it could be

shifted on the move. Other manufacturers soon rushed to copy International, and Allis-Chalmers's Power Director and Minneapolis-Moline's Ampli-Torc were different versions of the same thing. Case added a torque converter to produce the Case-O-Matic.

Meanwhile, power had been gradually increasing: 40hp had been the high horsepower class before the Second World War, but was now nothing special. The 1960s saw the tractor power race really take off, with Allis-Chalmers in danger of getting left behind until it produced the world's first production turbo-diesel tractor; the D19 of 1961 produced 25 per cent more power than the standard engine, offering gasoline power with diesel economy.

But the power race was so frenetic that within a few years the D19 had been eclipsed by a whole swathe of 100-hp machines, such as Allis-Chalmers's own D21, which relied on cubic inches rather than a turbocharger to produce its 103hp; it also needed a new set of implements to cope, including a seven-bottom plough. Not to be outdone, Case upsized its diesel engine to 451ci (7.4 litres) to produce its own 100-hp tractor, while International turbocharged its 361-ci (5.9-litre) engine for the powerful 1206.

However, increased power presented its own problems, chiefly that of transferring all that torque though just two wheels. The answer was four-wheel-drive, and though it was another ten years before this entered the mainstream, many specialist manufacturers began to fill the gap. The Steiger brothers, for example, farmers from Minnesota, built their own super-tractor, with four-wheel-drive, articulated steering, and a big diesel engine. It worked so well that neighbours were soon asking for replicas, and a new type of tractor was born. Steiger, along with Versatile, Big Bud, Wagner and others, specialized in giant tractors that catered to the vast expanses of wheat belt of the Midwest. Power outputs of 300hp or more and all-up weights of over 15 tons put them into a different league from conventional machines, with the result that super-tractors are an important part of the market to this day, particularly in North America.

Of course, all these advances had occurred with scant regard to the driver. By and large, tractor drivers were still exposed to

ABOVE
Case Comfort King.

LEFT
Versatile 875.

ABOVE
Caterpillar Challenger.

OPPOSITE
Massey-Ferguson 4365.

the elements, scorched in summer and frozen in winter, with controls that were often heavy and awkward to operate. Truck and bus drivers had far better working environments, but it wasn't until the early 1970s that serious attention was paid to tractor driver comfort and safety, and in this area John Deere took the lead. It had been building ROPS (roll-over safety system) into its tractors since 1966, but in 1972 unveiled the Sound Gard cab. This set a new standard in cab design, making them quieter with excellent visibility and even providing the option of a radio/cassette. Case had offered the rubber-mounted Comfort King cab from 1965, but this was something entirely new. Eventually, International and Allis-Chalmers came up with their own quiet, air-conditioned cabs.

Transmission design continued to advance in the 1970s, mainly through the number of ratios available. Ten-speed transmissions (a five-speed gearbox plus two ranges) become 12, then 16. Manufacturers added a third range, then a fourth, to further multiply the ratios, with Allis-Chalmers offering 20 speeds in its new 7000-series tractors of 1973.

Full powershifting (that is, the ability to shift on the move between all ratios) had yet to arrive, neither had the sophistication of electronic control, but in the meantime tractor transmissions were more adaptable than ever before. Shuttle changes, to allow quick transition between forward and reverse, were another boon for yard tractors, while an interesting spin-off was the hydrostatic transmission offered by International on a whole range of machines through the 1970s. Instead of a conventional gearbox, this provided pure hydraulic drive, giving an infinite variation of speed within a fixed range, which was useful for some jobs but less efficient than gear drives.

Meanwhile, intercoolers further boosted diesel power and four-wheel-drive entered the mainstream, available as an option on many small and mid-range tractors as well as the larger ones. The major manufacturers also began to offer bigger super-tractors to compete with those of Steiger and Versatile. John Deere's 50-series range was typical, with the same four-wheel-drive and articulated steering as the established giants; a 300-hp V8 8850 topped the range. Even the Case Magnum, ostensibly a mid-range tractor, offered over 200hp in the late 1980s. Another answer to the traction problem for high horsepower tractors was the Caterpillar Challenger, a crawler whose reinforced rubber tracks gave relatively high road speeds with crawler traction in the field. Announced in 1986, it was a giant leap forward in crawler technology, and brought Caterpillar back into the farm tractor market. Case-International Harvester went a step further in the late

4365
MASSEY FERGUSON

FAR RIGHT
John Deere 344H.

BELOW
Renault Ares 600-series.

1990s, replacing the four wheels of its 9350 super-tractor with four rubber tracks to produce the Quadtrac.

But as the 1980s gave way to the '90s, it was clear that sheer brute power was no longer necessary. The trend was away from a simple power race to one that sought to make the best use of the power available to increase efficiency in an increasingly competitive world.

The science of electronics made this possible, from its first tentative applications to top-of-the-range tractors in the 1980s to today, when all but the smallest and cheapest models make some use of the microchip. The applications are legion: a modern diesel engine's electronic 'brain' allows precise control of injection timing, to the benefit of power, torque and emissions. Electronic transmission control gives push-button operation as well as allowing the transmission to select the correct ratio itself, and even block an incorrect selection by the driver to prevent damage. The ultimate 'thinking' transmission is the fully automatic, in which the electronics make virtually all of the decisions. This is the age of information, and their most important function is to inform the driver of a huge range of variables. Systems like Datatronic from Massey-Ferguson keep an electronic eye on fuel consumption, wheel-slip, acreage worked – the list is endless. This can also be linked into control systems for engine, transmission and hydraulics to produce a tractor that virtually thinks for itself. One thing, however, is crystal clear. In the 21st century, scarce resources and concern for the environment make tractor design a more challenging task than it ever was before.

John Deere 5510.

RIGHT and OPPOSITE
The OilPull was the classic Advance-Rumely tractor, its smokestack topping the oil-cooled radiator. It continued well into the 1920s in various model forms.

ADVANCE-RUMELY

Like so many American tractor manufacturers, Advance-Rumely's roots lay in the 19th-century agricultural machinery industry. Unlike some, however, it failed to make the important leap from early heavyweight traction engines to modern, light tractors, and as a result it perished.

Dr. Edward Rumely's grandfather had set up the business in 1853, producing a variety of threshers, steam engines, and a dozen other machines over the years. Edward himself decided to build an internal combustion-engined tractor, one that would replace the great steam traction engines that had become an established part of big farms for decades.

The massive OilPull was launched in 1910 and bore more of a resemblance to a steam traction engine than any gasoline tractor. With 25hp at the drawbar, 45 at the belt, it was a powerful machine for its day, and weighed in at an elephantine 25,000lb (11340kg).

From the start, the OilPull was designed to run on kerosene, a cheaper, heavier and less refined fuel than gasoline. The problem with kerosene, however, was that it burned at higher temperatures, and in a narrower range, than gas. Rumely's answer was to equip his massive new OilPull tractor with oil cooling via a huge cooling tower between the front wheels, which would allow high cylinder temperatures without boiling away. Neither would it freeze in cold weather or allow the engine to rust from the inside. Kerosene was also prone to pre-ignition, so a Secor-Higgins carburettor atomized water along with the fuel to control any such tendency.

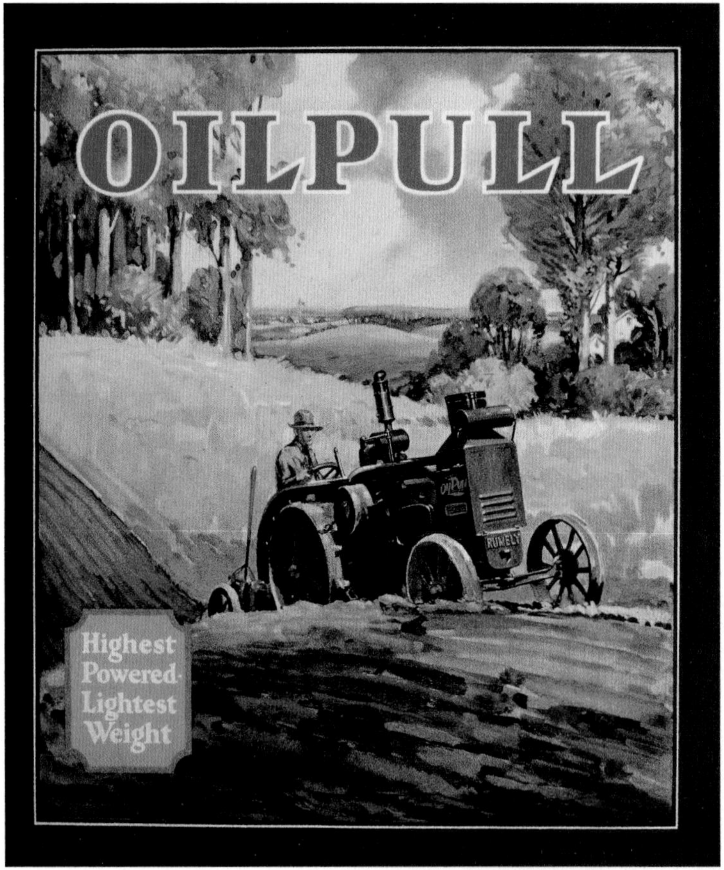

It wasn't exactly a nimble machine, but the OilPull proved to be quite a success. A little large for field work, unless the fields were on a similar scale, it soon proved a hit with the threshermen. The big 1884-ci (30-litre) twin-cylinder motor would gently chuff away all day long, giving out plenty of smooth, reliable, low-revving power. To prove

RUMELY
OILPULL
TRACTOR
GUARANTEED
WATER
IMPORTANT

The DoAll was Advance-Rumely's bid for the small tractor market, in production for three years.

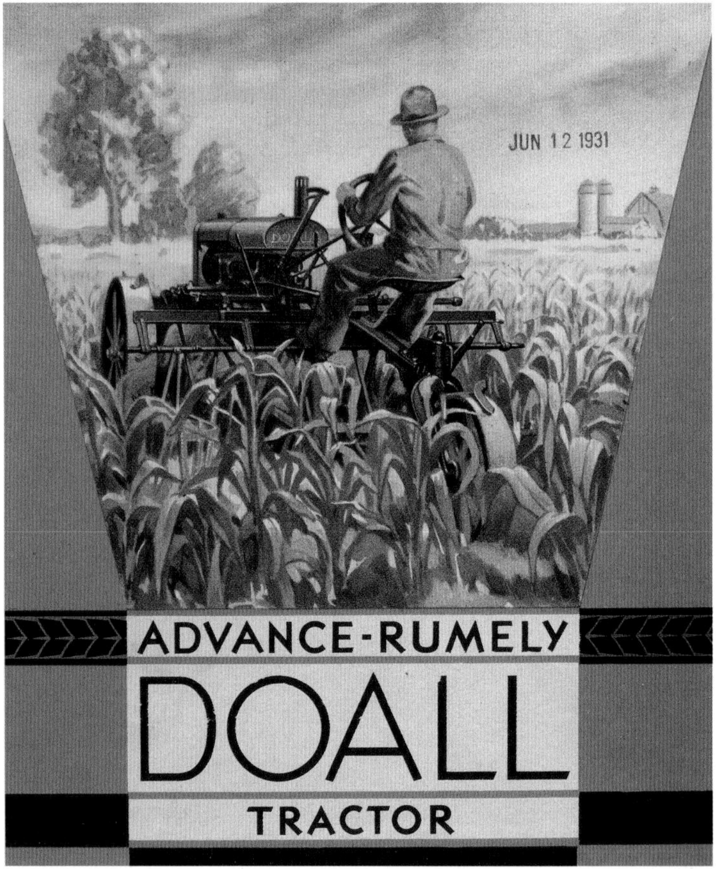

a point, Advance-Rumely hitched three of the big Model Es to a specially-made 50-bottom plough. Together, they could plough up an acre in four and a half minutes, and were able to cover 2,000 acres (800 hectares) in six days.

In fact, the OilPulls were in a class of their own, and continued long after other monster tractors had fallen by the wayside. A whole range was produced, including the relatively small 12/20 Model K. But it is the big ones, especially the biggest Model E, produced from 1910 to 1923, for which the Rumely OilPulls are remembered. Rated as a 30/60, the E actually produced 50hp at the drawbar, 75 at the belt! All the OilPulls were updated in 1924, with a lighter pressed-steel chassis, higher engine speeds, and a three-speed transmission.

By the late 1920s, however, it was obvious that the faithful OilPulls were out of tune with the times. The market now lay in smaller, lighter tractors, powered by conventional gasoline or kerosene engines. So Rumely bought up the Toro tractor and produced it as the DoAll, building just over 3,000 between 1928 and 1931. It was a neat little 20-hp machine, powered by a four-cylinder Waukesha engine; however, it was not a success and final stocks were sold off to dealers at little more than half the original list price.

Advance-Rumely's final attempt to produce a conventional tractor (and as it turned out, its final attempt at anything) was the 6A. It couldn't have been more different from the OilPulls, and used a modern Waukesha 504-ci (8-litre) six-cylinder engine to give 43hp at the PTO. It even had a six-speed transmission, unheard of at a time when most rivals had a mere three speeds. But despite this up-to-the-minute specification, the 6A's sales failed to live up to its promise. The last straw for Advance-Rumely was when it lost money on export sales to Russia, which was ironic, as some of the first OilPulls had been exported to Canada and South America, bringing in good business for the company. It was swallowed up by Allis-Chalmers in June 1931, which promptly ceased production of the DoAll, 6A and OilPulls and another famous name was no more.

AGCO

A dozen years ago, no one had even heard of AGCO, but within a few years of its set-up as a management buyout with no manufacturing capacity, it was claiming to be the largest tractor manufacturer in the United States. Now it is probably the biggest in the world. How did this happen, and how did such a success story emerge from the desperate slump in tractor sales of the 1980s?

The story begins in 1985 when Deutz of Germany acquired Allis-Chalmers. It closed

The AGCO 6690. Many early AGCOs were painted Allis-Chalmers orange, reflecting the company's roots.

880
ALLIS

down the Allis tractor factory and began to export its own machines to the States, badged Deutz-Allis. The intention was to start building tractors in America again, but in 1988 Deutz abandoned the idea, instead of which White was contracted from 1989 to build for them, using Deutz air-cooled diesel engines. This lasted only a year before the U.S. management of Deutz-Allis bought out the American end of the company and AGCO (Allis-Gleaner Co.) was formed.

At first, AGCO continued the arrangement with White, selling Deutz-engined tractors with U.S. chassis, but now badged AGCO-Allis and painted Allis orange instead of Deutz green. It also imported mid-sized and utility tractors from Deutz itself. So far, this was nothing very dramatic, but from 1991 AGCO began to expand by acquisition, building itself up into the giant it is today. First it bought the Hesston hay-maker business from FIAT, and the same year purchased the White tractor line; this was significant, as it gave AGCO its first tractor-making facility.

Nothing was bought in 1992, but a range of 15 tractors, 12 painted orange and badged AGCO-Allis was unveiled, the others painted silver and sold under the White name. The 15 were built for AGCO by SLH of Italy, the company that produced SAME, Lamborghini and Hurlimann tractors. This gave AGCO a complete, ready-made range which kicked off with the 4650 and 4660 utility tractors, powered by SAME air-cooled three-cylinder engines of 40-PTO-hp and 52-PTO-hp respectively. The mid-range 6670 and 6680 (63/72-PTO-hp) were similar, but with a 12-

OPPOSITE
The AGCO 8630 was built for AGCO by SLH (SAME/Lamborghini/Hurlimann) of Italy, the top of a new range.

LEFT
AGCO-Allis 2WD 5670.
As well as the more powerful four-wheel-drive tractors, AGCO-Allis offered the two-wheel-drive 4600 and 5600.

BELOW LEFT
In 1994, the AGCO-Allis 9435 and 9455 included ESC, electronic systems control and monitoring.

980
9650

OPPOSITE
The AGCO-Allis 9650: these biggest tractors still used air-cooled Deutz diesels, though they were phased out in favour of Cummins and Detroit diesels by 1996.

LEFT
An AGCOStar four-wheel-drive articulated.

RIGHT
AGCO-Allis 9650.

OPPOSITE
AGCO-Allis 8630.

speed transmission and cab. A bigger 7600-series ranged from the 89-hp 7600 to the 128-hp 7650, all with a 24-speed transmission. Finally, the 8600 offered no more power but had front-wheel-assist and optional 36-speed driveline.

The higher-powered 9600-series appeared in 1993, replacing the White-built 9100. Still using Deutz air-cooled engines, these ranged from a 9630 (133-PTO-hp) to the 9690 (584-ci/9.6-litre, turbo-intercooled engine, 191-PTO-hp). And AGCO had been out shopping again: this time it came home with White-New Idea (the implement section of White) and the North American arm of Massey-Ferguson. The following year, the rest of Massey-Ferguson followed, and in 1995 AGCO bought McConnell, makers of large four-wheel-drive tractors based on an old Massey-Ferguson design. McConnell production was moved to an AGCO factory and the tractors were renamed the AGCOStar range.

Meanwhile, the Deutz air-cooled diesels were gradually being phased out as the company bought in Detroit Diesel 40-series engines to power its top-end tractors. These ranged from the 9635 (135-PTO-hp) to the 195-hp 9695. By 1996, the Deutz diesels were gone, and the Deutz-Allis legacy was at an end. By the late 1990s, AGCO had

AGCO ALLIS
8630

AGCO-Allis 9690.

manufacturing plants in Britain and France as well as America. The smaller tractors – both Massey-Ferguson and AGCO-Allises up to 145hp – were built in the MF factories in Beauvais, France, and Coventry, England. The same went for the mid-range Whites, while the big machines were American-made, with row-crop machines up to 225hp wearing both AGCO-Allis and White badges.

It was not unusual to take advantage of economies of scale by having different factories specialize in what they did best and sell the results all over the world under a variety of well-known names and colour schemes. White's various parent companies had tried this in the past and failed. Now AGCO was making a success of it. This was underlined in 1999 when the latest update of the 9600-series, the 9755 appeared. It was part of a new four-tractor range, offering 160–225hp. Most telling was that all of them used AGCO-Allis' own 1300-series turbo-diesel engines. The company now had the resources to build its own power units, leaving behind the days when it had been necessary to buy in other manufacturers' engines, and even complete tractors.

In 2003, AGCO is able to claim that it sells tractors in 140 countries under 18 different brand names. These include the high-tech Fendt of Germany, which came under the AGCO wing in February 2000. A complete range of tractors range from a 24-hp compact to the 225-hp AGCO-Allises and Whites, not to mention, for the first time, a range of machines wearing the AGCO badge on its own. Some of these rebadged tractors are almost identical, but as a marketing ploy it works well. The Fendt Vario, meanwhile, offers fully automatic transmission in three tractor ranges, the 400, 700 and 900, while old implement and combine names such as Hesston, Gleaner and New Idea still feature. There is even a new marque, the Challenger. These are standard AGCO/Allis/White tractors (call them what you will) in

Caterpillar yellow, and constitute a full range of tracked and wheeled machines, balers and combines, all sold through Caterpillar dealers. AGCO seems unstoppable.

Unfortunately, the company is not totally immune to the vagaries of economics. At the start of the new century, two U.S. plants were shut down, and in the summer of 2002 it was announced that the Massey-Ferguson plant in Coventry, one of the largest tractor factories in Europe, would close within a year.

AGCO-Allis 9815.

The big Allis-Chalmers A replaced the long-running E, but when it appeared in the early 1930s, heavy tractors like this were already looking outmoded.

ALLIS-CHALMERS

Allis-Chalmers, although by the 1970s one of the top ten tractor manufacturers in the United States, wasn't always as powerful. It had never posed a challenge to John Deere or Fordson for market leadership, and until the 1930s was a very minor player indeed. But good, solid engineering, and a few well-timed technological milestones, contrived to secure it a place among the big boys.

Unlike all its major rivals, Allis-Chalmers did not emerge from an agricultural background: it once made industrial machinery, and only made the transition to farm tractors in 1913 when the market was evidently expanding and potentially lucrative. In fact, despite being best known for tractors, Allis-Chalmers became a large conglomerate, which made everything from air compressors to X-ray machines.

Its origins lay in the early 1860s, when

Edward P. Allis, an entrepreneurial New Yorker with a nose for a good deal, bought the defunct Reliance Works at Milwaukee. Although valued at $6,000, Reliance collapsed in the wake of the 1857 financial panic and, canny as always, Allis was able to buy the company for a reported $22.72!

The company thrived under Allis's sheer drive and determination, continuing its existing business of making sawmills, flour-milling equipment and castings. Within a few years it had outgrown its original site and moved into a new factory with its own foundry. This was the West Allis works, where tractors would be made right up to 1985. In 1869 Allis bought out his biggest rival, the Bay State Iron Manufacturing Co., and apart from near bankruptcy in 1876, the Allis company continued to thrive and expand, diversifying into steam engines and pumps. By the turn of the century, it was America's

The D15 was a powered-up version of the 1957 three-plough D14. It was Allis-Chalmers's mid-range tractor, sandwiched between the D12 and D17.

RIGHT
Allis-Chalmers made crawlers too, after buying Monarch in 1928. The Model K, shown here, came with petrol or oil engines.

OPPOSITE
The rear-engined Allis-Chalmers G was aimed at small farmers and market gardeners.

largest manufacturer of steam engines.

Edward Allis died in 1889 but the company survived, thanks largely to the leadership of Edwin Reynolds, a steam expert who had joined the company in 1877. In 1900, Reynolds had a chance meeting with William J. Chalmers of the Fraser & Chalmers company which built mining machinery and stamp mills. This led to a merger, which was good news for Chalmers, then in financial trouble. In 1901, the new Allis-Chalmers company was launched, an industrial giant which soon diversified into steam turbines and electrical generating equipment.

But behind the scenes, everything was beginning to go downhill. The U.S. economy was in trouble and while Allis-Chalmers may have been a giant, it was an unwieldy one, with factories scattered across the country. By 1912 it was close to bankruptcy and two receivers were called in to reorganize the company. One of these was General Otto Falk, who was to be president of the newly incorporated Allis-Chalmers Manufacturing

ALLIS-CHALM

The Allis-Chalmers RC was a combination of a WC chassis and a Model B power unit. It was short-lived.

Co. for nearly 20 years. General Falk (the military rank came from his time in the Wisconsin National Guard) proved to be the company's saviour, providing focused leadership and a determination to secure new markets, one of which was in tractors.

Falk owned a working farm in Waukesha, and he could see that the new market in gasoline- or kerosene-powered tractors was set to expand. These held the promise of lighter, cheaper and more compact machines when compared with the large steam traction engines then being built. The potential market for such machines was vast, as even then America was an overwhelmingly agricultural nation. Henry Ford's Fordson tractor had yet to appear, but he had already demonstrated the practicality of cheap gasoline transport with the Model T automobile. Surely all Allis-Chalmers had to do was design a tractor, make it, and wait for farmers to beat a path to its door.

Except that this didn't quite happen as planned. In those early days, no one knew

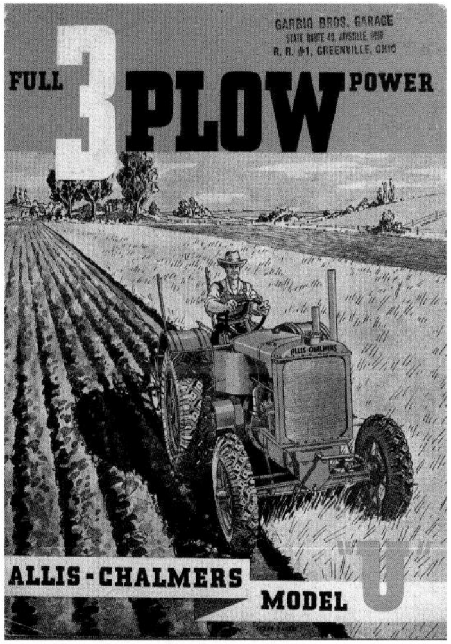

LEFT
Allis-Chalmers wasn't backward at promoting the benefits of its three-plough Model U.

what form the definitive tractor should take, a fact reflected in the early Allis-Chalmers experiments. Falk's first course was to buy in the Swiss-designed Monoculture rotary tiller, paying $10,000 for the right to make it. This was a three-wheeled device weighing 4,500lb (2041kg) and powered by a 30-hp engine, but only a few were sold before Allis-Chalmers abandoned the idea.

It next tried a huge half-track, a cross between a tractor and a truck that could allegedly haul 30 tons as well as cross rough terrain. But it was too cumbersome to be of much practical use.

It wasn't quite third time lucky, but Allis-Chalmers' next attempt was far more successful than the first two. The Model 10-18 was a simple three-wheeled tractor powered by a 303-ci (5-litre) twin-cylinder engine. It went into production in November 1914, and though not a great success was at least closer to what had been envisaged.

The 10-18 evidently pointed Allis-Chalmers in the right direction, for its next tractor, the little 6-12, was more conventional. It was a motor plough, with its four-cylinder engine mounted directly over the two front wheels to maximize traction. Motor ploughs were designed to hitch up to existing horse-drawn ploughs or binders, and as such were a cheaper alternative than conventional tractors, apart from the all-conquering Fordson, of course. The 6-12 cost $850 when launched in 1918, actually more than a brand new Fordson F, which was a 'proper' four-wheel tractor. Over eight years, however, less than 2,000 6-12s were built.

What Allis-Chalmers needed was a full-sized tractor, and this finally arrived with the 15-30, launched the same year as the 6-12 when the company's new tractor division was also set up. With the 15-30, Allis-Chalmers plunged straight into the mainstream of tractor design. The 15-30 had four wheels and a 461-ci (7.5-litre) four-cylinder motor built by Allis-Chalmers itself (the company had been building gas engines for over a decade by this time). Compared to a Fordson, the 15-30 was a heavyweight at 6,000lb (2722kg), and this was reflected in the price of over $2,000. The company claimed that seven years' work and $3 million had gone into the 15-30's development, adding that the vibration was 'no more noticeable than in the finest motor car or truck'.

More to the point for most farmers was the fact that the new Allis-Chalmers tractor had all the power it claimed, and more; early tests revealed that it gave 18hp at the drawbar rather than the claimed 15. One of the first Nebraska tractor tests produced just over 20hp at the drawbar, and 33 at the belt! At a time when many new tractors failed to live up to their extravagant claims, here appeared to be an honest one.

But the 18-30, as it was swiftly renamed, was still too heavy and expensive to take Allis-Chalmers into the big time. In part response to the Fordson, lighter mid-range tractors were selling well, and Allis-Chalmers came up with the 12-20, powered by a smaller 281-ci (4.6-litre) Midwest engine. Like its big brother, the 12-20 turned out to have an over-modest power rating, and it was soon renamed the 15-25. However, it never sold particularly well. Meanwhile, the 18-30 became the 20-35, due to a higher rated speed. Both Allis-Chalmers tractors were solid, well-engineered and too expensive. Neither was a big seller.

After over ten years of endeavour, it looked as though Otto Falk's tractor experiment had failed. Even the head of the tractor divison, George Gardner, recommended that his department be closed down altogether.

Falk would have none of it. He accepted Gardner's resignation and promoted his deputy, Harry Merritt, to the top job, a man destined to became a key figure in Allis-Chalmers tractor history. An energetic manager, he immediately initiated a ruthless cost-cutting exercise on the big 20-35; that same year the price was cut from over $2,000 to $1,885. The year after (1927) it was

ALLIS-CHALMERS

down again to $1,495, and another $200 was slashed the year after that. By 1934, a brand new 20-35 cost $970, less than half its original price! Sales rocketed, and over 19,000 Model Es (as the 20-35 became) were sold over 20 years. Otto Falk's faith in Harry Merritt and the Allis-Chalmers tractor had been vindicated.

But the Model E was a heavy four-plough tractor and the larger sales came from smaller two- and three-plough machines. Allis-Chalmers saw its chance when Henry Ford announced that he was pulling out of U.S. tractor production and a group of Fordson dealers banded together to form the United Tractor and Equipment Distributor's Association. They asked Allis-Chalmers to design a suitable three-plough tractor for them to sell, and it responded with the Model U. Sold both as a United and as the Allis-Chalmers Model U from 1929, the new tractor was up to the minute and much lighter than the Model E. But its real advance came in 1932 when Allis-Chalmers fitted rubber pneumatic tyres.

These were a milestone in tractor technology; first and foremost, they allowed much higher road-hauling speeds, with up to 15mph (24km/h) on the U's high-ratio fourth gear. Pneumatic tyres also made life far more comfortable for the driver and they were much more efficient in the field as well. Allis-Chalmers promoted the U's high-speed capabilities by fitting some demonstration tractors with ultra-high gear ratios, hiring well-known racing drivers and staging tractor races at county fairs. One even set a new tractor speed record of 67.877mph (109.2km/h) on the Utah Salt Flats. Once farmers were convinced that pneumatic tyres really were worth the extra $150 asked by Allis, they bought them. Within a few years, nearly every new tractor on the U.S. market was thus equipped.

Allis-Chalmers bought the Advance-Rumely concern in 1931, which filled in some large gaps in its dealer network. The Model U had raised the company's profile and given it a headstart on bigger rivals, so now the time was right to launch a mass-selling two-plough tractor, the WC. It certainly sold well: from 3,000 in 1934, sales more than tripled the year after, then rose to 18,000, then 29,000. The lightweight WC, which tipped the scales at less than 3,200lb (1452kg), cost only $625 on steel wheels: no wonder it went on selling well until 1948.

It was joined in the 1930s by two new machines that pointed the way tractor design was going at the time. The big Model A was an updated Model E, intended to power threshers via its big four-cylinder engine. But it was already outmoded, thanks to the first powered combine harvesters then being sold. More in tune with the market was the little Model B of 1937. This ultra-lightweight 14-hp machine cost a mere $495 brand new. Just like the Fordson of 20 years earlier, it made an affordable tractor available to thousands of small farmers. With its narrow-waisted, rounded styling by industrial designer Brooks Stevens, the B looked thoroughly modern into the bargain. The buying public agreed, and 11,000 were sold in its first year. A more powerful Model C version soon followed, 84,000 of which were built in a ten-year production run. There was no doubt about it: Allis-Chalmers had finally arrived.

During the Second World War, the company was busy, not only with defence contracts, but also with experimentation into new drive arrangements, a crawler personnel carrier, even fuel cells. In the late 1940s, the years of research and development were to bear fruit in a string of innovations. The WD tractor of 1948 replaced the successful WC, which, although superficially similar, boasted three new features: a second clutch allowed a live PTO and hydraulics; Traction Booster made use of a Ferguson principle; and power-adjust wheels used engine power to adjust the rear tread, making a laborious task simplicity itself.

At the other end of the scale, the little Model G was announced the same year. This was a new type of tractor, a tiny rear-engined device powered by a small 10-hp Continental motor, its light weight and excellent visibility making it a favourite with horticulturalists: over 30,000 were built over seven years. In essence, the G was the spiritual successor to the 6-12 motor plough.

Meanwhile, the C tractor was updated as the CA, with all the WD's advanced features; the WD itself received a 25 per cent power boost in 1953, with Allis-Chalmers's first diesel engine following the year after. According to Allis, these transformed the WD from a two- to a four-plough machine. The WD45 also had a Snap Coupler, which allowed in-seat hitching, making life very much easier for the driver.

It may have had plenty of advanced features, but the WD was still an update on

OPPOSITE
A milestone: even though pneumatic rubber tyres on the Allis-Chalmers Model U were expensive, they brought huge benefits.

BELOW RIGHT
The Allis-Chalmers WD represented a big leap forward, with live PTO and hydraulics, Traction Booster and power-adjust wheels.

OPPOSITE
The Allis-Chalmers One-Ninety.

the pre-war WC. Meanwhile, there had been a void at the bottom of the range since the demise of the little Model B and rear-engined G. Allis rectified this by renewing its entire range over two years. The new D-series kicked off with dual replacements for the WD in 1957: the three-plough D14 and four/five-plough D17. As well as brand new or substantially reworked engines, they shared a new feature called Power Director. This was Allis-Chalmers' take on the new move towards multi-speed transmissions, allowing on-the-go shifting. In this case, a second clutch ran at 70 per cent of engine speed, due to two reduction gears; it allowed on-the-move changes between these two ratios, and eight forward speeds in all. Roll-Shift was another new idea, doing for the front wheels what power adjustment had done for the rear. Finally, the D14 and D17 adopted the Ferguson three-point-hitch, which by now had become the industry standard. Without it, it was practically impossible to sell to the farmer with a barnful of implements only compatible with the Ferguson system.

The D14/17 were soon joined by the smaller D10 and D12, which were single-plough and two-plough respectively, with different tread widths but otherwise identical. Both used a 139-ci (2.3-litre) version of the D14's new gasoline engine, and although they were neat little tractors that could be had with all the advanced features of their big brothers, neither sold particularly well. Perhaps of more significance historically was the fuel-cell D12. Allis-Chalmers was mindful of its wartime fuel-cell research, and in 1959 unveiled a D12 powered by 1,008 fuel cells supplying a 15Kw electric motor. Although quiet and pollution-free, however, the fuel-cell D12 also weighed 75 per cent more than the standard tractor, but with much less power; this meant yet another return to the drawing board.

In fact, the search for more power, rather than radical forms of fuel, was to dominate the next ten years, and Allis-Chalmers was in imminent danger of falling behind. Its most powerful tractor in 1960 was the 46-hp D17, which no longer sufficed. A plan was hatched to boost it to a 60-hp D18 for 1961, but it was soon realized that this too was insufficient as John Deere and Ford, to name but two, were about to launch far more powerful machines.

So at the eleventh hour, D18 became D19 with a 71-hp gasoline engine or (and this was an important point) a turbocharged diesel. The Allis D19 was the world's first turbo-diesel farm tractor, so although its outputs of 62hp

ONE-NINETY
ALLIS-CHALMERS
LANDHANDLER

The Allis-Chalmers 6080 was FIAT-powered, as were all the 6000 tractors.

at the drawbar and 67hp at the PTO failed to set any new records, it made a huge impact. The turbocharger boosted the power of the existing 262-ci (4.3-litre) six-cylinder diesel by 25 per cent and made Allis-Chalmers the stuff of history books. Moreover, it appeared to be getting the hang of the horsepower race. Only two years after D19, it announced its first 100-hp machine, the D21. Instead of a turbo, this relied on sheer cubic inches, with a new 426-ci (7-litre) direct-injection diesel built by Allis-Chalmers itself. The D21 itself was turbocharged in 1965 to produce a 127-hp tractor.

As the 1960s progressed, the D-series was gradually replaced by the modern-looking 100-series, with its squared-off styling pioneered by the D21. The bigger ones were powered by a new family of engines – diesel, gasoline and LPG – with a new non-turbo One-Ninety replacing the D19. Inevitably, it was found wanting in the power department, so Allis-Chalmers turbocharged it. As the 93-hp One-Ninety XT it became the hot-rod favourite for a generation of tractor drivers, especially as the fuelling could be tweaked to produce 120hp (though Allis-Chalmers could not be expected to honour the warranty if you did!) Over 22,000 XTs had been sold by 1971, making it the most successful 100-series Allis.

Meanwhile, the D17 was replaced by the One-Seventy and One-Eighty, which offered a new cab option, reflecting increasing concerns regarding driver protection. In 1970, the new 200 tractor (which replaced the 190XT) had Allis-Chalmers's first cab with built-in roll-over protection. For the One-Seventy diesel, Allis-Chalmers broke with tradition and bought in an English Perkins engine of 236ci (3.9 litres), while the One-Eighty used the home-grown 301-ci (4.9-litre) six, with the fuelling turned right down for 64hp. But there was no attempt to design an American replacement for the smaller tractors. Instead, the 160 was imported from Renault of France, though it incorporated some Allis-Chalmers components. The company would soon be turning to FIAT for its smaller tractors.

Just as the D-series represented a wholesale change of strategy in the late 1950s, the 7000 Power Squadron did the same job in 1973, at least for the high-powered end of the range. All used Allis-Chalmers's familiar 426-ci (7-litre) diesel, which had first seen service in the 1965 D21. Now it came in 130-hp turbo or 156-hp turbo-intercooled form, which was enough to be competitive. Perhaps even more importantly, the Power Director transmission was uprated to 20 speeds in its top specification (the old 8-speed version had been looking very limited compared with rival 12- and 16-speed systems). Then following on from Allis-Chalmers's earlier development of cabs, the 7000-series tractors were made available with the Acoustacab, which was claimed to be the quietest on the market. New styling with a forward-sloping nose gave the 7000s a distinctive look, and they were later updated with a full-power shift transmission and small power increases.

The 7000s, of course, were Allis-Chalmers's top-end tractors, but they were joined in 1975 by the lower-powered 7000, a 106-hp 12-speed replacement for the 200. At the other end of the range, the 7080 (offered between 1975 and 1981) used both turbo and intercooler, plus a higher-rated speed than the similarly-engined 7060 (2,550rpm against 2,300). The result was 181hp at the PTO. It was soon joined by a four-wheel-drive version, the 7580, which in turn was supplanted by the much bigger 8550. This used a massive 855-ci (14-litre) diesel, straight out of one of the company's crawlers; for the first time, Allis-Chalmers was entering the super-tractor class with a machine of its own.

But for its smallest tractors Allis-Chalmers turned to FIAT for help. It already had a link with the Italian giant as the two had formed a joint venture in 1974 to produce construction machinery. So it was hardly surprising when Allis-Chalmers began to import FIAT tractor components as well. The 5040, for example, which sold between 1975 and 1981, came with a FIAT three-cylinder diesel engine of 142ci (2.3 litres) and a six-speed transmission, though a nine-speed was optional: the 5045 and 5050 were bigger-engined versions. Later, they were all replaced by the 6000-series, still FIAT-powered though built at the West Allis factory.

For the time being, Allis-Chalmers was still building its own big tractors. But this was to change in 1982 when the 7000-series was replaced by the 8000; the 8550 super-tractor was dropped in favour of the 4W220 and 4W305. The 8000, recognizable by its backward-sloping nose, continued with similar engines and transmissions to the 7000s, but with a larger, roomier cab and the option of front-wheel-assist. This cost an extra $7,500, but for a short time Allis-Chalmers actually offered this for nothing. The range consisted of the 8010, 8030, 8050 and 8070, all with a variation on Allis-Chalmers's faithful 426-ci (7-litre) diesel. In its final form in the range-topping 8070, it featured a turbo, intercooling, oil-cooled pistons, and a counterbalanced crankshaft, giving 170-PTO-hp at 2,400rpm.

These could all be regarded as the last true Allis-Chalmers tractors. The company was finding it increasingly difficult to survive the agricultural slump of the early 1980s in which tractor sales were hitting rock-bottom in the United States and showing little signs of recovery. In May 1985 it was announced that Allis-Chalmers's agricultural division had been sold to Deutz of Germany, which was more interested in selling tractors in North America than making them there; the West Allis factory was not part of the deal. So in December 1985 Allis-Chalmers finally closed its doors, and all tractors in stock were rebadged Deutz-Allis. In fact, the Allis name was to survive into the 21st century as part of AGCO, but for Allis-Chalmers tractors it was the end.

The 8000 replaced the 7000 in 1982, and is recognizable for its backward-sloping nose. A larger cab and the option of front-wheel-assist were the main improvements.

AVERY

The Avery brothers, Robert and Cyrus, set up together in business in 1874 to make planters and cultivators. Ten years later they had moved to Peoria, Illinois, and had begun to make steam traction engines and threshers by 1891. Their company, incidentally, is not to be confused with B.F. Avery & Sons of Louisville, Kentucky, which was the firm that was taken over by Minneapolis-Moline in 1951.

Inevitably, the Peoria-based Avery was eyeing up the upcoming tractor market with interest, though its first offering in 1909, the Farm & City, was more truck than tractor, albeit with a 6,000-lb (2722-kg) drawbar pull and round wooden plugs in the wheels to aid traction. A big single-cylinder machine with a 12-inch (305-mm) bore, 18-inch (457-mm) stroke and a promised 65hp, failed to meet expectations, but the twin-cylinder 20-35 which followed it was a success. The 20-35 also exhibited a unique Avery feature: to engage forward or reverse gears, the entire engine unit and radiator were shifted backwards or forwards!

A flood of new machines followed, from a motor plough and a little twin-cylinder 8-16 to massive machines like the 40-80, which weighed 22,000lb (9979kg) and had a drawbar pull of 8,600lb (3900kg). Its engine had the same bore and stroke as the 20-35, but with four cylinders. The 18-36 (replacing the old 20-35 in 1916), a 25-50, and a little 5-10, intended to compete with the Fordson, were other Averys of the early 1920s. But this multiplicity of models probably did more harm than good, and the company was

OPPOSITE
Avery made several smaller tractors, such as this 12-25, the little twin-cylinder 8-16 and the 5-10.

LEFT
The 40-80 was the biggest Avery of all, and weighed over 20,000lb (9980kg).

RIGHT
Belarus of Russia later built modern-looking machines, such as this 5380.

OPPOSITE
LEFT: Simple, value-for-money tractors, such as this 570, have long been part of the Belarus range,

RIGHT: Four-wheel-drive and a powerful turbo-diesel marked out the 1500.

bankrupt by early 1924. It was revived after a few months, then collapsed again in 1931, a victim of the Depression.

But still Avery refused to die. Reorganized yet again, it came up with the interesting Ro-Track, a two-plough tractor with a six-cylinder Hercules engine, notable for its tall, swivelling kingpins which allowed quick changes of front tread width. Sadly, production was halted by the Second World War and was never resumed afterwards.

BELARUS

Asked to name the world's most prolific tractor-producing nation, few would point to the former U.S.S.R. But before its political disintegration, Soviet Russia certainly was the biggest tractor producer on the planet. According to tractor historian Stuart Gibbard, the former Eastern Bloc countries still collectively produce more tractors than anyone else, and the massive factory at Minsk remains the largest in existence.

The Soviet tractor industry began to escalate soon after the Russian Revolution. A version of the Fordson was made in Leningrad from 1924 (many Fordsons had already been exported to Soviet Russia) and another plant in Stalingrad began to produce the STZ 15-30, a version of the International 15-30. Of these plants, only the Minsk factory was actually located in the region of Belarus (now an independent state), but most Russian tractors built for export have been sold under the Belarus name.

The first wholly Russian-designed tractor was a crawler built at Stalingrad, the STZ3 of 1937, though some components were still

influenced by Western exemplars, i.e. Caterpillar gearboxes, Krupp suspension and Vickers tracks. The STZ3 was most successful and over 20,000 were produced. During the Second World War many were used as artillery tractors while a forward-control military version, the STZ5, was supplied to the Red Army before war broke out. It was updated as the DT54 in 1949, with hydraulics offered as an option in 1957. It was finally replaced by the DT75 in 1963. Powered by a 384-ci (6.3-litre) four-cylinder direct-injection diesel, this too had a long production life and is even available today in improved form. It was exported to England for several years, where a British cab was often fitted.

Despite Russia's political and economic turmoil of recent years, production continues, and in 1996 a new Belarus crawler was announced with a four-cylinder turbo-diesel of 120-drawbar-hp, 150 at the PTO. Interestingly, it comes with both rubber and steel tracks which, on the VT-100, can be swapped over in less than two hours. There were also wheeled tractors, of course, and in the late 1990s the four-wheel-drive range included the 90-hp 862 and 130-hp 1221. The current MTZ Belarus range spans 6–12-hp mini-tractors, 20–35-hp compacts and 50–130-hp full-sized machines.

UMO GROUP
BELARUS 1500
The toughest bargain you can drive.

MUNKTELLS

BOLINDER-MUNKTELL

Three companies dominate the Scandanavian tractor industry: Valmet/Valtra, Volvo, and Bolinder-Munktell: but of the three, Bolinder-Munktell's origins in the industry go back furthest. Theofron Munktell, a clergyman's son from Eskiltuna, founded a machine shop in 1832, and went on to produce Sweden's first railway locomotives. Portable steam engines and threshers followed, then raw oil internal combustion engines from 1905.

In a rural country like Sweden it was inevitable that a tractor should follow, and Munktell's first was built in 1913, a massive 30-40 powered by a semi-diesel two-stroke engine. It was a giant twin-cylinder unit of 850ci (13.9 litres), which could run all day on just about any fuel that was to hand, which certainly included kerosene, naphtha or even tar mixed with alcohol. The 30-40 proved too big, however, so a downsized 20-24 soon followed, weighing a mere 4.2 tons and powered by a single-cylinder 779-ci (12.8-litre) engine. It also featured a transverse gearbox, which was a distinctive Munktell feature.

Meanwhile, the Bolinder brothers, Carl and Jean, had begun to make internal combustion engines in 1893. Like the early Bolinder motors, these were relatively crude two-strokes that could run on a variety of fuels. Hit by the Depression, the Bolinders merged with Munktell in 1932 to form Bolinder-Munktell. It was a good marriage, as the Bolinders were able to specialize in engines, leaving Munktell to concentrate on tractors. The first Bolinder-Munktell, the 25 of 1934, was powered by a 323-ci (5.3-litre) twin-cylinder engine of 32hp, still based on the two-stroke semi-diesel principle. Unlike its predecessors, engine speed could be varied, though rated speed was 900rpm. During the Second World War, nearly half the tractors in Sweden were converted to run on wood gas, though the semi-diesels were less suited to this than conventional engines.

Bolinder-Munktell merged with Volvo in 1950, and soon afterwards unveiled its first four-stroke full diesel, a three-cylinder direction-injection motor of 205ci (3.4 litres). This powered the Bolinder-Munktell 35 and 36 models, the 35 being the standard-tread, the 36 the row-crop, both with 43hp at 1,800rpm. Bolinder-Munktell's tractor range was also renewed in the 1950s; the old slim-hooded Bolinder-Munktell 10 was dropped in 1952, when two- and four-cylinder versions of the new diesel were introduced. The company flourished in the post-war boom, expanding capacity to 15,000 tractors a year.

But while Bolinder-Munktell was offering modern diesels, its transmission developments had fallen behind. The new T350 Boxer tractor of 1959 solved this, however, with a ten-speed (plus two-reverse) unit, independent PTO, and differential lock. Power came from the new 111 family, basically a bigger version of the existing diesel, with a 4.4-inch (112-mm) bore. In the T350, this produced 56hp, and 73hp in the larger T470 Bison, Bolinder-Munktell's first high-horsepowered tractor. A smaller model, the 40-hp Buster T320, replaced the outdated twin-cylinder Victor soon afterwards, though this utilized

OPPOSITE
Bolinder and Munktell merged in 1922, with Bolinder making the engines and Munktell the tractors. This is a 22HK.

LEFT
There is fancy chromework on this three-cylinder Bolinder-Munktell, with cab.

Early Bristols used Douglas motorcycle, and later Jowett car engines. After the Second World War, the choice was between Austin petrol or Perkins diesel units.

a bought-in three-cylinder Perkins diesel.

Bolinder-Munktell-Volvo's first 100-hp tractor was announced in 1966. The T800 used a Volvo rather than a Bolinder-Munktell engine, though like all Bolinder-Munktell Volvos it was built at the Bolinder-Munktell factory. With the six-cylinder diesel engine, eight-speed transmission, and modern U.S.-influenced styling, this was a conventional big tractor. The styling was extended to the smaller T600 (previously T350 Boxer) the following year. Two-speed powershift appeared belatedly on the updated Buster T430 in 1969, called Trac Trol.

Transmission development may have been tardy, but Bolinder-Munktell-Volvo was an early user of turbochargers. In 1968, the 113-hp T810 and T814 (the latter with four-wheel-drive) used the same Volvo D50 six as the T800, but with a turbo. A new mid-range tractor, the T650, was announced in 1970, with an all-new four-cylinder diesel of 256ci (4.2 litres) and advanced pressed steel cab.

A symbolic gesture was made in 1973 when the company name was changed from Bolinder-Munktell-Volvo to Volvo-Bolinder-Munktell. Effectively, Bolinder-Munktell was now merely a part of the Volvo empire.

BRISTOL

Bristol of England made miniature crawlers from the early 1930s up to the early 1970s. Designed by Walter Hill, who had already been involved with Fordson, Rushton and Muir-Hill tractors, it was powered by a Douglas horizontally-opposed twin-cylinder air-cooled engine of 74ci (1.2 litres); with a three-speed transmission, the little crawler was aimed at small farmers and market gardeners. As well as supplying the engine, the Douglas motorcycle concern also built the prototypes and was geared up to produce the Bristol in quantity. But in 1933 Walter Hill decided that not enough had been built and, after a few years of uncertainty, production of the Bristol was moved north, to Jowett Cars in Yorkshire.

The Jowett connection had occurred because the crawler was now powered by the car firm's own two- and four-cylinder opposed engines (the 61-ci/994-cc Victor Cub diesel was offered as well). After the Second World War, Bristol moved on to Austin gasoline car engines, notably the A70-engined

20 from 1949. It was updated as the 22 in 1953, and came with the option of a Perkins three-cylinder diesel and a drawbar pull of 4,100lb (1860kg) at 5.85mph (9km/h). Three years later, another update brought the 25, while 1960 saw the new D-series. Bristol continued to use the 32-hp Perkins P3 in the 1960s, now in its PD (Power Diesel) crawler, which boasted a drawbar pull of 5,000lb (2268kg). Bristol was later taken over by the Marshall company, which built crawlers under the Track-Marshall name. Bristol's last crawler, the Track Marshall 1100, was produced during the early 1970s.

BUCHER

During its long history, Bucher only briefly made full-sized farm tractors, though it has been producing cultivators for decades. It began as a blacksmiths in 1807, and the company went on to build powered machinery for hay-making and horticulture, most probably in the 1920s.

Between 1950 and '57, a range of farm tractors was offered, powered by German MWM diesel engines. For some reason, however, the line-up was not pursued, and Bucher concentrated instead on its well-established range of mowers and cultivators; to date, Bucher has produced 100,000 of the latter. A later example of a Bucher mower was the Tractomobil TM800 of the late 1970s. This used a Kubota three-cylinder engine of 68ci (1.1 litres), offered an eight-speed transmission (with four reverse), featured hydraulic lifts at both ends, and a number of PTOs. The 1979 four-wheel-drive TR-range came as tractors or load-carriers,

Bucher made farm tractors for only eight years, powered by MWM diesels.

Typical of small German post-war tractors was the Bungartz, which came with a variety of diesel engines.

powered by 22-hp Kubota or 33- and 43-hp Leyland diesels.

Among Bucher's current line-up is the Duro, a four-wheel-drive multi-use military vehicle. Available as a troop-carrier, ambulance, fire engine, or even an armoured vehicle, the Duro uses an Italian VM turbo-diesel of 254ci (4.2 litres).

BUNGARTZ

A German company, Bungartz began life as the Bungartz & Co. Maschinenfabrik in Munich, and built its first tractor in the late 1930s, using a DKW engine. Over the years, although Bungartz did make some of its own power units, it also bought in engines from Fichtel & Sachs, Hatz, MWM and Deutz.

An example of a Hatz-powered Bungartz tractor was the 1958 T5, fitted with a 42-ci (6.9-litre) single-cylinder engine and a seven-speed transmission with three reverse speeds; this may also have been exported to Italy as the Tigrotto. Compact tractors like this, of less than 35hp, were the focus of Bungartz attention. One unusual feature of them was the extraordinary ability of the front wheels to rotate 90 degrees, enabling the little Bungartz to turn in its own length. This was made possible by specially extended king pins, which placed the steering joints above the front wheels.

From 1960 Bungartz tractors were exported out of Germany, including to America, where imports were handled by the Burton Supply Company. The company was eventually taken over by Gutbord/Moto Standard in 1974, which dropped the tractor line and concentrated on the Bungartz line-up of municipal mowers, which they had been making since the 1960s, some powered by VW engines, and load-carriers.

CASE

Jerome Increase Case had that rare combination of talents: business acumen, inventiveness and sheer perseverance, which were to make him the largest employer in Racine before he was 30. In mid-19th-century America, Horace Greeley's advice to 'Go West, young man, and grow up with the country' was sound, and this is exactly what Jerome did. The great plains of the Midwest were being opened up to create huge farms, but there was a shortage of manpower and a crying need for mechanical assistance.

The young Case, the son of a farmer, bought six Pitts Groundhog threshers on credit and set off for Chicago. Arriving during the 1842 harvest, he proceeded to Racine, Wisconsin demonstrating the threshers and selling them to the more prosperous farmers. His plan was working, as far as it went, but Case could see that the Groundhog was ripe for improvement. So in 1843 he set up shop in Racine to build a new version that incorporated a fan to separate the corn from the chaff, which was a huge success. Within a few years, the J.I. Case Company was established as a major manufacturer of threshers, with a modern factory using steam power. This wasn't enough for Jerome, however, who also found time to inaugurate the Racine Manufacturers' National Bank; he also served two terms as town mayor and one as a Wisconsin state senator!

The secret of his success lay in attracting competent people to his company: Robert Baker headed the collection department (many Case machines were sold to farmers on credit); Manessa Erskine was boss of the mechanical department; and Case's own brother-in-law, Stephen Bull, became Jerome's personal assistant. Together, they were known as the

Ever-cautious, Jerome Case delayed the unveiling of a production tractor until 1911. This smaller 12-25 followed two years later.

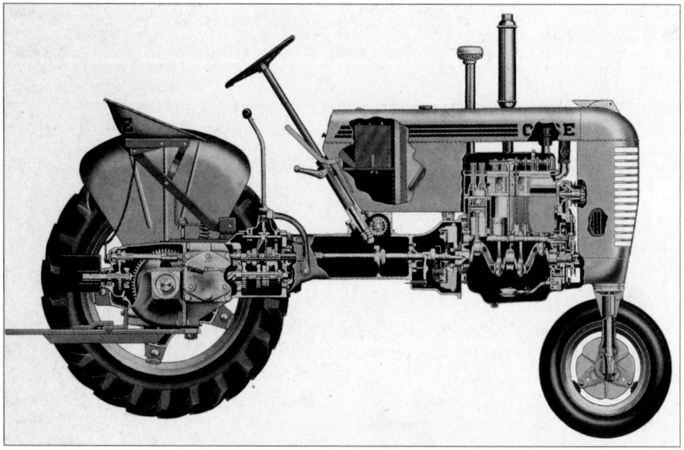

ABOVE
High clearance and a single-wheeled front end distinguished this Case row-crop machine.

RIGHT
The Case Model C was a smaller version of the L, one of the new generation of tractors that replaced the Crossmotor.

OPPOSITE
The Crossmotor saw Case through a difficult decade and served the company well. Its four-cylinder engine was mounted transversely, hence the name.

Big Four, and became equal partners in J.I. Case & Co.

Meanwhile, Case had acquired a trademark: Old Abe, the famous eagle perched on a globe ('The Sign of Mechanical Excellence the World Over') was the company's instantly recognizable symbol for over 100 years, though it is thought that the original Abe had been the mascot of Company C of the Eighth Wisconsin Regiment. It is said that Jerome Case had been so impressed by the sight of it, perched alongside the company colours, that he determined to adopt it himself. Attachment to the eagle became so strong that when it was suggested that the logo be modernized in 1956, long-running president Leon Clausen rose up in his chair in anger; no one dared to mention the matter again until Clausen died in 1965 and Old Abe was finally retired.

Meanwhile, Case was not resting on its laurels, and continued to introduce bigger, improved threshers. The new Eclipse of 1869 was able to thresh 100 bushels of grain per hour, but what it really needed was steam power. With all that talent and capital in-house, buying someone else's steam engine seemed unthinkable, so Case built its own, announcing it the same year as the Eclipse. Case steam engines were a success and were used for hauling and ploughing as well as belt work, and the company carried on building them up to 1924.

But the Case soon realized that the new technology of internal combustion had potential advantages over steam, so in the early 1890s the company employed William Paterson to investigate. Paterson's engine was unusual in that it mounted two opposed pistons in one cylinder, with a complex linkage connecting them to a single crank. The complete Case Gas Tractor was a big, heavy machine, producing 30hp for threshing. Unfortunately, it also had the drawback of primitive carburation and ignition, as did most early gas engines, and was consequently unreliable. Unwilling to take a risk with unproven technology, Case abandoned its first

CASE
CASE

The Case Model L was a three- or four-plough machine, powered by a 503ci (8.2-litre) engine.

attempt at building a tractor, and went back to steam. It was a far-sighted move: many companies had prematurely espoused the tractor business, expecting an immediate success and huge profits. In fact, it was another 20 years before the U.S. tractor market really took off and Jerome Case didn't live to see it; he died the same year that William Paterson designed the gas tractor. However, the J.I. Case Threshing Machine Co. was in safe hands and Jerome's partner, Stephen Bull, took over as president..

J.I. Case Threshing, of course, was not to be confused with the J.I. Case Plow Works. Both were owned by Case, but there was no love lost between the two. Back in 1876, Jerome had financed Ebenezer Whiting to produce his 'centre-draft' plough, and a factory was set up next to J.I.'s own. But the company soon ran into trouble, so Case took it over, changing its name to the J.I. Case Plow Works. The two firms were legally separate and regarded themselves as rivals, especially after the original company moved into ploughs itself. It got to the point where all mail, whichever the company, had to be delivered to the Plow Works! Moreover, in 1915 Case Plow Works took Case Threshing to court for using its brand name on a new line of ploughs. This absurd situation wasn't finally resolved until 1928, when Massey-Harris of Canada bought the Plow Works (which now produced Wallis tractors as well). One of Massey's first actions was to sell all rights to the Case name to J.I. Case, thus ending 'decades of confusion and animosity'.

Ten years after the abortive Paterson prototype tractor, Case showed no signs of being tempted into this new market. But some American companies were – names that would become bywords of the tractor industry. In fact, Charles Hart and Charles Parr began building tractors in 1902, the same year that International Harvester was incorporated. Slowly, J.I. Case came around to the idea that the time was ripe for a second attempt at tractor building. The Gasoline Traction Department had been working on just such a project, and demonstrated its prototype to the company's board in 1910. Given the go-ahead, work proceeded apace, and the Case 30-60 tractor was finally launched in late 1911. It was heavy and massive, like most early tractors, owing as much to steam traction engine dimensions as anything else, and at $2,500 cost about the same as a steam engine. But its horizontal twin-cylinder engine (very different from William Paterson's opposed piston design) had the power to cope, with 30hp at the drawbar, 60 at the belt.

A smaller 20-40 soon followed, with a horizontally-opposed twin-cylinder engine – a flat twin. Again, this was quite different from the Paterson design, but was a success, winning two gold medals in the 1913 Winnipeg Trials for fuel economy and remaining in production for eight years.

But other tractors like the Little Bull and Wallis Cub were pointing the way ahead, being smaller, lighter and much cheaper than these monster machines. Unlike these, the new breed of small tractors promised to replace a team of horses on the average small farm and was also the route to achieving mass-market sales. Case responded with its 12-25 in 1913, though at 9,000lb (4082kg) it was no lightweight, and also cost considerably more than a Bull or Wallis. Not a huge success, it was dropped after five years.

The breakthrough came in 1916, the year that Frank Bull (son of Stephen) became chairman of Case's board. It was typical of Case that, well after Jerome's death, the same dynasty should still be carrying on, and it was fortunate that a new generation of Case tractors – the Crossmotors – existed to see the company through the difficult 1920s, when Henry Ford's cheap and trusty Fordson F was putting countless tractor manufacturers out of business.

The Crossmotor was born out of Case's involvement with the automobile business, which had come about almost by default. The Pierce Motor Company was partly owned by top Case managers, so when it ran out of money, a takeover by the tractor company

Flambeau red arrived with the 1939 Model D.

CASE
CASE

seemed the obvious solution. Case bought Pierce in 1912 and remained in the car business for the next 15 years.

This is how the Case Crossmotor 10-20 came to use a modified car engine, a four-cylinder overhead-valve unit of relatively advanced design. The engine was mounted crossways in the chassis (hence the name), which itself was of cast steel, making a far stronger and more rigid structure than a conventional riveted chassis. The 10-20 was a three-wheeled tractor, the engine driving just one rear wheel most of the time, the other wheel clutching into the power train when the going got tough. Best of all, the 10-20 was far lighter and cheaper than any previous Case.

Under the leadership of D.P. Davies, who was in charge of development, Case went on to produce a series of Crossmotors. The little 9-18 of 1916 was more conventional than its predecessor, having four wheels and a differential. Powered by a 236-ci (3.9-litre) four-cylinder engine, nearly 5,000 9-18s were sold in just three years. This could hardly match Fordson mass-production figures, but was enough to keep the price of the 9-18 down to a reasonable level. The 9-18B of 1918 introduced a cast-iron frame which included the engine block; in other words, an early type of unit construction. Later the same year it was uprated into a 10-18 by increasing the engine rated speed by 150rpm. The engine was quite advanced, with a water pump and a sight gauge so that the circulating oil could be easily checked.

But the most successful Crossmotor was still to come. The 15-27 of 1919 was built along the same lines as its little brother, but

OPPOSITE
Like all pre-war Cases, the four-cylinder Model R was chain-driven.

LEFT
The Model RC was the row-crop version of the R, with a twin-wheeled tricycle front end and 'chicken roost' steering arm.

CASE

with a larger 382-ci (6.3-litre) four-cylinder motor. It was built to last, with pressure lubrication and a three-bearing crankshaft of massive dimensions, which partly accounted for its high price of $1,700, when a Fordson cost just $395. This was particularly embarrassing for Case, for with high compression and running on gasoline, the little Fordson could produce the same belt horsepower, though it always had less pulling power. Fortunately for Case, however, many farmers seemed to recognize the 15-27's other qualities, and over 17,000 were sold in five years. In 1925 it was re-rated as the 18-32 and that too sold well, with 15,000 leaving the works. There was no doubt about it: Case had survived the Fordson test.

The 10-18 was updated too, as the 12-20, with a new disc clutch replacing the internally-expanding type. Moreover, it went on selling despite costing twice as much as a

OPPOSITE
To the casual observer, the Case Model S looks identical to the D, but was a smaller version.

LEFT
The Case 300 replaced the S in 1956 with a new colour known as Desert Sand. There was a choice of a 149-ci (2.4-litre) petrol or 157-ci (2.6-litre) diesel.

CASE 600
CASE

OPPOSITE
The eight-speed 600 topped the range for 1957. Note that 'Old Abe' the eagle was still Case's proud symbol.

LEFT
The Case Model VAC; the V had replaced the R in 1939, and broke with tradition by using gear final drive instead of chain.

Fordson. But Case really wished to sell much bigger Crossmotors, as its big steam engines were now obsolete, and unveiled the 22-40 in 1919. This was its most powerful tractor yet, with 40-belt-hp from its imposing 641-ci (10.5-litre) engine. The 22-40's purpose in life was to power the big threshers that Case also built, and the two were often bought as a working outfit that could cost over $6,000.

Big farms could afford big machines, which at fast work rates would soon pay for themselves. That was also the logic behind the biggest Crossmotor of all, the 40-72. Like the 22-40, it had its own very strong riveted chassis housing a massive four-cylinder engine, this time of 1,232ci (20.0 litres). It weighed 22,000lb (9979kg) and could empty its big kerosene tank, which held 52 gallons (236 litres), in the course of a single day's work! It was a prodigious worker which could pull a 12-bottom 14-inch (36-cm) plough.

The Case 400 of 1955 was the first all-new Case for 26 years: it had diesel power, gear final drive, and eight-speed transmission.

Possibly it was just too big for most, especially at $4,100 (some say nearly $5,000), and in a four-year production run only 41 40-72s were built.

By the mid-1920s, however, Case was in trouble. The pace of tractor development was such that the Crossmotors were already looking out of date, with lighter, general-purpose machines such as the Farmall pointing the way to the future. But one man turned the company round – Leon R. Clausen – another farmer's son, though reputed to be inflexible and authoritarian; it was said that he preferred to tell customers what they needed rather than to pay heed to their requirements. But he was to have a huge influence over the company, right up until his death in 1965. It was Clausen, remember, who forbade any interference with Old Abe.

Clausen was also a great organizer, and by the age of 41 had been vice-president of manufacturing at John Deere, joining Case in June 1924 as president and setting to work with a will. The Case automobile division was shut down, and manufacture of steam engines (a proud part of the Case heritage, though long since outdated) was phased out. More significant to our story, Clausen ordered D.P. Davies to design replacements for the complete range of Crossmotors.

There were two of them, both launched in 1929; the four/five-plough Model L to replace the 18-32 and 25-45 Crossmotors, and the smaller Model C, which did the same for the 12-20. Both were exactly what Case needed at the time, being simple, straightforward, yet thoroughly up to date. With their four-cylinder motors, now mounted longitudinally as part of their Wallis-style unit construction, the new generation of Case tractors looked as conventional as in fact they were.

The Model L was usefully more powerful than its close rival, the John Deere D, with 44hp at the belt and 30 at the drawbar. Its simple four-cylinder 503-ci (8.2-litre) engine was designed (just like previous Cases) to be reliable and long-lived. It also had a three-speed gearbox, where the John Deere had only two, and a rear PTO to complement the latest shaft-powered binders and combines. The Model C was really a scaled-down version of the same thing, with a smaller 324-ci (5.3-litre) motor. It was just as advanced as the L's, however, with pressure lubrication, three-bearing crankshaft, and removable cylinder liners. It shared the three-speed gearbox and chain final drive layout, but was a two/three-plough machine. According to its first Nebraska test, the C produced just under 30-belt-hp, and nearly 20 drawbar, making it competitive with the Fordson.

Both L and C were standard-tread tractors, and as such could not compete with the all-round utility of new general-purpose machines like the Farmall and John Deere C. Case's response was a general-purpose version of the Model C (named CC). It had at least some of the right ingredients, such as crop clearance, adjustable rear tread and so on, but the CC was really too heavy and expensive to compete. The Case sales force was clamouring for a lighter, cheaper version. Clausen's response? 'The purpose of Sales,' he said, 'is to sell what you've got!' But reluctantly, he acceded, giving the go-ahead for the little 132-ci (2-litre) RC, launched in 1932. But Clausen refused to make too much of the RC in case it attracted sales away from the L and C.

The year 1939 saw the beginning of a new era at Case with the introduction of the colour Flambeau red. Until then, all Case tractors had been painted grey, but the late 1930s saw a new interest in style that was influencing tractor design. Flambeau red was in tune with the optimistic mood of an industry that was finally leaving the Depression behind; it was well timed, as the same year saw a wholesale modernization of the range: Models R, RC, CC and L respectively became D, S, V and LA.

The D was little more than a restyled C, though a mechanical Motor Lift was added (to aid the attachment of implements) with hydraulics, disc brakes and a live PTO, all added before production ended in 1953. The S appeared identical, but was really all-new – a two-plough machine to the Model D's three. Like the D, it came in several versions, including SC general purpose, SO orchard, and SI industrial. All were powered by the same 133-ci (2.2-litre) four-cylinder engine running at a relatively high 1,550rpm. Again, like the D, it ran through to 1953.

The Model V was the smallest of the new 1939 generation. For years, Case had disregarded the market for small single-plough tractors, now revitalized by the Allis-Chalmers B and John Deere L. And once again, Leon Clausen proved an obstacle. He had been vindicated in part when the RC had failed to sell well, but his sales force insisted it needed a baby Case to compete. Again, he eventually relented, and the Model V of June 1939 was launched with a 124-ci (2.0-litre) Continental engine of 22-belt-hp. Unfortunately, it was far heavier than the competition, weighing 4,290lb (1946kg), or twice as much as an Allis B. It was more powerful as well, but that was missing the point of a lightweight; it was an affordable single-plough tractor.

During the Second World War, Case built over 15,000 tractors for the military, including a special LAI adapted for desert use. With a top speed of 40mph (64km/h), it had a folding windscreen, air brakes, and blackout lights. The company also built howitzer shells, aircraft wings, and aftercoolers for the Packard-Rolls-Royce aero engine. When war ended, the Case tractor range carried on as before, though the little V had by then been replaced by the VA, with an in-house 124-ci (2.0-litre) engine.

The VA was also the first to offer Case's reply to the Ford-Ferguson three-point-hitch. Named the Eagle Hitch (presumably in honour of Old Abe) it had easy and quick snap-on attachment points. On the other hand, it was without draft control and was incompatible with the three-point implements that many farmers were buying. John Deere and Oliver both adopted hitches which complied with this need.

In fact, Case, although rated fourth in the industry behind International, Ford and John Deere, was technically slipping behind. Imperfect as it was, however, the Eagle Hitch was launched a decade after the three-point-equipped Ford 9N. Diesel engines were the coming thing in U.S. farm tractors, and John Deere, International and Oliver all offered them well before Case, and had more transmission speeds as well. But Leon Clausen was still keeping an iron grip on the company's direction, and by now the entire Case board consisted of old men. Belatedly, Case did introduce a six-cylinder diesel engine for the updated Model LA, now renamed 500. It was strong and reliable, with 64-belt-horsepower. But there was still no draft control, live power take-off or power steering. More radical changes were needed.

They came in the 1950s with the advent of Marc Rojtman. Like Leon Clausen, and indeed Jerome Case himself, Rojtman was a strong, charismatic leader who was highly influential on Case the company. Just as Clausen had transformed Case in the 1920s, so Rojtman did the same 30 years later. He

With four-wheel-drive, the four-wheel-steered 2670 was one of the new breed of super-tractors, with 221bhp and an intercooled turbo-diesel engine.

had arrived in the United States as a refugee from the Nazis (though some say that he was actually born in Russia and fled the Bolsheviks with his family as a small boy). Whatever the case, Marc Rojtman was remarkable in his way, 'a 38-year-old human dynamo', according to tractor historian Robert Pripps, 'talkative and domineering ...a cross between P.T. Barnum of circus fame and Bill Lear of aircraft fame'.

Rojtman came to Case via the American Tractor Company, where he had been selling TerraTrac crawlers with great panache. In 1956, Case absorbed this firm, and part of the deal was that Rojtman should become vice-president of both concerns. Like Clausen before him, Rojtman jumped straight in at the deep end, introducing new blood to engineering, finance and sales. The difference was that he was not facing an outdated line-up of tractors, as work had already begun on the renewal of almost the entire line-up.

The Model 400, which had been unveiled in 1955, sporting the new colour scheme of Desert Sunset sheet metal over Flambeau red chassis, was one such example, and used a four-cylinder version of the 500's six-cylinder diesel. From the start, this engine had been designed as part of the whole family, and in the 400 it came in 251-ci (4.1-litre) form, powered by gasoline, LPG or diesel. All this made the 400 a 50-hp four-plough tractor. There was also a new eight-speed transmission, where Case had previously made do with a mere four speeds, plus a three-point-hitch with draft control; the old chain drive was finally pensioned off in favour of a modern gear differential. The 400 was soon joined by the smaller 300 and 350, both three-plough machines. Meanwhile, the 500 was updated as the 600 with new six-speed transmission.

Although this process of renewal had been initiated before his arrival, Rojtman certainly brought new drive and showmanship to the company. To launch the 1958 range, he invited every single Case dealer and their spouses on a three-day trip to Phoenix, all expenses paid. There, as well as seeing and trying out the latest tractors, if they wished, everyone was wined, dined and entertained on a lavish scale. No agricultural equipment manufacturer had done anything quite like this before, and while the extravaganza cost $1 million to finance, the orders that flowed in afterwards were valued 100-fold, with 30,000 tractors sold as a result.

There were less radical changes in the tractors themselves, though all adopted the same corporate styling, with headlamps in the

hood and a plain, aggressive grille. The greatest technical change was Case-O-Matic, a torque converter that allowed a clutch-free start and infinitely variable speeds; it could also be locked out to provide 16 fixed ratios. There was more power across the range, due to higher rated speeds, but few other changes. The new 900 (which replaced the 600) even retained the old hand clutch and chain drive, which dated back to the 1929 Model L. A 700/800 replaced the 400, and the 200/300/400/500/600 replaced the 300 and 350. It was, to put it mildly, all rather confusing, and one pitied the Case dealers' parts clerks.

For 1960, all the tractors were given a '30' suffix, so 900 became 930 and so on.

LEFT and BELOW
Case brochures of the 1980s, displayed the Case-IH logo, adopted after the merger with International Harvester. The big Internationals were dropped in favour of the Case 94-series.

RIGHT
A typical modern 1990s mid-sized tractor from Case-IH, well-equipped with four-wheel-drive and a roomy cab.

OPPOSITE
The Case-IH 1394 with four-wheel-drive, one of the smaller tractors built at Doncaster, England.

There were more transmission options, including triple ranges and shuttle-shift, while factory cabs were offered for the first time. That was all very well, but there were battles in the boardroom. Marc Rojtman had made some powerful enemies among the older, more conservative members of the Case management. So when in early 1960 he offered his resignation following an argument concerning production levels, the board accepted and Rojtman departed. In four years he had turned Case into a major manufacturer, despite the fact that the company had been perilously short of cash after all the expensive model launches of the 1950s. Fortunately, its saviour arrived in 1967, when Tenneco Inc., of Houston, Texas, took Case over, providing financial stability by backing up its now extensive range of tractors, implements and construction equipment.

After all the activity of the late 1950s, in which the Case tractor line-up had been brought up to date, the 1960s proved a quieter time, though the Comfort King was launched in 1965. It was aptly named, with the driver's platform mounted on rubber to minimize vibration; this greatly improved comfort whether or not the optional cab was fitted. Case could not ignore the power race, and 1966 saw its first row-crop tractor break the 100-hp barrier. The existing diesel engine was enlarged to 451ci (7.4 litres), thanks to an extra quarter-inch on the bore. Rated at 2,000rpm, it produced 102hp, which was competitive but not class-leading (Allis-Chalmers had launched a 100-hp tractor three years earlier).

After the Tenneco takeover, the new parent company's chairman, Nelson Freeman, also became chairman of Case, and like previous new brooms – Clausen in the 1920s, Rojtman in the '50s – set about making big organizational changes. Old Abe was one of the first casualties, replaced by a brand new logo – 'CASE' – stamped out of a tyre print. It was stronger and more dynamic, but many mourned the passing of the eagle.

The late 1960s once again saw a renewal of the range, with the 70-series. This kicked off with the small 470 and 570 in 1969, available as general-purpose, standard-tread and low-profile forms. However, they actually failed to last very long, as Tenneco took over the English tractor maker David Brown in 1972, and from then onwards, most smaller Case models were rebadged David Browns. But the bigger 70-series was still made at the Clausen Works in Racine. All had a rubber-mounted platform, which was continued from the Comfort King, and there was a choice of three different seats with adjustable suspension. Case's six-cylinder diesel now

CASE
BRILLION

The most significant Case of the 1990s wasn't this mid-sized 5140, but the bigger Magnum of 1988, which was the backbone of the range.

used the more efficient direct-injection system, with gasoline an option on all tractors apart from the big 1070, though the LPG alternative was dropped.

The transmission was more sophisticated now, with powershift (on-the-go shifting) available right across the range. This offered four standard gear ratios and three powershift speeds, giving 12 forward gears altogether and four reverse; the powershift system was composed of a planetary gear train and four disc clutches. Case 70-series tractors also featured hydrostatic power steering, self-adjusting disc brakes, and a two-speed PTO of 540 or 1,000rpm.

The 70-series also included the Black Knights, which had been carefully tuned and weighted for ultimate performance, making them collectors' items to this day. But Case's most flamboyant tractor of the 1970s has to be the 1570 Spirit of '76. The Americans are a patriotic people, and to celebrate the bicentenary of their independence from British rule, Case painted its top two-wheel-drive tractor in red, white and blue stars 'n' stripes, topped by a cab with tinted windows. The 1570 was the most powerful two-wheel-drive tractor available, powered by Case's own 504-ci (8.2-litre) six-cylinder diesel, with the benefit of a turbo that produced 180bhp at 2,100rpm.

But these hot-rod two-wheel-drive tractors were rapidly being overshadowed by the new breed of four-wheel-drive machines. Pioneered by manufacturers such as Steiger and Versatile, they were increasingly becoming part of the mainstream, though Case had actually launched its own big 4 x 4 tractor back in the early 1960s. The 1200 Traction King was a suitably massive tractor with four-wheel-steering as well as four-wheel-drive. It was powered by a turbocharged version of the Case 451-ci (7.4-litre) diesel, to give 120hp.

In 1969, the Traction King became part of the 70-series, renamed the 1470 and now with hydrostatic steering on the front wheels and hydraulic steering at the rear. These two systems were independent, and enabled the driver to switch between crab-steering, four-wheel-steering, and front- or rear-steering alone. The 1470 was re-engined, too, with a new turbocharged direct-injection diesel of 504ci (8.3 litres). There was even more power in 1972, when the biggest Case was replaced by the 176-hp 2470 and 221-hp 2670, the latter with intercooling as well as a turbo. It was obvious that the Tenneco regime was working, as that same year it announced a best-ever sales performance of $610 million.

With subsidiary factories in England and France making smaller tractors, Case itself was increasingly specializing in the big ones, and in 1978 replaced the 70-series with the 90. The smallest four-wheel-drive super-tractor, the 2590, continued to use the faithful 504-ci six-cylinder diesel, though the biggest 4 x 4 had been using a bought-in engine from the mid-1970s. Micro-electronic controls were added to the 4 x 4s in 1981 and mechanical front-wheel-drive was offered as an option on the two-wheel-drive 2090 and 2290 the following year. In 1983, the entire range was replaced by the 94-series, first as two-wheel-drives ranging from 43bhp to 180bhp. The 4 x 4s, which were launched soon afterwards, ranged from the 4494 to the 4994, and covered 210–400bhp. The big 4994 was powered by a V8 turbo-diesel, with Hydra Shift semi-automatic transmission. Much of the tractor industry was following Massey-Ferguson in its development of electronics; consequently, Case's 'Intelligence Center' monitored time, acreage worked, and wheel position.

But events of importance were to happen in 1984, when parts of International Harvester, the large-scale rival that Case had never quite been able to match, were taken over by Tenneco. International had been hard hit by the collapse of tractor sales in the early 1980s, and now found itself the junior partner in a reconstituted Case-International Harvester. Its own big tractors (almost all 95-hp-plus models) were dropped in favour of the Case equivalents, and International Harvester began increasingly to specialize in transmissions within the group. The combined range of tractors was reduced from an unwieldy 50 models to around a dozen.

All of this put Case in a strong position; it suddenly found itself ranked second in the industry, with a full range of tractors and a large dealer network. It was reinforced still further when Tenneco bought Steiger in 1986. The company now had tractor factories in Racine and Fargo (U.S.A.), St. Mary's (Australia), Doncaster and Meltham (England), St.-Dizier (France), and Neuss (Germany). In short, it had become a truly global player. This brought economies of scale, and it was able to cut costs further by a joint venture with Cummins to produce a new range of diesel engines branded CDC.

The Case Magnum, launched in 1988, used CDC engines coupled with International transmissions. Essentially an upper-mid-range tractor with standard four-wheel-drive, it ranged from 130 to 195hp, and by 1997 had been uprated to 155–264hp. The Magnum became the backbone of the Case-IH range, though in 2002 guise it was no more powerful than those 1997 machines, underlining the fact that advances in transmissions, electronics and engine efficiency were now proving more useful than sheer brute power. Meanwhile, the smaller Maxxum Plus was introduced to take over in the 90–125-hp class, and in 2002 covered 67–145hp. With the Magnum, Maxxum and the STX Steiger range, Case now had the high-power tractor market well sewn up, but also offered a range of DX Compact

One size up from the 40-series was the 50. This is a 5150, seen here with front and rear implements attached.

'She crawls along like a caterpillar,' exclaimed a bystander as Benjamin Holt's prototype crawler rumbled past in 1908. The name stuck.

tractors (21–39hp) and CX Utility machines (40–83hp).

However, not everyone was a winner. The ex-David Brown plant in Meltham, England, was closed in 1988 after several years of rumour and redundancies; in fact, Case-IH was to lose all its English production capability, and in November 1999 merged with New Holland to form CNH Global. This huge corporation was also part-owned by FIAT-Geotech, making Case part of a global consortium, as the name suggests, and a U.S.-based outfit no longer. Concerned with the size of CNH, the anti-trust authorities ruled that the company should dispense with the ex-International Doncaster factory, not to mention New Holland's ex-Versatile plant in Winnipeg, Canada. For the people who worked in these factories, globalization was therefore a mixed blessing; but Case, as part of CNH, survived.

CATERPILLAR

Caterpillar was the offspring of two bitter rivals in the crawler business and grew to be a world leader. It pioneered the use of diesel engines in U.S. tractors, and while the use of Caterpillar crawlers for farm work was a sideline for most of the 20th century, in 1986 the company announced a revolution in the form of rubber tracks, which offered crawler traction in the field, and something close to the speed of rubber tyres on the road.

The Best brothers, Samuel, Daniel, Henry and Zechariah, were wheat farmers in 19th-century California. Daniel was an inveterate inventor, and was responsible for the design of a successful harvester, cleaner and thresher: in other words, a 'combined harvester'. At about the same time, Charles Holt came out West from New England, set up in the wagon-wheel business, and was later joined by his three brothers. It wasn't long before they branched out into the same business as the Bests, making steam-traction engines and harvesters. From then onwards, the two clans were to be bitter rivals.

Best and Holt steam engines both used huge, wide driving-wheels in an attempt to spread the load of these weighty machines. It was Benjamin Holt, however, who recognized the potential of a continuous crawler track: the idea wasn't new, but he applied it well, and as the wood-and-metal-tracked prototype

The Best company was a pioneer of crawlers, though Holt got there first. This Best 60 had a big four-cylinder engine.

THIRTY
CATERPILLAR TRACTOR CO.
CATERPILLAR

rumbled home after a successful test run, a wondering onlooker gasped, 'She crawls along like a caterpillar'. The name stuck, and by 1908 Caterpillar tractors with gasoline engines were being produced in the Holt factory. That same year, Daniel Best sold his company to the Holt brothers, which didn't suit Dan's son, C.L. 'Leo' Best, who soon had a new Best company up and running. Within a few years he was building a crawler similar to Holt's, but with improvements. The old rivalry was still strong.

But Holt found itself in a superior position following the First World War, having concentrated on the civilian market while Best was supplying the military. The early 1920s tractor slump made it clear that there was no room for two crawler makers, so in 1925 the two companies merged and the Caterpillar Tractor Company was born. It actually worked very well: Holt's premier crawler was the small T-35, or 2 Ton, while Best had the big Thirty and Sixty, so the best of each line-up combined nicely. The 2 Ton was aimed at farmers and had the unique feature of an overhead-camshaft engine, at that time usually restricted to exotic cars. It was affordable, though, and at one point the price was cut to just $375. The Best Sixty, meanwhile, was a surprisingly agile monster of 35-drawbar/55-belt-hp, powered by a 1,128-ci (18.5-litre) four-cylinder engine.

New models followed, notably the little Ten and Fifteen crawlers, but in the early 1930s Caterpillar was forced to consider something more radical. Competition from Cletrac, and the Monarch crawler line from Allis-Chalmers, was hotting up. So there were power boosts for all the gasoline Caterpillars; the Ten became the new Fifteen,

OPPOSITE
The Caterpillar 30: all Bests and Holts became 'Caterpillars' following the merger.

LEFT AND BELOW
The massive Best/Caterpillar Sixty, from the 1920s, boasted 55hp at the belt from its 1,128-ci (18.5-litre) motor.

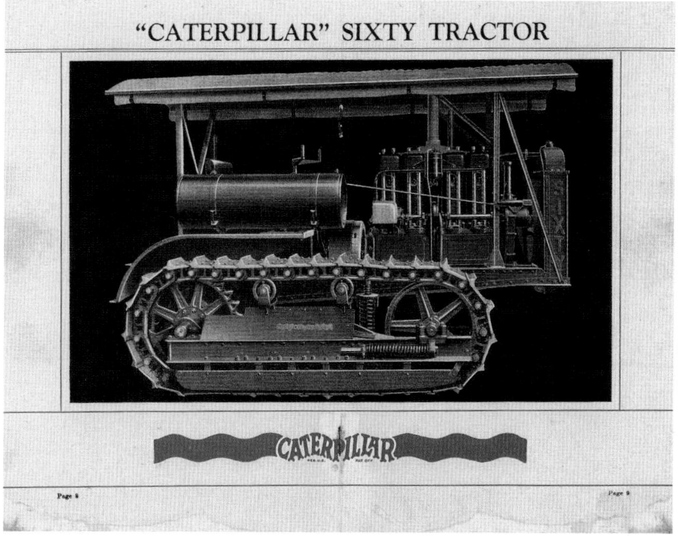

A 1931 poster featuring the Caterpillar Sixty.

the Fifteen the Twenty, and so on. But the problem with all these gasoline engines was their thirst: a Caterpillar Sixty could easily burn 10 gallons/45 litres of fuel an hour when working hard. A diesel engine was able to cut this by half.

Both Best and Holt had been looking at diesel before the merger, and 1931 saw the world's first production diesel tractor delivered to a customer. It was also the first Caterpillar finished in the famous Highway yellow, replacing the dour grey of earlier machines. Whatever its colour, the Cat's new diesel was a success, and within three years the company was building more diesels than every other North American manufacturer combined. The 1,090-ci (17.9-litre) diesel used Bosch injection equipment and a twin-cylinder donkey engine for starting. This Diesel Sixty was soon replaced by the Seventy, then the Seventy-Five. Smaller diesels joined them from 1933, notably the four-cylinder Fifty and three-cylinder Thirty-Five. They were so successful that Caterpillar made no gasoline crawlers at all after the Second World War; even though it had lost money in 1932, the company's faith in diesel had been justified.

Caterpillar was kept busy during the Second World War, supplying the military with bulldozers and building aircraft engines, but from 1946 it was business as usual, with the D2, D4, D6, D7 and D8 pre-war crawlers continuing in production. All were replaced by the U-series in 1947, basically similar but with mostly bigger engines. Both the four-cylinder D2 and D4 had an extra quarter-inch on the bore (giving 350ci/5.7

The little Caterpillar 10 was aimed at farmers.

RIGHT
The Caterpillar R2, now updated with the overhead-valve gasoline engine from the Twenty-Two. The 'R' designation meant that it was a special U.S. Government order.

OPPOSITE
The breakthrough! Caterpillar was a pioneer of diesel power in crawlers, and within three years of its 1931 introduction was building more diesel engines than anyone else in the world.

Caterpillar
68
Caterpillar Diesel
CATERPILLAR
D4

RIGHT
The Caterpillar RD6.

OPPOSITE
A rare wheeled Caterpillar with high-flotation, low-pressure tyres.

litres on the D4), while the D6 used a six-cylinder version of the D4 motor. The new D5 used this engine too, with the same running gear as the D4 apart from a five-roller track. D7 and D8 shared big cylinders measuring 5.75 x 8in (146 x 203mm) – four of them on the D7, six on the D8. All U-series crawlers had a five-speed transmission, and starting was by electric motor or a donkey engine.

A turbocharger was added in 1954 to the D9, producing 50 per cent more power than the D8 on which it was based. There were transmission advances, too. The D9 had power clutch controls, while four years later

CATERPILLAR
CATERPILLAR

CAT
CATERPILLAR

OPPOSITE
One of the old school: big steel-tracked crawlers like this D8H were rarely used for farm work.

LEFT
A Caterpillar model of 2001 used for farm work.

RIGHT and OPPOSITE
After the success of the original Challenger, Caterpillar swiftly launched the smaller 35, 45 and 55, aimed at row-crop work.

the D8H offered a three-speed powershift and torque converter. Construction machinery was Cat's biggest market now, but it hadn't forgotten the farmers, and in 1966 the D4, 5 and 6 were unveiled in SA (Special Application) form, specially for field work. The engines were mounted further forward to provide better balance for drawbar work, and automatically gave an extra 35 per cent more power in third, fourth or fifth gears (an electric switch moved the injector rack stop). A D7 SA was added in 1977 and D8 SA in 1984.

CAT
CHALLENGER 65B
AGRICULTURAL TRACTOR
The Total Field Machine
■ Innovative Mobil-trac System (MTS) — the best of wheels and tracks.
■ Differential Steering — Automotive-type steering for precise, constant steering response.
■ Direct-Drive, Powershift Transmission — designed and built by Caterpillar specifically for agricultural tillage applications.
■ State-Of-The-Art Agricultural Cab — comfort and style, conveniently placed controls assure high productivity.
■ Power Applied Efficiently — converts more engine power to drawbar power than wheel tractors.
■ 30% Torque Rise — provides lugging power needed for heavy drawbar applications.
■ Total Customer Support System — parts or service..."when and where" you need them.
Cat® 3306 DITA diesel Engine
Gross power ....212.5 kW/285 HP
Drawbar power at 1900 RPM* ....168 kW/225 HP
PTO* ....186 kW/250 HP
Operating weight ....14 060 kg/31,000 lb
to 17 690 kg/39,000 lb
Featured machines may include additional equipment applicable only for special applications. See your authorized Caterpillar dealer for available options.
* Manufacturers estimate based on Nebraska OECD Tractor Test 1613-Summary 053 on Challenger 65
CATERPILLAR

Sealed and lubricated tracks were introduced in 1976, greatly reducing track wear. But for farmers, this was really missing the point. More than ever before they were looking for reasonable road-hauling speeds and greater comfort, neither of which steel tracks could provide. The breakthrough came in 1986 with Caterpillar's Mobil-trac system, which consisted of tough rubber tracks with the traction and flotation of steel tracks, but with something closer to the comfort and speed of rubber tyres. Fitted to the new Challenger tractor, they were a huge success, and a whole range of Challengers followed, notably the smaller 35 and 45 aimed at row-crop work, with tracks adjustable between 60 and 90 inches or 80 and 120 inches (152 and 229cm and 203 and 305cm). By 1999 there were three of them: the 175-hp 35, 200-hp 45 and 225-hp 55. All had a 16-speed electronically-controlled powershift transmission.

So successful was the concept of the rubber track that conventional manufacturers soon began to follow Caterpillar's lead. John

CAT
CATERPILLAR
35

Chamberlain began with twin-cylinder kerosene engines, but soon transferred to conventional diesels, such as the one used in this Super 70.

Deere and Case-IH both produced rubber track conversions of their wheeled machines, while Claas of Germany assumed the distribution of the Challenger in Europe. Finally, AGCO paid the company the ultimate compliment by buying the manufacturing rights and selling its own tractors through Caterpillar dealers and in Cat colours.

CHAMBERLAIN

Once Australia's leading tractor manufacturer, Chamberlain is now part of the John Deere empire, involved exclusively in the manufacture of tillage and seeding equipment. A.W. Chamberlain founded the company in 1947 with his two sons, though it was another two years before the first 11 tractors were produced in the former munitions factory. These utilized horizontally-opposed twin-cylinder engines, which ran on kerosene and were designed by Australian engineer Phil Irving, who went on to play a key role in the Vincent motorcycle company. There were 40-, 45- and 55-hp versions; a diesel was tried, but was unsuccessful.

Chamberlain's first diesel appeared in 1952: the 60DA was powered by one of General Motors' high-revving two-strokes, the three-cylinder GM 3-71, and the General Motors-powered Chamberlains remained in production right up to 1967.

A smaller, cheaper alternative was the Champion, a Perkins L4-powered tractor, available from the mid-1950s. It was extremely popular, and over 20,000 were built over the next 20 years. The simple Perkins diesel was supported by Chamberlain's own robust six-speed transmission, a three-speed gearbox with twin ranges.

One of these tractors took part in a 6,000-mile (9656-km) round-Australia motor rally in 1955, and ended up rescuing no less than 30 less fortunate competitors, who had crashed or managed to get themselves stuck in sand. Two years later, it was driven 11,140 miles (17928km) in 11 days – a remarkable feat for a tractor.

By European or American standards, Chamberlain was still small, with a production capacity of just 3,000 tractors a year, but it

Chamberlain, Australia's most successful tractor manufacturer, produced this Super 90, a compact and powerful machine.

A Chamberlain Sedan, contemporary with the John Deere era. Tractor production ceased in 1986, but Chamberlain still makes implements.

was growing. In the 1960s, sales increased from A$7.6 million to A$19.3 million and the company offered its first 100-hp tractor, the Countryman, powered by an English Meadows diesel. In 1970, John Deere bought a 49 per cent share in Chamberlain, later taking over altogether, and the range split between the traditional Chamberlain yellow machines and John Deere-derived or imported machines in Deere green, though still badged as Chamberlains. The 80-series of 1975, for example, used Deere engines from Saran in France, from the four-cylinder 68-hp 3380 to the six-cylinder turbocharged 119-hp 4480. A bigger 90-series was unveiled in 1982, with 12-speed collar-shift transmission and 94–154hp.

But in May 1986 John Deere brought all production in Chamberlain's Welshpool plant to a halt, preferring to export complete machines. From then on, Chamberlain concentrated on making implements.

CLAYTON

Clayton & Shuttleworth of Lincoln, England, was a maker of steam engines from 1845 and by the turn of the century was offering oil-fired steam engines. The company also did plenty of trade with Eastern Europe and had a factory in Vienna; it was this continental connection that made Clayton instrumental in the forming of HSCS, the Hungarian tractor manufacturer.

Clayton's first internal combustion-engined tractor was unveiled at the Norwich Royal Agricultural Show in 1911. With a big four-cylinder engine producing 80hp on paraffin (kerosene) and 90hp on gasoline, it was intended for ploughing. Speeds achieved were 4mph (6km/h) on the road (a fast walking pace) and 2.5mph (4km/h) in the field (a slow one). Five years later, a crawler was launched as the Clayton Chain Rail Tractor, powered by a 386-ci (6.3-litre) Dorman engine. A bigger crawler, the Multipede, was powered by a 100-hp National motor with three-speed transmission and speeds of up to 6.5mph (11km/h). Steering was by a single front wheel, plus individual brakes on each track differential.

But tractor production did not last long: Clayton was taken over by Marshall in 1926, and production ceased two years later, though the company later pioneered combine harvesters in Britain.

Clayton had been an early maker of crawler tractors until it was taken over by Marshall in 1926.

Best known for its crawlers, Cletrac also made a few wheeled tractors.

CLETRAC

Caterpillar may have been the best known crawler manufacturer in the world, and was certainly the biggest, but it was not the only one. Rollin H. and Clarence G. White set up the Cleveland Motor Plow Company in 1916, specifically to produce crawlers for farmers. The name of the company was rather a mouthful, but fortunately there was also a brand name which could be used – Cletrac.

The early Cletracs were all small, from the first Models R and H to the successful 12/20-hp W, launched in 1918 and in production for 14 years. A smaller 9/16 Model F followed in 1921, though it was short-lived, and the bigger

Cletrac once made the smallest crawlers on sale in the United States.

OPPOSITE
The Oliver OC-3 after the 1944 takeover, Cletracs were often badged as Olivers.

LEFT
The 27/37hp BD was aimed at farmers, and was powered by a Hercules diesel.

15/25 was unveiled in 1926. What made these Cletracs different from Caterpillars (or indeed from any other crawlers) was the steering system. Other crawlers steered by declutching the inside track, allowing the other to power pull round the outside. With power delivered only to one crawler, traction was obviously compromised. Cletracs steered via a planetary gearset with a brake at each drive cog. Consequently, variable amounts of power could be sent to each track as required, while both were still driving the machine.

Most Cletracs were relatively small (under 30hp), and reflected the requirements of ordinary farmers. But the 1930s saw the advent of much larger machines, built for the construction and road industries, with up to 100hp, also a diesel aimed at farmers was

Cletrac-Oliver built big crawlers to rival the full-sized Caterpillars, such as this 80.

produced in 1935; the 27/37-hp BD, powered by a Hercules six-cylinder diesel of 298ci (4.9 litres), proved a hit with big farms in the West, while the bigger FD used a 707-ci (11.6-litre) Hercules with up to 97hp at the belt. Cletrac also made the smallest crawler available in the United States; the HG of 1939 weighed only 2,900lb (1315kg), and with drawbar power of 11hp was aimed at orchard and speciality crop growers. There was a choice of 42- or 68-inch (1067- or 1727-mm) track gauge, and the light, manoevrable little HG proved to be a great success. Cletrac made just one wheeled tractor, the gasoline GG, with another Hercules motor giving 11/17hp. Only 7,500 were sold in three years and the design was eventually sold on to B.F. Avery.

In 1944, Cletrac was bought by Oliver, which was keen to add crawlers to its line of wheeled tractors. So the old Cletrac line carried on after the Second World War, rebadged as Olivers from 1953 and painted Oliver green; the HG became the Oliver OC-3. Oliver, by now owned by White, which of course had started Cletrac in the first place, halted the production of crawlers in 1965.

COCKSHUTT

Contrary to popular belief, the Massey-Harris was not the only tractor to come out of Canada. For nearly 20 years, Cockshutt built some beautiful little examples, and it was one of the first manufacturers to offer live hydraulics and PTO.

J.G. Cockshutt set up the Cockshutt Plow Company at Brantford, Ontario in 1877. Unlike many contemporaries who eventually found their way into the tractor business, Cockshutt concentrated on implements, resisting the temptation to build self-powered steam or gasoline tractors. It wasn't until the 1920s that Cockshutt salesmen came to the conclusion that demonstrating a plough was a golden opportunity to sell a tractor at the same time. There was no question of Cockshutt building its own tractors, so it began to sell Hart-Parrs in Canada instead, alongside its ploughs. It did transfer its allegiance to Allis-Chalmers in 1929, but this evidently didn't work out, as it was soon back with Hart-Parr; the tractors were badged and painted as Cockshutts, even though they had come straight from the Hart-Parr factory.

By the end of the Second World War,

Cockshutt of Canada produced its neat-looking line of small tractors for nearly 20 years following the Second World War.

The 40 was Cockshutt's mid-size tractor, with a six-cylinder Buda engine added to the same live PTO and hydraulics as the 30.

however, Cockshutt finally decided to build in-house, and the following year unveiled the Model 30, an exceptionally good-looking tractor with streamlined sheet metal in cream and red. Better still, it had one of the first live set-ups for the hydraulics and PTOs. Until then, when the driver declutched, he disconnected power from the PTO and hydraulics as well as the rear wheels, which could be most inconvenient. Now they kept running for as long as they were needed, and other names in the tractor business (far bigger than Cockshutt) soon followed suit.

The 30-hp Model 30, which used a four-cylinder Buda engine of 153ci (2.5 litres) was given a diesel option in 1949 (another 153-ci Buda) while a new six-cylinder Model 40 was announced. Like the 30, it was Buda-powered, with a six-speed transmission; the bigger engine produced 39hp at the belt, 30 at the drawbar, though there was no diesel option until 1954.

The new tractors were a success, performing as well as they looked, and Cockshutt broadened the range with the 20/26-hp Model 20 in 1952 and five-plough Model 50 with a 50-hp 273-ci (4.5-litre) Buda later the same year. All shared the same fresh styling, and all were sold as Co-Op tractors as well.

In 1958, the whole range was replaced by five all-new tractors, complete with styling by Raymond Loewy. But were the great man's squared-off lines really more attractive than the pretty original? Engines now came from Continental, Perkins or Hercules as Allis-Chalmers had taken over Buda, thus denying Cockshutt its main supplier. The new range consisted of the 540 (26/31-hp utility tractor), 550 (26/34-hp row-crop or standard-tread), 560 (35/43hp) and 570 (40-drawbar-hp).

Attractive and capable as they were, though, they heralded the company's swansong; a group of short-term investors bought a controlling interest in the company in the late 1950s, and used the name as a means of selling FIAT tractors in America. However, the arrangement didn't last long, as is often the case, and Cockshutt was taken over by White in 1962. From then on Cockshutts increasingly became Olivers under another name. By the early 1970s, the Cockshutt name had disappeared for good.

CO-OP

Over the years, several farmers' co-operatives have sought to supply their own tractors by contracting out to established manufacturers. The Allis-Chalmers U-model,

A four-cylinder, three-wheeled Co-Op tractor.

for example, was originally built at the request of a Chicago-based farmers' co-operative, and only after the deal collapsed did it become an Allis-Chalmers model. However, it is not clear whether or not the Co-Operative Manufacturing Company of Battle Creek, Michigan, had such a function, though it was offering three tractors in 1938, with four-cylinder Waukesha and six-cylinder Chrysler engines.

Canada's farm co-operatives got in on the act as well, selling the Canadian Cockshutt 30 as the CCIL. In fact, Cockshutt did well out of the co-ops: the little 30 was also sold by the American Farmers' Union as the E3. The E3 came resplendent in Pumpkin orange, but was otherwise identical to other Cockshutts. The Pumpkin deal evidentally worked, as all other Cockshutt models were sold by the American Farmers Union as well. The Co-Op E4 was its version of the six-cylinder Cockshutt 40, while the little Cockshutt 20 was sold as the E2. The AFU also marketed the biggest Cockshutt as the E5.

A later Co-Op tractor, this time with standard tread.

The David Brown VAK1A, complete with the distinctive fairing which was designed to keep at least some of the wind and rain off the driver!

DAVID BROWN

It was never David Brown's intention to make tractors at all; nevertheless, the engineering firm, based in the north of England, expanded to become one of the major British manufacturers in the field. However, it was taken over by Case in 1972 and built only Case-badged tractors from 1983 until the parent company closed it down five years later.

The original David Brown company had begun in 1860, making wooden gears in the town of Huddersfield, Yorkshire. It gradually diversified, turning its attention to cast iron, steel gears, and finally complete automotive gearboxes. The company appeared to be prospering under the second David Brown (grandson of the founder) in the 1930s when it was approached by Harry Ferguson. The Irish engineer had developed his revolutionary three-point-hitch, and now needed someone to build the tractor he had designed around it; David Brown responded enthusiastically to the idea. Like Ferguson, Brown was a proficient engineer, and could immediately see the

BELOW RIGHT
The company also made a few crawlers: this is a 50TD.

OPPOSITE
When David Brown quarrelled with Harry Ferguson, he decided to build his own tractor, the VAK1.

potential of the Irishman's proposal; unfortunately, two such strongly individual characters were bound to clash sooner or later, and eventually they did.

David Brown lost no time putting what was known as the Ferguson-Brown into production. It was a squat little machine, powered by a Coventry Climax engine of 20hp, and of course fitted with the hydraulic three-point-hitch. The Ferguson system was a genuine milestone in tractor development, and gave automatic depth control as well as an hydraulic lift for attaching and detaching implements. It was so efficient that it allowed low-powered tractors to out-perform bigger-engined machines with a conventional hitch.

At first, all went well: production of the Ferguson-Brown went smoothly enough, with David Brown responsible for building the machine and Ferguson for selling it. But the strain soon began to tell. Sales were disappointing because of the tractor's high price tag, while Harry Ferguson refused to contemplate any design improvements,

DAVID BROWN

ABOVE
The Cropmaster: the classic David Brown of the 1950s.

OPPOSITE
The David Brown TVO model. TVO stood for 'Tractor Vapourizing Oil', a cheaper form of tractor fuel used in Britain.

blaming poor quality control at the David Brown factory instead. Relations became so strained that Harry Ferguson took himself off to America to demonstrate his hitch to Henry Ford; however, he did this without telling David Brown. Meanwhile, David Brown had decided to design another tractor in secret. By the outbreak of the Second World War in September 1939, the Ferguson-Brown agreement was in tatters, though David Brown's own tractor, the VAK1, was ready for production. Although VAK1 had a three-point-hitch, the company was careful not to infringe any Ferguson patents; the four-cylinder ohv engine was built by the David Brown company itself. Many VAKs were built during the war, in crawler form and as aircraft tugs, also as farm tractors.

After the war, the VAK1 continued with a few updates, but still with that distinctive flared sheet metal fairing to partially protect the driver. It was replaced in 1947 by the famous Cropmaster, a most popular tractor; in fact, David Brown had made nearly 60,000 of them by the time production ended in 1954. There was a wide range of implements, and from 1949 a 32-bhp diesel option was offered.

The simpler, cheaper DB25 and DB30 were brought on stream in 1953 in response to fierce competition from Ferguson (now building his own tractors) and Fordson. Alongside these was the higher-powered VAD6, with a 50-hp six-cylinder diesel

NYD 471

engine; again, this was designed and built by David Brown. Meanwhile, a new 40-hp 900 was produced, intended to slot between the two ranges, though unfortunately problems with the CAV fuel pump gave it a poor reputation. In response, David Brown brought forward the 950 replacement in 1958, which was far more successful with 43bhp and, on the Livedrive model, live PTO and hydraulics. It was later joined by the smaller 850, which was also sold in the United States as the Oliver 500, and the three-cylinder 880.

The 950 was replaced by the 53-bhp 990 in 1961, which turned out to be the most successful tractor David Brown ever made. It was later uprated to 55hp, and in 1967 was joined by the larger 1200, itself soon uprated to 72hp. At this time David Brown was focusing increasingly on the U.S. market in reply to requests from ex-Ford tractor dealers to sell David Brown tractors. With this in mind, an experimental 100-hp machine with semi-automatic transmission was built. David Brown planned to devote a great deal of financial resources to develop U.S. models, and built a factory extension in which to assemble them; but the necessary funds was not forthcoming. The company had overextended itself and was forced to sell its tractor division to Case in 1972.

Meanwhile, tractor developments continued, such as the semi-automatic Hydrashift transmission in the 1212, and powershift on all the smaller machines. There was a 91-hp turbocharged 1412 in 1974, a new quiet cab in '76, and David Brown's first 100-hp production tractor, the 1690, in '79. In fact, the 90-series constituted a complete range: 48-hp 1190, 58-hp 1290, 67-hp 1390, 83-hp 1490 and the 1690. Despite minor problems, such as high cab temperatures, the 90-series was briefly the best-selling tractor in Britain.

In 1983, the 90 was replaced by the 94-series, which sadly also saw the disappearance of the David Brown badge. From then on, all David Brown tractors would be badged Case (later Case-IH). A closer look, however, would have revealed the words 'David Brown' still visible on the engine block casting! The range now kicked off with the 1194 (still 48hp), then the 61-hp 1294, 72-hp 1394 (now turbocharged), 83-hp 1494, 95-hp 1594 (with de-rated six-cylinder engine) and a new 1694 with low-pressure turbo-diesel and optional four-wheel-drive.

In fact, these 94s were to be the last tractors to leave the production line at Meltham; the newly-merged Case-IH found itself with two factories in England, and decided that it preferred the ex-International plant at Doncaster over the David Brown factory at Meltham, which was closed in March 1988. It was a sad end for a dynamic manufacturer which, had it been given more flexibility in terms of finance, might still have been making tractors today.

OPPOSITE
Fuel pump problems earned the 40-hp 900 a poor reputation; it was swiftly replaced by the 950.

LEFT
The 91-hp 1412 was David Brown's first turbocharged tractor and was launched in 1974. This particular example is the company's 500,000th machine.

In 1927 Deutz was the first company in the world to offer a diesel tractor. This is a post-war F2L.

DEUTZ

Not only did Deutz of Germany produce the world's first diesel tractor, it was also responsible for pioneering the internal combustion engine, for it was in his workshop at Deutz, near Cologne, that Michael Zons helped Nikolaus Otto to build the first four-stroke gasoline engines. Other automotive pioneers, such as Gottleib Daimler and Wilhelm Maybach – even Ettore Bugatti – later joined the company, which by the mid-1870s had a workforce of 240, turning out the four-stroke motors in series production.

But it wasn't until 1907 that the company made its first agricultural machine. During the First World War, massive 100-hp artillery tractors were built, leading to a line of forestry machines such as the 40-hp Deutz Trekker of 1919, which was half-tractor, half-truck. The first true tractor, the single-cylinder MTZ 222, came in 1926, with a diesel version the following year. The diesel's single-cylinder produced 14hp and was water-cooled, using a simple hopper system rather than a radiator, which was rather unexpected, given Deutz's later predilection for air-cooling.

The Deutz tractor line evolved slowly, but by 1937 it was building one of the world's first mass-produced mini-tractors. This too was powered by a single-cylinder diesel engine, this time of 11hp, and had a 540-rpm PTO. Now merged with engineering firm Humboldt and engine maker Oberursel, and operating under the name Klockner-Humboldt-Deutz, the company made a variety of vehicles during the Second World War, most of which used air-cooled diesel engines. Deutz's air-cooled conversion was complete by 1951, when its final water-cooled model, the F1M 414, was dropped. After the war, tractor mass-production resumed, and by 1954 the firm had made its 50,000th, not to mention 275,000 air-cooled diesel engines of all types. Deutz tractors were also the best-selling German tractors in France, with 15,000 sold between 1945 and 1960, which put them ahead of Fordson and underlined how keen the continent still was in the early post-war years on the concept of a simple, single-cylinder diesel tractor. An 11-hp model still featured in 1960, but now had the facility for the driver to face forwards or backwards as required.

Deutz linked up with implement maker Fahr in the 1960s, and the two merged in 1968/9. Two years earlier, the company had begun to export tractors to the United States alongside its range of diesel engines. Being air-cooled made Deutz tractors unusual in America; they found more favour in the colder north, where they could not freeze up, rather than in the warm south, where overheating was not unknown if the cooling fins clogged with dust. In 1971, the U.S. line-up included the D5506 (49-hp four-cylinder engine) and D8006 (73-hp six). Another side effect of the air-cooling, of course, was that Deutz tractors were noisier than the opposition; a D8006 recorded an ear-splitting 98dB(A) when tested at Nebraska.

Deutz-Fahr went into Italian ownership in 1995 when it was bought out by SAME for £65 million. But it was no lame duck, and Deutz went on to produce a string of high-tech tractors in the late 1990s. The milestone, of course, was the Agrotron. Launched in 1995, the futuristic machine seemed positively space-age compared with the older Deutzes or most other contemporary tractors. A completely new range of water-cooled diesels, developed by Deutz itself, powered the new tractor, which had the steeply-sloping nose that typified late-1990s machines. Covering the 68–150-hp range, they drove through new transmissions developed jointly by Deutz and gearbox specialist ZF; both sychronized versions have powershift with forward/reverse shuttle. The high-visibility

Deutz was unusual in that it persisted in using air-cooled engines when all its rivals were using water-cooling. Although they were cheaper to make and less likely to freeze up, the Deutz air-cooled tractors fared less well in hot, dusty conditions.

Deutz made a great leap forward with the 1995 Agrotron. Its low bonnet line was later copied by many rivals.

cab had a massive 70-sq ft (6.5-m^2) expanse of glass, and there was an electronically-controlled hydraulic lift. The Agrotron was certainly not without its teething problems, but it marked a turning point for Deutz. It was joined the following year by the simpler Agroplus, based on the SAME Dorado tractor but with Deutz engines of 60–95hp. The diesel pioneer had survived.

DEUTZ-ALLIS

Deutz-Allis was the result of a marriage between two long-established names which sadly failed to survive. By the mid-1980s, Deutz had been exporting tractors to America for nearly 20 years, and the opportunity to acquire the ailing Allis-Chalmers could not be ignored. Not only would Deutz be able to make use of a well-known and respected brand name in the United States, it would also gain access to Allis-Chalmers's big dealer network, which consisted of 1,100 across America at a time when Deutz had only 400.

But there were no immediate plans to build tractors in America, so the old West Allis works was closed down, and the first Deutz-Allis machines were a combination of German imports and the surplus inventory from West Allis. Consequently, the Deutz-Fahr DX-range (launched in America the year before) became the Deutz-Allis 6200-series for 1986, ranging from the 43-PTO-hp 6240 to the 71-PTO-hp 6275. All five models were powered by Deutz air-cooled diesels. From the old Allis-Chalmers line came the rebadged Deutz-Allis 5015, 8010, 8030, 8050, 8070 and 4W-305. There were also two compact tractors imported from Toyosha of Japan, the 21-PTO-hp 5220 and 26-PTO-hp 5230.

In subsequent years, the Deutz content was increased as the old Allis stocks ran low. For 1987, the 7000-series came straight from Germany, offering up to 144hp from the air-cooled diesels. The plan was to begin building larger tractors at one of the plants Deutz had acquired as part of the deal, but early in 1988 it announced that White-New Idea would build a range of 150-hp-plus tractors on Deutz-Allis's behalf. These appeared the following year as the 9130, 9150, 9170 and

The Deutz-Allis 6265 was basically a rebadged Deutz-Fahr DX, sold through Allis-Chalmers dealers.

9190, all powered by Deutz engines covering the 150–193-hp range. All had an 18-speed transmission with three-speed powershift. Painted Deutz green, these four finally replaced the old West Allis stock.

But the following year Deutz-Allis was bought by the new AGCO corporation; one of the first announcements was that the big 9100-series would now be painted in Allis orange rather than Deutz green! In any case, the 9100 was brought in-house in 1991, when AGCO bought up the White tractor concern. Finally, in 1992, AGCO announced that it would be badging its tractors AGCO-Allis, and Deutz-Allis's short career as a tractor marque was over. However, it would be another four years before AGCO-Allis tractors stopped using Deutz engines.

OPPOSITE LEFT
The Deutz-Allis 7145 came directly from Germany as stocks of the old U.S.-built Allis-Chalmers line ran dry.

OPPOSITE RIGHT and LEFT
From 1988, the Deutz-Allis range was topped out by the 9130, 9150, 9170 and 9190. They were built for Deutz-Allis by White, though they were still Deutz-powered.

EAGLE MFG. CO.
APPLETON WIS.
GASOLINE
EAGLE
20 35

OPPOSITE
'Built right, works right and is priced right' – the Eagle 20/35.

LEFT
In 1930, Eagle's elderly twin-cylinder machines were supplanted by the modern 6A.

EAGLE

The Eagle Manufacturing Company had been in the farm machinery business from 1906, but lost no time building its first tractor. It was a heavyweight twin-cylinder machine, rated at 32hp. The cooling system was novel in that water flowed out of a tank and over a screen, the liquid cooling purely by evaporation. However, the first Eagle tractor, dating from about 1911, made little impact, and it was another five years before the next one appeared, a bigger four-cylinder machine claiming 45hp at the drawbar, 56 at the belt. Speed was 2.5mph (4km/h).

Smaller tractors followed, such as the 8/16 of 1916, which was governed to 400rpm, unusually low for a relatively small tractor. The 16/30, another twin-cylinder machine, was offered between 1916 and 1932. A 12/20 twin was produced from 1917, later uprated as a 12/22, then a 13/25. But it was the 20/35 that really excited the Eagle copywriters: 'You take no chances when you buy an Eagle tractor … tested and tried out in every condition of field and belt work … Built right, works right and is priced right … any man can run it and keep it in repair without help … Write today for

RIGHT and OPPOSITE
Eicher made suitable tractors for the German market – small, simple and diesel-powered.

illustrated folder and full details.'

Oversold? Well, no more than many other tractors of the time, and probably less than some. But there was no denying that the Eagle's heavyweight twin-cylinder construction was looking increasingly outdated as the 1920s wore on, though the company was to persevere with the 20/35 until 1934 and the even bigger 20/40, with its massive 9-inch pistons with a 10-inch (250-mm) stroke, until 1938.

Eagle's response in 1930 was the startlingly modern 6A, complete with six-cylinder Hercules engine and a more up-to-date chassis. A Waukesha six of 28-drawbar-hp and 40 at the belt soon replaced the Hercules, while the 6A was joined by a row-crop 6B and utility 6C. Both of these used a slightly smaller Hercules engine. Eagle continued to build tractors into the 1940s, but production was suspended during the war due to a shortage of engines, and never resumed.

EICHER

The Eicher brothers of Germany came relatively late to the tractor business and started in a small way, building 1,000

MÜ
L 334

The Model L was Emerson-Brantingham's first small tractor.

machines between 1936 and 1941, all of them Deutz-engined. All were small and simple, similar to the machines produced by its compatriot Fendt and, of course, Deutz itself.

After the Second World War, Eicher developed its own range of air-cooled diesels, offering two-, three- and four-cylinder versions from 1948. Typical Eichers of the 1950s were the EKL11, powered by a 92-ci (1.5-litre) Deutz single-cylinder engine, and the 26-hp twin, using Eicher's own 159-ci (2.6-litre) diesel. By 1968, it was building a six-cylinder diesel for the big Wotan tractor.

Water-cooled Perkins diesels were also used for a time in the 1970s, due to the fact that Massey-Ferguson's Canadian arm had acquired a stake in Eicher, and Massey-Ferguson then owned Perkins. The company later specialized in building four-wheel-drive machines and built its 120,000th tractor in the mid-1980s, at which time it was producing 2,000 machines a year. Eichers are still made in India.

EMERSON-BRANTINGHAM

John H. Manny of Rockford, Illinois, was the inventor of an effective horse-drawn reaper in the mid-19th century, and in 1852 formed a company to build it, with the help of investors Waite Talcott and Ralph Emerson. Manny

The Fendt Xylon was a high-tech systems tractor, with four-wheel-drive, reversible cab, and 44-speed transmission.

died four years later, but his benefactors carried on with the renamed Talcott-Emerson Company. It thrived, and in 1895 several extra lines were added, including tillage tools, though the firm showed little interest in building steam traction engines. In the meantime, a young grocery clerk named Charles Brantingham had so impressed Ralph Emerson that he was taken on and by 1909 was president of the newly reorganized Emerson-Brantingham Company.

The company expanded rapidly by absorbing other firms, one of which was the Gas Traction Company, which made the giant Big Four tractor. This was a massive machine in the traction-engine tradition; Emerson-Brantingham inherited the Big Four 30, a 21,000-lb (9526-kg) four-cylinder behemoth with 99-inch (2515-mm) driving wheels and a claimed 60hp at the belt. It was followed in 1913 with the six-cylinder 45 (23,000lb/10433kg, 45 drawbar and 90 at the belt), which only lasted a couple of years. Emerson-Brantingham had by now taken over Reeves & Co., which came with a 40/65 tractor as part of the deal; the company persevered with it until 1920.

Possibly realizing that the days of such giant machines were numbered, Emerson-Brantingham went on to design its own, smaller tractors. The first was the 1916 Model L, a three-wheeler (two front, one rear) of 12/20hp and three-plough pulling power. It was soon replaced by the more conventional four-wheel Model Q 12/20, whose major flaw was the exposed gear drive when most manufacturers were going over to enclosed drives; nevertheless, it was in production until 1928. Using the same engine, the 1918 Model AA was nearly a ton lighter and had slightly more power; it too lasted until 1928. In 1917, the little 9/16 was aimed at the Fordson, though by 1918 it cost $1,125 – too expensive to compete with Henry Ford, and was soon dropped. There were other EBs, such as the 20/35 of 1919, a big 10,000-lb (4536-kg) machine powered by an L-head four-cylinder engine.

But in the end, Emerson-Brantingham was unable to survive the difficult 1920s, and in 1928 was taken over by J.I. Case, which soon put a stop to all Emerson-Brantingham tractor production, though it retained the implement line.

FENDT

Fendt, known today for the high-tech innovation of its automatic transmission and Xylon system tractor, began by making very simple machines indeed. Hermann Fendt was a mechanic, part of a family of blacksmiths in Weimar, Germany. In 1928, at the age of 17, he built a mower which was little more than a stationary engine with a basic transmission mounted on wheels. Simple it may have been, but this was the basis of the Dieselross

Fendt also built conventional four-wheel-drive tractors for many years, such as this 309LSA. One unusual feature was the Turbomatik stepless transmission, which Fendt pioneered.

('Diesel horse'), a concept to which Fendt remained faithful right through to the 1960s.

A tractor version soon followed, and early Dieselross machines used hopper cooling for their simple diesel stationary engines. But by 1937 the more sophisticated F18 was offering an independent PTO, and the following year the F22 was powered by a twin-cylinder Deutz diesel, with a conventional radiator replacing the simple hopper. During the Second World War, fuel shortages encouraged Fendt to develop tractors which could run on almost any combustible fuel, including wood gas.

Fendt went straight back into full production after the war, churning out over 1,000 Dieselross machines in 1946. Then the company gradually transferred its allegiance from Deutz to MWM for its engine supply; one of the last Deutz-powered Fendts was the 18-hp F18H of 1949, using a 110-ci (1.8-litre) single-cylinder engine. In contrast was the more powerful Dieselross F28, powered by a twin-cylinder MWM diesel of 144ci (2.4 litres), though both remained faithful to the Dieselross concept.

Meanwhile, production of the little F12 and F15 soared: Fendt built 50,000 machines by 1955 and had produced 150,000 ten years later, building its half-millionth tractor in the mid-1990s. The first departure from the Dieselross came in 1958 with the single-cylinder Fix tractors, the twin-cylinder Farmer and three-cylinder Favorit, some of which were air-cooled. But a technical breakthrough came in 1968 with the Turbomatik, which provided a stepless automatic transmission. By now, Fendt was building far more powerful tractors with MAN six-cylinder engines, and by 1979 could offer one of the most powerful machines available – the MAN-engined 262-hp Favorit 626. By 1980, the relatively simple Farmer range could now be had with Turbomatik, suspension cabs and four-wheel-braking. The power range was 50–86hp.

Fendt survived the 1980s and continued to prosper; in fact, it was the best-selling make in Germany by the mid-1990s, with 17 per cent of the market. But a total output of 10,000 machines a year still made Fendt tiny in world terms, and vulnerable to takeover, which happened in January 1997 when it came under the giant AGCO umbrella.

Why should AGCO have been interested in such a relatively small German manufacturer? Because Fendt had become an innovative, high-tech company, a fact underlined by two important tractor launches in the mid-1990s. The Fendt Xylon carried on where the famous MB-Trac left off. Like the Mercedes, it was a systems tractor, with a mid-mounted cab and the ability to carry front and rear implements simultaneously. In fact, it had four mounting positions, giving it the potential to perform several operations at a single field pass. With four-wheel-drive and near-equal-sized wheels, the Xylon was powered by a turbo-intercooled MAN four-cylinder diesel, offering up to 140hp. This had a Variofill turbo clutch which brought the turbo in and out of engagement as required. The complex transmission gave 44 speeds (20 crawler speeds and 24 for other work), allowing up to 31mph (50km/h) on the road. With front-axle suspension, a quiet cab, and four-wheel-braking, the Xylon was a thoroughly modern tractor that took many of its components from Fendt's conventional Favorit range.

Fendt's other major release of the 1990s was the Favorit Vario. Remember the Turbomatik of the 1960s? This too had automatic transmission, though there the resemblance ends. In its 2002 guise, it offered infinitely variable speeds within two ranges – 1–20mph (2–32km/h) and 1–31mph (2–50km/h). In theory, the Vario system would also allow road speeds of up to 44mph (70km/h), but in practice the purpose was to allow relaxed cruising of 1,680rpm at 31mph. In fact, the 2002 version was said to be much easier to use than the original Vario, with more constant efficiency and fewer losses. And it remained the only stepless automatic available on tractors of this power; the 926's six-cylinder turbo-intercooled MAN produced 271hp and 849lb ft. Fendt had come a long way since the Dieselross.

A young driver enjoying the experience of trying out a four-wheel-drive Fendt Farmer.

RIGHT and BELOW RIGHT
The Ferguson-Brown was the joint project of Harry Ferguson and David Brown.

BELOW
A field demonstration of the Ferguson three-point-hitch, a landmark in tractor design.

OPPOSITE
After quarrelling with both Brown and Henry Ford, Ferguson decided to go it alone, producing his own range of tractors in both Coventry and Detroit. This is a TE20.

FERGUSON

Harry Ferguson deserves his place in tractor history. His revolutionary three-point hydraulic hitch, designed in the 1920s and now used by almost every tractor in production, was a milestone in tractor technology. Together with Henry Ford, he can justly be regarded as a pioneer of the modern farm tractor.

Ferguson possessed that rare combination of skills: he had near-genius as an inventor and engineer, and was an astute businessman as well. Not only did he invent the three-point-hitch, and later developed four-wheel-drive systems for cars, he also mass-produced

OPPOSITE
An idyllic setting for this little grey Fergie with grass tyres and roll-over bar.

LEFT
The ingenious Ferguson Road Roller, which used the little Fergie's power and weight to good advantage.

There was diesel power and a traction-boosting wheel cage for this T20.

his own tractors and made a profit in the process. But Harry could also be stubborn and irascible and it was not surprising that the three major partnerships of his tractor-building career, with David Brown, Ford, and Massey-Harris, ended in acrimony and recrimination.

Like Henry Ford, Harry Ferguson was a farmer's son and well aware of the difficulties of life on a small farm. Consequently, the last thing he wanted was to stay at home and spend his life working the land. He chose instead to help his brother in his cycle repair business in Belfast, Northern Ireland; Harry's aptitude for all things mechanical was obvious, and the brothers soon progressed to repairing cars, which in turn led to Harry's interest in motor racing. By 1909 he was the first person in Ireland to have built and flown his own aircraft.

With such formidable talent at his disposal, it is possible that Ferguson could have pursued any branch of engineering he chose, possibly in England. But the advent of the First World War re-ignited his interest in tractors. Britain was under a grain blockade, and was desperate to grow more food. This was where Ferguson's business acumen came in; he began selling the Waterloo Boy tractor through the garage in Ireland, and eventually

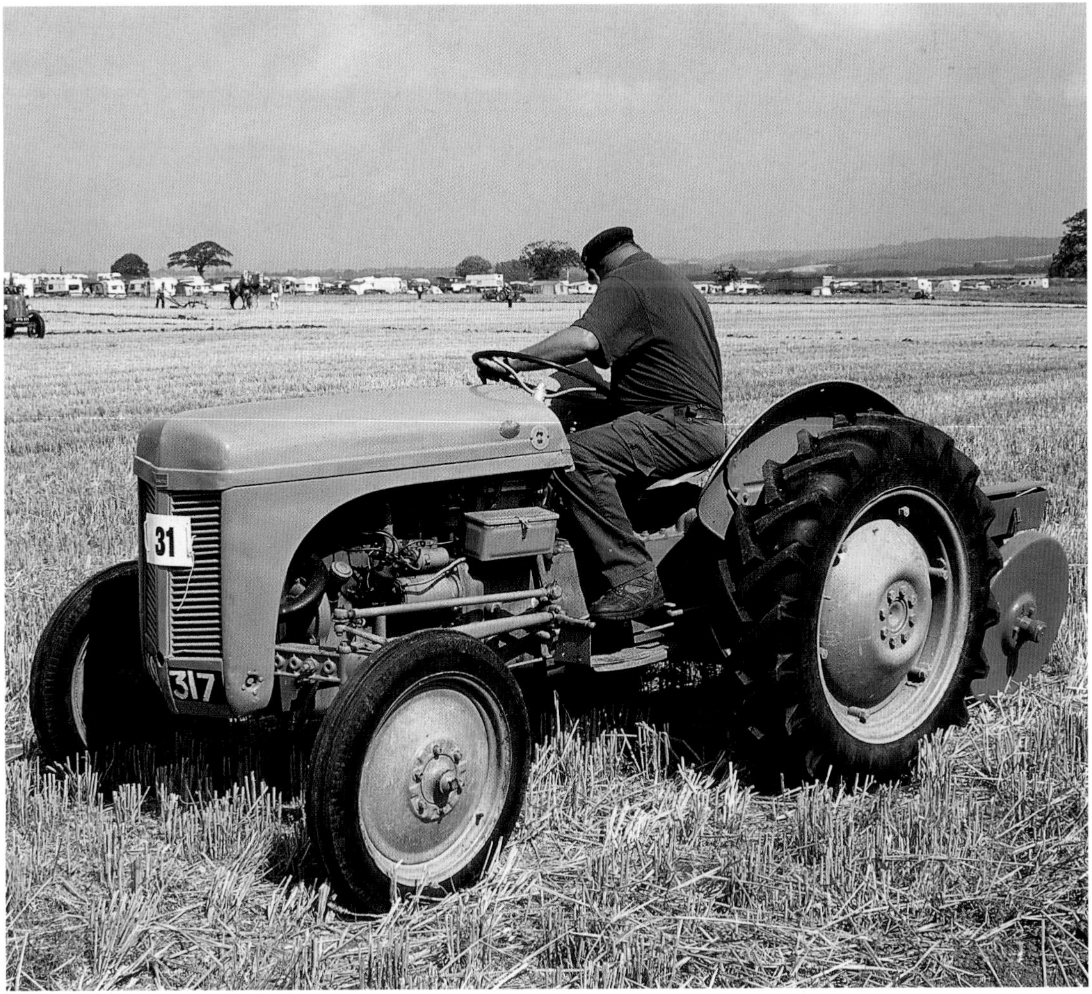

Neat, simple and workmanlike: the ubiquitous little grey Fergie.

JWU 215

Go years ahead
The FERGUSON SYSTEM
With FERGUSON
Greater output per man-hour
with an even more efficient
Ferguson System

sold it all over Britain and Ireland as the Overtime.

The Irish Board of Agriculture invited Ferguson to visit the farmers himself so that he could advise them on getting the best out of their recently acquired machines. This, in turn, sparked his interest in implements and the ways in which they could be attached to tractors, and barely five months after returning from his tour Harry had patented an improved plough. He then set to work to develop a plough specifically for the new Fordson F; significantly, this could be attached to the tractor by means of a pair of struts which helped maintain a more even draft (working depth) and reduced the tendency for the tractor to flip over backwards, which was a particular tendency of the Fordson. This was actually the famous three-point-hitch in embryo.

In the late 1920s, the hitch really arrived, now with three attachment points and hydraulic operation. The third point allowed automatic draft control where, on standard attachments, the tractor would bog down and stall if the plough encountered a sticky patch. The Ferguson System, as it came to be known, was able to sense this and hydraulics raised the implement just enough to maintain speed, lowering it again when the going became easier. The geometry of the three-point-hitch was also carefully arranged to bear some of the implement's downforce onto the rear wheels of the tractor, thus maximizing traction. It was this combination of hydraulics, draft control, improved efficiency and stability that made the Ferguson System such a great leap forward.

To demonstrate his system, Ferguson

OPPOSITE
Unusually, the Ferguson TEA20 was powered by a car engine.

LEFT
This was no idle claim – the Ferguson System really was years ahead of its rivals.

designed a tractor to go with it. The Ferguson Black was an unusual-looking, low-slung machine, powered by a Hercules engine with gears cut by the David Brown company. David Brown was impressed by both tractor and hitch, and a partnership was struck in which David Brown would build the Ferguson Type A, or Ferguson-Brown, as it came to be known, while Harry would sell it. At first, all went well. The Ferguson-Brown went into production in 1936, now with a 20-hp Coventry Climax engine and three-speed gearbox; with the three-point-hitch it was easily able to outperform larger more powerful competitors.

The trouble was, it was also more expensive than most of them. To add salt to the wound, anyone wanting a new Ferguson-Brown also had to buy a whole new range of implements to suit its unique three-point-hitch. Tensions began to grow, especially when David Brown asked for improvements, such as more power and a four-speed transmission. Ferguson refused to comply, and

TO (Tractor Overseas) was the Americanized Fergie, built in Detroit.

blamed the poor sales on Brown's quality control. He would submit the David Brown factory to his super-critical eye, convinced that this was where all the troubles lay. Tractor historian Alan Earnshaw later wrote: 'Harry Ferguson was undoubtedly a genuis, but he had his eccentricities which were difficult to understand, and quite often absolutely unacceptable to more ordinary people … Such was his obsession with ordinary bolted components that he could frequently be seen ... literally hanging (with his feet off the ground) onto a specially made five-foot extension welded on to an engineer's spanner – making sure the nut was securely tightened!'

Such antics only served to sour the Ferguson-Brown relationship, which eventually led David Brown to develop his own tractor, the VAK, without telling Ferguson what he was doing. For his part, Harry Ferguson secretly crossed the Atlantic with a tractor and plough to demonstrate his system to Henry Ford. Ford was impressed, and the two men exchanged their famous handshake agreement then and there: Ford would design and build an all-new light tractor to suit the Ferguson three-point-hitch and Harry would market it (*see* Ford).

This, of course, meant the end of the Ferguson-David Brown liaison, but by 1947, after thousands of Ford 9Ns and 8Ns had been built, Ferguson was party to another acrimonious split. Ford was losing money on every tractor it was making; thanks to the handshake agreement it was only able to sell tractors to Harry Ferguson, who creamed off the profit by selling implements to suit the 9N. Ford finally served notice that from July 1947 their agreement would be at an end. Ferguson was furious, and sued Ford for patent infringements and damages, the total claim being a huge $340 million. However, after a three-year legal battle, all he ended up with was a 'mere' $9.25 million.

So the end of the association wasn't the blow it might have been, and Harry was encouraged to build his first Ferguson-badged tractors, contacting the Standard Motor Company, which had a large modern factory with spare capacity at Banner Lane, in Coventry. In yet another agreement, Standard was to produce the new Ferguson TE20, while Harry would be responsible for design and marketing. The TE20 (TE stood for Tractor England) actually wasn't new at all. It

FE35 was an updated, powered-up version of the original T20.

BELOW
A TE20 in Surrey County Council colours, fitted with grass tyres.

OPPOSITE
The Ferguson TED20, which ran on vaporizing oil.

was very similar in concept and styling to the Ford N-series, and at first even used an American-made engine until Standard's own 113-ci (1.8-litre) unit was ready, a modern overhead-valve four-cylinder engine that was also used in the Standard Vanguard car, and which produced 25hp at 2,000rpm.

This was the 'little grey Fergie', familiar to generations of European farmers, and the British equivalent of the original Fordson or a John Deere. A diesel version followed in 1951; the TEF20 used a 133-ci (2.2-litre) four-cylinder engine, while other models were designed to run on TVO, a vaporizing oil which was a blend of kerosene and lamp oil.

Meanwhile, and after all that had occurred, Harry Ferguson was determined to take on Ford tractors on their home ground. At first, the TE20 was exported to the United States, but it wasn't long before Ferguson made other arrangements. Typically, this was all done at top speed; Harry bought a plot of land near Detroit in January 1948, began to build a new factory in February, and just five months later was driving the first TO20 off the production line. TO20 (Tractor Overseas) was an Americanized version of the TE, which retained the Continental engine but used several other American components.

Despite, or because, of this lightning pace, Harry's tractor business flourished on both sides of the Atlantic. The TO20 was soon updated as the TO35, with more power, a six-speed transmission, and improved hydraulics with position control. (After the

TYB 922

merger with Massey-Harris, it would be enlarged, rebadged and sold as the Massey-Harris 50.) Meanwhile, at Banner Lane, the TE35 aquired a three-cylinder Perkins diesel to replace the Standard in 1959. Despite the Massey merger, it was still badged solely as a Ferguson, as was the Ferguson 40, really a repainted Massey-Harris.

There was never a larger Ferguson, but a prototype Ferguson 60 was produced at Banner Lane. Designed to accept engines of up to 100hp, though the prototypes were of 45–60hp, it was intended to take Ferguson into the four/five-plough class. There was a five-speed transmission, patented dual clutch, two-speed PTO, and improved hydraulics. But after three years of testing, and very promising results, the TE60 was dropped. Massey-Harris management was in charge now, and it considered the prototype unsuitable for the North American market.

In truth, the 'merger' between Massey-Harris and Ferguson in 1953 was more of a takeover, and Harry resigned once he realized that his control was at an end. However, he later set up a research company to develop four-wheel-drive systems for both road and racing cars. For all his faults, the world would have been a duller place without Harry Ferguson.

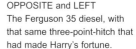

OPPOSITE and LEFT
The Ferguson 35 diesel, with that same three-point-hitch that had made Harry's fortune.

The 702, FIAT's first production tractor.

FIAT

John Deere, Massey-Ferguson, Case-International Harvester: these are all well-known, major tractor manufacturers. But what of FIAT? Strange as it may seem, the Italian giant has been one of the largest tractor makers in the world for many years, with plants all over the world. In the 1980s, it was producing 100,000 tractors a year, and was big enough to take over Ford-New Holland; but even before that it was the largest manufacturer in Europe and the fifth largest in the world. So large, in fact, that when it merged with Case to form CNH Global, antitrust laws precluded such a monopoly and certain plants were sold off before the deal could go ahead.

However, FIAT started life in a very small way. In 1899, 33-year-old Giovanni Agnelli and a group of businessmen set up a company to produce those new-fangled automobiles.

FIAT made a large range of construction and agricultural crawlers, as well as wheeled tractors.

Not as well known as the little FIAT 500 car, this 500 Special was a typical FIAT tractor of the late 1960s/early '70s.

FIAT's giant range of crawlers, small tractors, and big 4 x 4s not only reflected its dominance of the big home market, but also the healthy state of its exports. This is a 505C Montagna crawler.

Fabbrica Italiana di Automobili Torino (FIAT) did well, and under Agnelli's guidance diversified into trucks, aircraft, railway rolling stock, and marine engines. The first tractor was being developed by 1910, actively encouraged by the Italian government, which was keen to see a home-grown tractor in production. But the project was hindered by the First World War, and it was eight years before a prototype could be shown to the public.

After a year or so of trials, the FIAT 702 eventually went into production, the first Italian tractor to do so, and certainly the first designed specifically for farmers. The 702 was a mixture of old and new: it was of advanced unit construction, in which the engine and transmission were stressed members, part of the chassis, making it a strong yet light structure. But the 702's four-cylinder engine came straight out of FIAT's existing 3.5-ton truck. Measuring 380ci (6.2 litres), it produced 30hp at 900rpm on gasoline, 25hp on kerosene.

An uprated 702B arrived in 1924 and had 35hp, due to an extra 200rpm on the governed speed. And there was a 703 industrial model, which also used the higher-speed 35-hp engine. The 702 was exported to the Americas (North and South), as well as to other parts of Europe: FIAT was destined to export a major part of its tractor production. The 702 did quite well, being tough and reliable, though it was, of course, far more expensive than the smaller Fordson. In Britain, the FIAT cost £595 at a time when it was possible to buy nearly five Fordsons for that price.

The 702 was replaced by the slightly less powerful and much smaller 700-series in 1927. This went on to spawn both crawler and wheeled versions, with gasoline and diesel options. In fact, it wasn't until the 700C-crawler of 1932 that FIAT had a real success on its hands. This was strengthened by buying up tractor-making rivals such as Ansaldo, Ceriano, SPA and OM. FIAT also began to use the Boghetto design of diesel, which started on gasoline, switching over to diesel when it had warmed up (a similar system to that used by International on some of its tractors at about the same time).

The company remained active in wartime, and despite booming demand for small cars, in which it was expert, FIAT was finding tractors difficult to sell. Only 32 FIAT tractors found buyers in 1945, and a little over 200 the

FIAT built its own big tractors, including this 100-90, but in the early 1980s it also sold Versatile super-tractors, rebadged as FIATs.

following year. Italy was then still a nation of small farmers, but most tractors were simply too big and expensive. So why not extend FIAT's car expertise to tractors? Why not make a FIAT 500 for the field?

This is precisely what FIAT did. The 18-hp 600 tractor of 1949 proved to be a real breakthrough; sales rocketed to 4,000 that year, to nearly 12,000 in 1953 and over 20,000 by the end of the decade. A diesel option later added to La Piccola's appeal. FIAT had finally hit the big time, and 20,000 Piccolas were sold between 1956 and '58 alone. In what was to become a FIAT tradition, many were exported as well; moreover, a joint venture with SIMCA of France in the early 1950s produced the SOMECA tractor. Overseas ventures also blossomed over the next couple of decades, with FIAT tractors produced in Romania, Turkey, Yugoslavia and Argentina.

The home-produced range was huge, covering crawlers, four-wheel-drives, and all sizes of tractor apart from U.S.-style super-tractors. Even this was addressed from 1979 when the company began to sell Versatiles in Europe, painted and badged as FIATs, in 280-hp 44-28 or 350-hp 44-35 form. The home-produced mid-range consisted of the DT-series, which included the four-wheel-drive 1000DT (FIAT's first 100-hp wheeled tractor) and the 150-hp 1300DT. At this time, exports to the United States were helped by the purchase of implement maker Hesston; in fact, for a time FIATs were sold as Hesstons in the United States.

In 1980, FIAT made its half-millionth tractor, and five years later was claiming to hold 45 per cent of the home market and 13 per cent worldwide. The 90-series tractors were launched that year, ranging from 55 to 180hp, and offering powershift on the larger models. Buying Ford-New Holland in 1991 merely served to strengthen FIAT's position in the large modern tractor sector. The Ford-New Holland 70-series, for example, was sold in some markets as the FIAT G-series, but FIAT red or New Holland blue, the tractor was the same. It went the other way too, as FIAT itself continued to specialize in smaller machines; the little FIAT L-series was also sold as the New Holland 5635. The 66S-series of the mid-1990s ranged from 35hp to 60hp, all with three-cylinder diesels, and with transmissions ranging from 16- to 20-speed. There were bigger four-cylinder 66s (65–80hp), while the half-a-class bigger 93-series offered up to 85hp from its turbocharged four.

As majority owner of the truly massive CNH Global group, FIAT is now bigger than ever. Is it the Italians who say that size isn't everything? With FIAT behind them, probably not.

Don't be fooled by the New Holland badge: this is really a FIAT L-series, also sold as a New Holland.

FORD

When Henry Ford closed his American tractor production line in 1928 (*see* Fordson), one could have been forgiven for thinking he had proved his point. He had produced the world's first cheap, mass-produced tractor, and had achieved his ambition to mechanize thousands of American farms. Perhaps it was time to return to the serious business of making cars.

Not a bit of it. Henry was of farming stock – it was in his blood – and transferring tractor production from America to Ireland, then England, was only a temporary measure. Through the 1930s he and his engineers built and tested prototype tractors. One was powered by a V8 truck engine, and Ford actually got as far as demonstrating it to the farming press. He intended to get back into tractor production as soon as he could. 'I don't care if we don't make a cent of profit,' he said, 'the main thing is to get something started.' Little did he know how prophetic those words would be (the 9N tractor would lose Ford $25 million in its early career). But Ford's words also indicated a genuine commitment; for him, tractors were as much a matter of the heart as of the head.

It was at this point that Harry Ferguson came along. The two men got along instantly, having much in common. Both had connections with the land; both were instinctive engineers and astute businessmen; and both were practical, hands-on types. A photograph of the time illustrates this perfectly: it shows Ferguson and Ford, accompanied by half a dozen engineers, posed in a field with an early 9N. The engineers are sharp-suited and serious-faced, looking more like business tycoons. But there, on the very edge of the picture, in unbuttoned tweed jackets and scuffed shoes, are Ford and Ferguson. Ford leans nonchalantly against the tractor, while Harry Ferguson stands, hands on hips, obviously impatient to get all this publicity business over.

So when Harry demonstrated his three-point-hitch to Ford in 1938, they struck an immediate deal, sealing it with the famous handshake. Ford agreed to build a new tractor incorporating the three-point-hitch, and Ferguson would sell it. Millions of dollars were involved, but there was no paperwork, no lawyers, just a gentlemen's agreement made in a field by two men who understood one another. But what seemed like a brave gesture at the time was destined to end in a multi-million dollar lawsuit.

But this was still in the future. Ford's team designed a new tractor to accommodate the three-point-hitch with incredible speed, and the 9N was in production by June 1939, just eight months later, and was just as innovative as the Model F had been 20 years earlier. Built low, with a low centre of gravity, it was a new type of tractor: the utility. Everything was geared to make it comfortable, safe and user-friendly for first-time drivers. The 120-ci (2-litre) side-valve four-cylinder engine (based on half a Ford V8 car engine to save time and money) was quiet and docile. There was an electric starter and pneumatic rubber tyres, and the driver sat low rather than perched on high. Just like its Fordson predecessor, the 9N relied on low weight to make the most of its modest 23hp, and weighed a mere 2,340lb (1061kg). The Ferguson three-point-hitch allowed it to outperform much larger, more powerful machines, and being a Ford, was cheap in America at $585.

Farmers seemed delighted to be able to buy a Ford tractor again, and 10,000 9Ns were sold in its first half-year; while in 1941 over 40,000 found homes. Then the war intervened and Ford was forced to reduce the specification because of shortages. Out went the rubber tyres and electrical system, in came a simple old-fashioned magneto. This was called the 2N, but in 1946 the full-specification 9N was back in production, and over 74,000 were built that year. Unfortunately, building these great little tractors was far less profitable than selling them. While Harry Ferguson was making good profits as the sole distributor of 9Ns and the implements to fit them, Ford was losing money on every tractor built. In fact, the whole company was in bad shape. So when Henry Ford II took over the running of the firm from his grandfather, he quickly set up an in-house distribution company and informed Ferguson that with effect from July 1947 he would no longer be supplied with tractors.

Harry's response was to set a full-scale lawsuit in motion (*see* Ferguson), but in the meantime Ford introduced its own update of the 9N. The new 8N of 1947 brought a four-speed transmission, a position control for the hydraulic lift, and better brakes. It proved even more successful than the 9N, with over 100,000 sold in 1948 – ten times more than its nearest rival. From now on, Ford would continue to make a profit on its tractors.

Ford's 2N was the austerity wartime version of the 9N. It was without electrics or rubber tyres, though most were subsequently upgraded, including this example.

BELOW
The masters with their masterpiece. From left to right: Harry Ferguson, the Ford 9N, Henry Ford.

But something else had changed. Old Henry had made very few alterations to the Model F in its lifetime, adhering to a one-model policy. Under the new regime, there would be regular updates, and (eventually) a complete range of tractors. It took time, though; the NAA, the radically updated 8N, didn't arrive until 1953. Built along the same utility lines as the 8N, it had Ford's first overhead-valve tractor engine, a 134-ci (2.2-litre) unit which increased power to 27.5hp. There were live hydraulics and PTO. The NAA was also known as the Golden Jubilee, in honour of Ford's half-century.

The range was broadened the following year with the 600- and 800-series, the 600 basically an updated NAA with the option of a five-speed transmission, while the 800 offered a large 172-ci (2.8-litre) motor. But Ford still didn't have a row-crop tractor of its own: that came in 1954, with the two-plough 700 and three-plough 900, based on the 600 and 800 respectively. There was still no diesel option, but this gap was filled by importing English Fordsons, and in 1958 the bigger Fordson Power Major gave Ford a 48-PTO-hp machine.

American-made diesels came in 1959, along with LPG, for the whole range of U.S.-

OPPOSITE RIGHT
'Less Work, More Income Per Acre.' Ford made implements as well as tractors.

LEFT
Neat, compact, advanced and hard-working – the Ford 9N was an instant hit.

built tractors, as well as a smaller 500-series, which with Power Major gave a good range of machines, though big row-crop tractors were still absent. That same year also brought the Select-O-Speed transmission – not one of Ford's better ideas. It was an early type of powershift, allowing shifting through all ten speeds without stopping the tractor. But it proved woefully unreliable in service, and did great damage to Ford's reputation, even though it persevered through to the late 1960s.

The year 1961 brought a big change when the U.S. and English tractor ranges were finally integrated. The Fordson badge was dropped, and all Ford tractors now wore the same badge and came in the same blue-and-grey colour scheme. To mark the occasion, the entire range was renumbered in 'thousands':

Ford
85

OPPOSITE
Ford's 8N replaced the 9N in 1947, and ended the company's commitment to Ferguson.

LEFT
The NAA replaced the 8N in 1953, but was also named the 'Golden Jubilee', to celebrate Ford's 50 years in the business.

Ford 501 OFFSET WORKMASTER

the little Fordson Super Dexta became the Ford 2000 Diesel; the 600/700s became the 2000, and 800/900s 4000s; the Fordson Super Major was now the 5000. At the top, there was an all-new U.S.-built 6000. With 66hp, this took Ford into the big row-crop market for the first time. It came with a 223-ci (3.7-litre) gasoline or 242-ci (4.0-litre) six-cylinder diesel; the only transmission was Select-O-Speed, so the 6000 was subject to frequent recalls and updates.

The smaller tractors were updated in 1965, with a six- or 12-speed transmission on the 2000 and more power for the 4000 from a new three-cylinder engine. A new 3000, using the same three-cylinder diesel in 37-hp form, was brought in to plug the gap. All these tractors came with the new family squared-off appearance. The 9N's friendly curves were out – aggression for the new power decade was in.

Ford wasn't at the front of the power race but it was keen to keep up. In 1968, the 8000 was unveiled as its first 100-hp-plus tractor. It came as a wide-fronted row-crop machine with a new 401-ci (6.6-litre) six-cylinder diesel and the choice of eight- or 16-speed transmission. According to Nebraska, this produced 106hp at the PTO and 87hp at the drawbar in third gear of eight. The test tractor weighed 9,980lb (4527kg) and had a relatively poor fuel economy of 13.37hp/hr per gallon. It is interesting that twin rear wheels were an option, these now being necessary to transmit 100hp to the field without excessive wheelslip.

They were even more necessary on the turbocharged 9000, announced the year after the 8000. Based around the same six-cylinder diesel, this produced 131-PTO-hp at Nebraska, 110 at the drawbar. It also proved

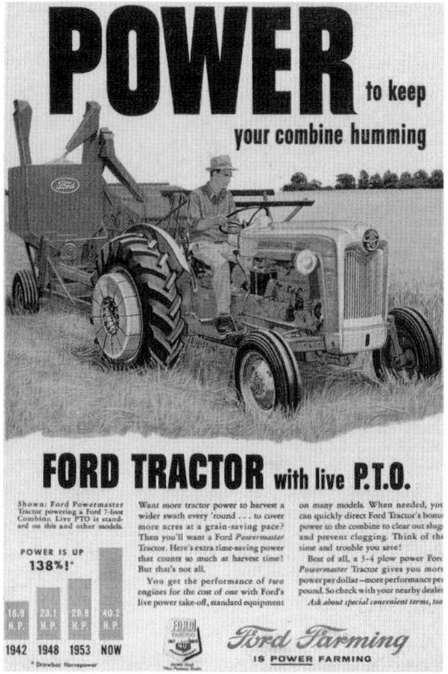

OPPOSITE
A Ford 501 Workmaster. In the 1950s, Ford accepted that a single tractor was not enough.

FAR LEFT
The live PTO for 1954 underlined Ford's determination not to get left behind in the technology stakes.

LEFT
Part of the new unified range for 1961, the Ford 4000 was an updated 800/900.

RIGHT and BELOW
The 66-hp 6000 took Ford into the high-power row-crop market for the first time, though its Select-O-Speed transmission proved to be a headache.

OPPOSITE
The 8000 was Ford's first 100-hp tractor.

far more efficient than its non-turbo brother, with 16.32hp/hr per gallon.

The thousands were to take Ford well into the 1970s: in the meantime, however, Ford was turning its attention to the growing market for compact tractors, which were becoming increasingly popular in the United States with landscapers and hobby farmers. Japanese companies were the best and most prolific players in this class, so Ford imported its first compact machine, the 23-hp twin-cylinder diesel 1000, from Japan in 1973. So successful was this line that by the end of the decade Ford was offering an entire range, from the 11-hp 1100 to the 27-hp 1900. John Deere and International decided to follow Ford's example by also importing compact tractors from Japan.

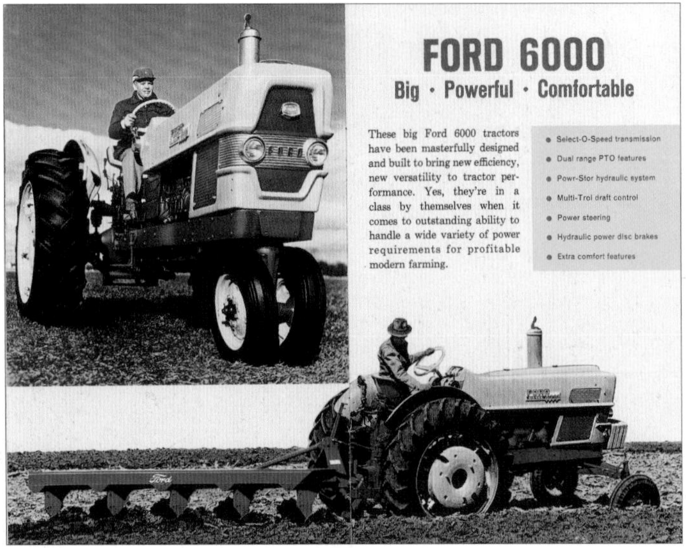

FORD 6000
Big • Powerful • Comfortable
These big Ford 6000 tractors have been masterfully designed and built to bring new efficiency, new versatility to tractor performance. Yes, they're in a class by themselves when it comes to outstanding ability to handle a wide variety of power requirements for profitable modern farming.
Select-O-Speed transmission
Dual range PTO features
Powr-Stor hydraulic system
Multi-Trol draft control
Power steering
Hydraulic power disc brakes
Extra comfort features

The same year that Ford's first mini-tractor was unveiled, it upgraded the big 8000 and 9000 as the 8600 and 9600. PTO was now up to 111 and 135hp respectively. In fact, there were power increases across the range in 1974, when the other Ford tractors received the '600' tag, becoming the 32-hp 2600, 40-hp 3600, 52-hp 4600, 60-hp 5600, 70-hp 6600 and 84-hp 7600. The latter two were supplanted by the 6700 and 7700 in 1977, both with a higher driver's platform mounted on top of the transmission. The others retained the lower utility tractor position, with driver astride transmission.

Despite their extra power, the big 8/9600s still weren't big enough to compete with the four-wheel-drive super-tractors, so from 1978 Ford sold Steiger machines as its own. The Ford FW-20, FW-30, FW-40 and FW-60 produced 210, 265, 295 and 335hp respectively, all courtesy of Cummins V8 diesels. The arrangement only lasted four years, however, and Ford dropped its big FWs, though five years later it returned to the super-tractor market after purchasing Versatile of Canada. Meanwhile, its own two-wheel-drive tractors were creeping up the power graph as well. The 8/9700s were replaced in 1979 by the TW-series, offering up to 163hp at launch and later up to 170hp in the 1983 TW-35. All the TWs still used the venerable 401-ci (6.6-litre) six-cylinder diesel, originally seen on the 1968 8000, though now in turbo-intercooled form. In

FORD
FORD 8000

RIGHT
In the 1980s '10' denoted Ford's smaller and mid-sized tractors, now with optional cabs, four-wheel-drive, and front-wheel-assist.

BELOW RIGHT
The 40-series formed Ford's backbone in the 1990s, especially the immensely successful 7740 and 7840.

FAR RIGHT
Turbocharging transformed the 100-hp 8000 into the 131-hp 9000, Ford's most powerful tractor yet.

OPPOSITE
The 7840 was the mid-sized 40-series Ford, with 90hp. The range was topped by the 106-hp 8340; both this and the 7840 used six-cylinder engines.

fact, Ford was getting value for money out of that engine; it was still using it in the 86-hp 7810 and it would carry on into the 1980s.

All Ford's smaller tractors now carried the '10' badge, denoting three-cylinder diesels for most of the mini-tractors and a 16-speed option for the mid-range machines, among other changes. Cabs, four-wheel-drive, and front-wheel-assist were other options.

In 1985, Ford bought New Holland, the implements manufacturer, giving it a full line-up (big 4 x 4 machines apart) of tools and tractors. But it also announced its intention to pull out of tractor building in the United States altogether. Smaller machines would be transferred to the Basildon, England factory, and larger ones to Antwerp in Belgium. 'The Ford Motor Company,' according to tractor historian P.W. Ertel, 'was clearly looking for a graceful way out of the tractor business.'

But not just yet: in 1987 Ford took over the Versatile Farm Equipment Company, introducing a range of super-tractors to what was now known as Ford-New Holland Inc. Versatile's existing machines became Ford Versatiles in Ford blue, ranging from the 193-hp 846 to the 360-hp 976. Like the Ford-badged Steigers of the previous decade, these were powered by Cummins V8s.

Compact tractors were becoming ever more sophisticated and Ford responded with the 20-series. The 1120 to 1520 all featured a nine-speed transmission, while front-wheel-assist and hydrostatic transmission were among the options. The mid-range machines numbered up to the 30-series, which arrived in 1990. The four smallest models now all

used three-cylinder diesels, with 192ci (3.1 litres) for the 3230 and 3430; 201ci (3.3 litres) in the 3930 and 4630. Standard transmission was eight-speed, with a 16-speed (two-range powershift) optional. The biggest two-wheel-drives, the TW-series, were replaced by the 8530, 8630, 8730 and 8830 (105hp to 170hp) with 16-speed

In 1983, Ford's big tractors were updated as the TW-series. This TW-15 was powered by a 121-hp turbo version of Ford's faithful 401-ci (6.6-litre) diesel.

standard. In this case, extra money bought a clever 18-speed, which was electronically controlled with full powershift.

Finally, in 1991, Ford effectively made good its promise of the previous decade. It sold 80 per cent of Ford-New Holland-Versatile to FIAT of Italy. Three years later, FIAT-Geotech, as the tractor business was now called, bought the remaining 20 per cent. Part of the deal was that FIAT should go on using the Ford name on its products until 2000, though in the late 1990s this was done sparingly. So Ford fell far short of a century of tractor production, but 74 years is still more than respectable, especially when it was

In terms of tractors, however, it is still the post-Fordson age. Henry Ford's Model F, which had its first customer in 1917, really was that significant. It was probably the most important tractor ever made, though this was not because of its technical innovation, which may have been impressive but was hardly ground-breaking. It was, in fact, the F's sheer affordability that made it so special, possible through Henry Ford's inventive use of mass-production. When launched, the Model F cost $750, and in typical Ford fashion the price was cut still further later on. At $385 a brand new F was eventually about one-third the price of comparable tractors, and Henry later slashed the price again, to an all-time low of $285. It made possible for countless small farmers to buy their first-ever tractor.

Long before he finally went into production, Henry Ford was building prototype tractors: Left above: The 1906 Automobile Plow; Left below: A later machine with reversible seat; Below: A prototype, based on the Model T car.

FORDSON

There is a tendency to divide history into neat packages of time, wrapped around significant people or extraordinary events. For many people, 'pre-war' and 'post-war' will always refer to the period before and after the Second World War, while pre- and post-Gorbachev is a convenient dividing line in Russia's turbulent history. Most recently, and poignantly, the world will never seem the same again after the horrific events of nine-eleven, when freedoms that had been taken for granted seemed irreparably lost.

BELOW
A water pump, a governor, and a high-tension magneto were useful updates on the Model N Fordson, but in the United States it never proved as popular as the original F: even when launched it looked outmoded.

OPPOSITE
The tractor that changed the world: the Fordson F.

was now accessible to thousands of farmers who would never previously have even contemplated buying a tractor and the start of mechanized farming for the masses. Fordson got its iconic status and farming would never be the same again.

But it wasn't only the price that was so attractive. The little tractor may have had its flaws, but it was also reliable and actually worked first time.

There was good reason for this. Henry Ford had grown up on a farm in Michigan and knew all about the day-to-day drudgery of working the land. With his extraordinary vision and engineering talent, he could see how a simple, cheap tractor could transform the lives of ordinary small farmers. Moreover, he had time and money to consider how best this might be done. With the huge profits from the Model T rolling in, Henry was able to indulge his interest in tractor design, and take his time to get it right.

His first prototype was built in 1907, ten years before the Model F finally made it to production: it is said that about 50 different prototypes were built and tested before the F reached its final stage. It was not possible to call his tractors plain Fords as the name was already in use by the Ford Tractor Co. of Minneapolis; moreover, his shareholders did not approve of the new tractor venture, so Henry simply set up a new company, Henry Ford & Son Inc., over which they had no control. This was soon shortened to 'Fordson' to save time and money when transmitting telegraph messages. That first Fordson relied

FORDSON

Fordson
Fordson

NEW! Fordson Dexta Diesel
ONLY $1.60 FOR FUEL – PLOW ALL DAY!*
Fuel bills running high? Then try a Fordson Dexta Diesel tractor. Now you can reduce your fuel bills as much as 50 percent—and even more! In addition, you can enjoy the extra lugging ability of a diesel engine. And you can save on upkeep and repair expense, too – the Fordson Dexta Diesel tractor is an "easy keeper."
But here's the best part: The new Fordson Dexta Diesel tractor is in the same price range as comparable gasoline tractors of other makes—yet it usually cuts fuel costs in half, and more. A typical Ford value!
The Fordson Dexta Diesel comes fully equipped, too – including standard hydraulic system and 3-point hitch for Ford tools, six-speed transmission, power take-off, Proof-Meter, lights, and much more. Live PTO is also available.
So see your nearby Ford tractor and implement dealer and get the facts. Better yet, try out the new Fordson Dexta Diesel on your own farm. The sooner you put it to work, the sooner you can start saving on fuel bills! Convenient terms can be arranged – up to four crop years to pay. Ask your dealer.
Also See World's Largest Selling Diesel Tractor
FORDSON POWER MAJOR
Full 4-plow power. Used by more farmers the world over than any other diesel tractor. See your Ford tractor dealer and find out why. Save plenty!
Tractor and Implement Division • Ford Motor Company • Birmingham, Michigan
FORD
LOW COST FARMING AT ITS BEST!
*Based on 10-hour day; 16¢ fuel; average soil.

heavily on Ford car parts to keep costs down; right from the start, it was to be a small, light, simple machine, and costs needed to be pared to the bone. It was little more than a transverse-mounted four-cylinder engine on wheels, but it worked. The engine and planetary gearbox came from a Model B car, the steering gear from a Model K. It also had a chassis which failed to survive the long transition to Model F; instead, the engine, transmission and differential were bolted together to form a rigid structure on which everything else was mounted. This made the little tractor relatively light at 2,710lb (1229kg), so that it could have a small 251-ci (4.1-litre) side-valve engine of low power and still do useful work. As well as unit construction and four cylinders, the transmission was three-speed and fully enclosed; in fact, compared with some of its contemporaries the Fordson was in many ways quite advanced.

Although ready for production, Henry was loath to proceed. The impetus to do so, however, came from the British Government. Britain was at war with Germany, and with a grain blockade on its hands was finding it necessary to produce as much food as possible at home. Moreover, thousands of men and horses had departed for the trenches of Flanders, causing a severe shortage of labour: tractors would seem to be the solution to the problem.

On 8 October 1917 the first Fordson Model F rolled off the line at Dearborn. The British Government put in an order for 6,000, and Ford was in the tractor business at last. Fordson understandably received tremendous kudos in Britain, where the Fordson name on

OPPOSITE
Perkins diesel power (note the four-ring badge on the radiator) transformed the Fordson N.

LEFT
The U.K.-built Dexta diesel sought to seduce American farmers with its sheer economy; there could be no argument with $1.60 a day!

TVS 160

U.K.-produced tractors continued long after America reverted to plain Ford.

Capitalist though he was, Henry Ford was also something of a philanthropist, and felt there was something he could do for post-revolutionary Russia. He was also a pacifist, and recognized that a productive U.S.S.R. was more likely to embrace peace. As a result, 26,000 Model Fs were shipped to Russia, and thousands more were made there under licence. It was estimated that by 1927, 85 per cent of tractors and trucks in Soviet Russia were Fords.

Back at home, the Model F was selling in such numbers that many rival tractor manufacturers were being forced out of business. They were finding it simply impossible to compete with Ford on price, so they either specialized (as International did with the Farmall) or gave up the fight altogether. Of course, the Model F wasn't perfect: it suffered from excessive wheelslip (either because of lack of weight over the rear wheels or inadequate lugs) and consequently poor drawbar performance. In 1920, when tested at Nebraska, it gave the worst fuel efficiency rating of the whole year. Moreover, the light weight and short wheelbase made it liable to turn over backwards, which was highly dangerous as far as the driver was concerned.

On the other hand, it was reliable, dirt cheap to buy, and cost peanuts to run, which for countless small farmers was quite enough.

OPPOSITE
The Super Major was the biggest Dagenham-built Fordson.

BELOW
Many Fordson Ns were converted as half-track or full-track crawlers by Roadless.

Fordson
Major
Fordson
WSV

After 11 years, nearly 750,000 had been produced.

In 1928, Henry Ford decided to stop making tractors in America. His Model A car, the long-awaited replacement for the Model T, was almost ready, and Henry wanted to clear the production decks of everything else to make room for it. Instead, Model F production was transferred to a new factory in Cork, Eire, from whence Henry's grandfather had emigrated to America, and which remained an area of high unemployment. (It was probably a case of a grandson who had done well in a new country wishing to express gratitude for his good fortune.)

The F emerged from its new home as the mildly updated Model N. The F had been looking outdated in some respects, so the N boasted more power and stronger front wheels. It also had a water pump, a governor, and a high-tension magneto replaced the F's primitive ignition. Unfortunately, the decision to produce tractors in Eire didn't work out too well. The Cork factory was isolated from the two major markets for Fordson tractors – the United States and Britain. Moreover, all raw materials had to be imported (anathema to Ford), which inflated production costs.

So in 1933, the Fordson was moved again to Ford's massive new complex at Dagenham in England. There were few technical changes this time, but the colour was changed to dark blue, the U.S. originals having been grey. But changing the colour wasn't enough. It still sold well in England, but Fordson sales slumped in America compared to younger, more useful rivals such as the Farmall, John Deere GP and the rubber-tyred Allis-Chalmers. There was a belated attempt to measure up to them with the Fordson All-Around, a general-purpose row-crop tractor with more power and a bright orange colour scheme, but this too failed to impress American farmers.

The story of Ford tractors now split in two. Ford's English arm declined to build the new 9N in 1939, preferring to persevere with the old Fordson; the English tractor market was far less competitive than the American, and

OPPOSITE
The Perkins P6 diesel gave the Fordson E27N a new lease of life. Over 20,000 were made, many exported to the United States.

LEFT
The Fordson Dexta was later sold in America as the Ford 2000: the days of separate Ford (U.S.) and Fordson (U.K.) tractors were over.

ABOVE
Fordson E27 Major.

OPPOSITE
Fordson Major.

Fordson still had a loyal following. During the Second World War, Fordson at Dagenham made up more than 90 per cent of U.K. tractor production, and around 80 per cent of working tractors were Fordsons.

So in 1945, while Dearborn was busy churning out the successful (but shortly to be litigious) 9N, Dagenham produced its update on the Model F theme, the E27N. Power was up again, to 27hp, and the F's old worm-wheel final drive was discarded in favour of a helical gear differential. Moreover, the colour was changed back to dark blue, having been green during the war. More to the point, the E27N was soon followed by a diesel version, powered by the modern Perkins P6, a six-cylinder engine that delivered a solid 45hp. It gave a final lease of life to the E27N, which had had its roots in the 1917 F, and 23,000 were sold. Some were exported to America as the Major, having the diesel option and high clearance that the U.S.-built NAA lacked.

Its replacement was the New Major of 1952. Bigger and heavier than the E27N, the New Major was all-new, notably with its family of engines. Diesel, gasoline and TVO versions all used the same cylinder block and crank, though the diesel was slightly bigger at 220ci (3.6 litres); the other two were 199ci (3.3 litres). A six-speed transmission was common to all (three-speed gearbox plus two ranges), as was a hydraulic three-point-hitch, though with no draft control and the hydraulics weren't live. This was rectified with the 1958 Power Major, which brought a 22 per cent power increase to 43hp, live power take-off and optional power steering. The Super Major, and New Performance Super Major which followed, had all that plus disc brakes, a differential lock and, finally, draft control. All were built at Dagenham, though the Super Major was sold in America as the Ford 5000. The smaller Fordson Dexta, with 31hp at the PTO in diesel form, was also shipped across the Atlantic.

These were the last tractors to bear the Fordson badge. In 1961, Ford consolidated its U.S. and British tractor arms and the two ranges were integrated, with the same colour scheme and badging. And the legacy lives on: the Fordson continues to be regarded with as much affection in Britain as it is in the States.

MCT 528
TONY DICKINSON
FORDSON
MAJOR

GARNER

England went though a period of austerity in the years following the Second World War, but desperately needed new tractors to replace its ageing, mostly pre-war fleet. Consequently, a new breed of small utility tractors appeared to meet this demand. They were invariably simple, single-cylinder machines, which disappeared when the demand for 'austerity tractors' diminished in the early 1950s.

The Garner was one such, built from 1947 in an ex-truck factory in north London. Powered by a 6-hp JAP air-cooled engine, it was targeted at horticulturalists, and was soon joined by a 7-hp four-wheel version. Fifteen a week were being made at the peak of its production, and Garner also produced an

intriguing ballasted version, with full bodywork, for towing canal boats. But demand gradually petered out, and Garner Mobile Equipment turned its attention to light trailers and tractor cabs. The company closed in 1968.

GIBSON

Gibson was only in existence for a few years, but in that time produced a full range of tractors. It was formed by Wilbur Gibson in 1946, whose father originally built railcars but had already begun to experiment with tractors. It was the intention of the new company to profit from the massive demand for tractors in post-Second World War America.

A new factory was built at Longmount, near Denver, and Gibson's first product was the single-cylinder Model A, powered by a 6-hp Wisconsin air-cooled engine. Like all the small Gibsons, steering was by levers, though a conventional steering wheel was optional. It weighed in at just 875lb (397kg), so was ideal for small-scale horticulturalists. Transmission was three-speed, and there were two independent rear brakes.

But Wilbur Gibson must have been keen to extend this market, and twin-cylinder tractors such as the Super D2 were rapidly added. In 1948, Gibson announced its first four-cylinder full-size tractor, the Model H, which was powered by a 25-belt-hp Hercules engine. Finally, the six-cylinder Model I was introduced, with 40hp at the belt, able to pull two- or three-bottom ploughs. Gibson now had a range to rival that of John Deere or International, at least at the lower end of the market.

The biggest model, the I, came with tricycle front end, the IFS with fixed front axle, and the IFA with adjustable front axle. But not many were built, probably less than 500 of each. However, another estimate puts the number of small Gibsons at over 50,000.

Tractors weren't Gibson's only product, but that didn't prevent it from being taken over by Helene Curtis Industries in 1952. By then, tractor production had apparently already ceased.

GRAHAM-BRADLEY

The Graham-Bradley tractor was a short-lived attempt by the Graham Brothers to find a new market when their Graham-Paige car sales slumped. They had had a varied career, starting out as farmers, then making bottles for a while before going on to build commercial bodywork. That led in 1919 to the complete Graham Brothers truck, though they sold out to Dodge in 1926.

OPPOSITE
LEFT: An early pre-war Garner.

RIGHT: From 1947, Garners were mini-tractors aimed at market gardeners.

LEFT
Not a well-known name, Gibson only produced tractors for six years, but in that time built everything from single-cylinder mini-tractors to the full-sized six-cylinder Model I.

The Graham brothers turned to tractor building in 1938, to counteract falling sales of their Graham-Paige cars.

The brothers' next project was the Paige-Detroit car factory, where they began building Graham-Paige cars, changing the name to plain Graham in 1931. But things were going badly for the latest Graham enterprise: they had sold over 70,000 cars in 1928, only 19,000 in 1936 and less than 9,000 over the last three years before America entered the war, which is the reason why they turned to tractors in 1938, hoping for a buoyant new market. To make best use of what was already available, the Graham-Bradley Model 32 used the car's side-valve six-cylinder engine, with a four-speed transmission, electric starter, pneumatic tyres, PTO and hydraulic lift.

In 1939, it was replaced by the Model 104, which used the same engine but had a wider speed range of 2 to 20mph (1 to 32km/h), quite a high road speed for the time. But despite being available through existing Graham car dealers, and even via the Sears

Roebuck catalogue, sales were disappointing, and production ended in 1941. The factory was turned over to war work, making aircraft and marine engine parts, and also some Alligator amphibious military tractors. Three years later, it was sold to the Kaiser-Frazer Corporation, while the Graham brothers went into real estate. There were no thoughts of retirement for them.

GRAY

In the early days of tractor production, various ideas were tried to maximize traction and minimize soil impaction. Many companies tried four-wheel-drive, while the Holt and Best companies, later to merge as Caterpillar, pioneered crawler tracks. The Gray tractor offered a unique solution with two very wide rear-drive wheels, close-coupled to produce a rear-drive roller as wide as the machine itself.

It was not W. Chandler Knapp's original intention to go into the tractor business at all: he merely required a suitable machine to work his orchards. He built his first in 1908 which, by the following year, had those wide drive wheels, though it was another six years before the Gray tractor was finally offered for sale. By now, the two drive wheels had been replaced by a one-piece 54-inch-wide (137-cm) drum with closed-off ends, as the wide spoked wheels had a tendency to fill up with dirt and mud. The original twin-cylinder engine had gone too, replaced with a transverse-mounted Waukesha four-cylinder unit. The spur gear transmission had proved troublesome, so this was replaced with in-line spur gears and twin roller chain on each side of the drive drum, working via a four-speed transmission. A final change was to bolt a corrugated iron canopy over all the works; there was no sheet metal bodywork.

Two Grays were offered for 1916, the 15/25 and 20/35, though a later 18/36 proved the most popular, using a 478-ci (7.8-litre) Waukesha four. Unfortunately, none of them was very manoevrable, as the twin-chain drive allowed for no differential, so the Gray was steered by a complicated system of rods and levers. The company was reorganized in 1925, after which time just one model, the 22-40, was available. Production ceased in 1933.

GULDNER

Based in Aschaffenburg, Germany, Guldner started out as an engine manufacturer and only later diversified into tractors. The

The unique Gray tractor used a 54-inch-wide (137-cm) roller, in place of rear wheels, to minimize soil impaction and improve traction.

GULDNER G30

company was set up in 1904 by Dr. Hugo Guldner (himself a personal friend of the famous Rudolf Diesel) and Professor Carl Von Linde. Under these two men, Guldner the company concentrated on two-stroke diesel engines of up to 500hp. After they died (Guldner in 1926, Linde six years later) four-stroke diesels joined the range.

The first Guldner tractor was launched in 1938, a simple 20-hp single-cylinder diesel similar to other small German machines like the Fendt. Various twin-cylinder machines followed, built in conjunction with the Deuliewag company. In fact, from then on much of Guldner's work would be in close partnership with other German firms.

During the Second World War, Guldner supplied engines to Fahr and was part of a wartime consortium of engineering firms. After the war, many of Guldner's tractors were twin-cylinder machines, such as the 1948 AF30 (30hp, water-cooled) and the late-1950s ABL (112ci/1.8 litre, air-cooled). The Europa, a joint venture with Fahr, was launched in 1959, including the 15-hp twin-cylinder Spessart and a rare four-wheel-drive articulated version, still with the same 15-hp twin-cylinder diesel.

By this time, the company was offering larger machines as well, powered by Perkins three-cylinder and Daimler-Benz four-cylinder diesels. By the mid-1960s, the range had extended to a 50-hp four and 75-hp six, some with four-wheel-drive. Typical was the 1967 G45, with a 45-hp air-cooled diesel of 192ci (3.1 litres).

But Guldner was no longer independent. It had merged with Fahr in 1962 and was finally taken over by Deutz in 1968/9, which spelt the end of the Guldner name. The company had made over 100,000 tractors.

ABOVE
Guldner specialized in small utility tractors such as this 15-hp model, popular on small German farms.

OPPOSITE
There were bigger Guldners too, using the company's own twin-cylinder diesels. The top models were powered by bought-in units from Perkins and Daimler-Benz.

HANOMAG

Hanomag (otherwise Hannoversche Maschinenbau AG) was in business for decades before it branched into tractors. It began in heavy engineering in 1835, progressing to steam locomotives and ships. Trucks joined the product range in 1905 and motor ploughs in 1912, using Baer, Kamper or Korting engines.

The first full-sized tractors, in both crawler and wheeled forms, didn't appear until after the First World War, at first using gasoline power units of 25hp. But, being a German company, it wasn't long before Hanomag launched a diesel tractor. In fact, it could claim to have offered the first full diesel tractor in 1930 (the Deutz pre-dated it in 1926, but was a semi-diesel machine). It was also more sophisticated than the Deutz, using a 333-ci (5.5-litre) four-cylinder engine producing 40hp, which was to

RIGHT
Some Hanomags bore as close a resemblance to trucks as they did to tractors.

OPPOSITE
The Hanomag R25. Despite their conservative appearance, Hanomag tractors often pioneered new technology. The company offered the world's first full diesel tractor in 1930, and applied turbo and supercharging to tractors in the 1950s.

remain in production for 35 years. Six years later, and there was a six-cylinder 545-ci (8.9-litre) version.

Hanomag was a pioneer of both supercharging and turbocharging for tractors (in 1953 and '57 respectively) and offered a five-speed transmission from 1942. The 1950s range included tractors of 16 to 55hp, plus crawlers of up to 90hp. So far, all Hanomag tractors had used four-stroke engines, but it began to make small two-stroke diesels around this time; the 12-hp R12 single-cylinder was launched in 1953 and a twin-cylinder version followed soon afterwards.

The company advanced to become a major producer and had built 100,000 tractors by 1954. But it was not big enough

HANOMAG
R 25

The Hanomag Granit. By the late 1960s, Hanomag had been taken over. It launched an all-new range of machines, but these were not a success.

Hanomag eventually stopped making farm tractors, but its name lived on in the construction business.

to evade takeover, and Hanomag came under the Rheinstal group's umbrella in 1961. This made a modern Borgward diesel of 109ci (1.8 litres) available, though the company was still producing its traditional big four-cylinder models, some of which were used as aircraft tugs. An all-new range was unveiled in 1967, with direct-injection diesel engines, nine- or 12-speed transmissions, and even four-wheel-drive. Despite the up-to-date features, however, it didn't sell well, and production ceased in 1971 after 250,000 tractors of all types had been built. The company was split up and was eventually taken over by Kubota in 1989.

HAPPY FARMER

The company with the most cheerful name in the business was a short-lived attempt to rival the Waterloo Boy. Like the Waterloo, it too had a bucolic logo, in this case a grinning farmer, while its rival sported a smiling, rosy-cheeked field hand. It was designed by D.M. Hartsough, who had also drawn up the Big Four tractor.

The Happy Farmer was on a much smaller scale, with a 255-ci (4.2-litre) twin-

ABOVE
A pioneer tractor with a cheerful name: the Happy Farmer.

OPPOSITE
The Hart-Parr 12/24E was one of the new breed of Hart-Parrs that succeeded the original heavyweights.

cylinder engine mounted horizontally in the frame. Unusually, it used overhead valves (though the valvegear was exposed) and the chassis consisted of a single large-diameter tube. Like the Waterloo Boy, the transmission gear teeth were exposed. (The Happy Farmer shown here is a four-wheeled tractor with longitudinally-mounted radiator, though a contemporary picture shows a three-wheeler, with transverse radiator.)

Launched in 1916, it was announced that 500 Happy Farmers would be built on a sub-contract basis by the H.E. Wilcox Motor Company and another 1,500 by the La Crosse Tractor Company. But by late 1916 (some say the early '20s), the Happy Farmer was out of production, though it lived on as the La Crosse until 1921.

HART-PARR

John Deere, Jerome Case, Henry Ford, Harry Ferguson: all practical, self-made men and founders of tractor dynasties which sprung from either agricultural or engineering

HART
PARR
CHARLES CITY IOWA U.S.A.
12 24

The Hart-Parr 28/50, based on two 12/24 engines. The company later merged with Oliver.

backgrounds. But America's best claim to have produced the world's first practical internal combustion-engined tractor appears to be the invention of two college students: Charles Hart and Charles Parr.

The pair were students of engineering at the University of Wisconsin, and after graduating moved to Charles City, Iowa, and founded the Hart-Parr Gasoline Engine Company. They built their first tractor in 1901, were conducting field tests the following year, and went into production in 1903, when 15 tractors were built.

In the race to build the first production tractor, it therefore appears to be an honourable draw, with Englishman Daniel Albone producing his Ivel tractor that same year. But it was Hart-Parr's sales manager, W.H. Williams, who could claim to have coined the term 'tractor'. 'In 1907 I began to use the term "tractor" in our advertising,' he recalled. 'In 1912 I began to use the term "farm tractor", and the term seemed so appropriate that it has stuck with us ever since.'

The first Hart-Parrs were big, heavy machines, really intended for threshing instead

of heavy drawbar work, the transmissions being unequal to the demands of two cylinders, each one measuring over 800ci (13 litres). Even 4-inch (10-cm) steel axles broke when subjected to hauling heavy loads, though a 5-inch axle solved that problem. But that wasn't the end of Hart-Parr's troubles: in 1910, over $100,000 were paid out in free repairs after many crankshaft failures, when it was discovered that the cranks had been incorrectly heat-treated.

But generally, the huge, slow-revving Hart-Parrs were well-regarded and included the 30/60 'Old Reliable' built from 1907–18. One of Hart-Parr's biggest tractors of this period was the monster 60/100; it weighed 26 tons all told, and had 9-ft (2.7-m) diameter wheels.

However, the future lay in smaller, lighter machines which Charles Ellis, a business partner in the firm, insisted was the only way to survive. In the end, Hart and Parr resigned in disgust!

But Ellis was right, and the 'New Hart-Parr' of 1918 was a twin-cylinder 12/25, with a conventional front-mounted radiator and four-wheel chassis. It was soon joined by a 30-hp 15/30 Type A and the smaller 10/20 Model B. An updated 10/20, the 12/24 Model E, replaced it in 1924. The latter weighed only 4,300lb (1950kg), had a disc clutch (replacing the old band type) and force-feed lubrication, with excess lube directed to the enclosed final drive. One intriguing variation was the four-cylinder 22/40, powered by two 10/20 twins mounted side by side, with individual carburettors but common magneto ignition. It later grew into the 28/50, based around two 12/24 motors.

But by 1929, Hart-Parr could no longer survive on its own, and decided to merge with the Oliver Chilled Plow Company, plus two smaller concerns, to form the Oliver Farm Equipment Co.

HATZ

The German Hatz brothers set up their company in 1880, and engine manufacture was soon their speciality. One hundred and twenty years later, Hatz is a well-established producer of industrial diesel engines, its

Hatz, a long-established diesel engine manufacturer, also built tractors in the 1950s and early '60s. Most were small utility machines like the Hanomag and Porsche.

HSCS of Hungary had English connections, but from 1938 concentrated on its own version of the Lanz Bulldog.

tractor-making days in the 1950s and '60s being just brief interludes in a long history.

The company was an early producer of diesels (something of a tradition in German engineering), making its first semi-diesel in 1910 and a full diesel eight years later. The company began building marine diesels during the First World War and later developed air-cooled diesels, experience which formed the basis of Hatz tractors, which were introduced in either 1950 or '54. All of these were small utility tractors, similar to those produced by other German manufacturers of the time, such as Hanomag and Porsche. The early Hatz tractors had one or two air-cooled cylinders, though three-cylinder machines producing up to 40hp were offered from 1964.

Hatz found the tractor business too highly competitive, however, and decided to pull out not long after the three-cylinder range had been announced, returning to its core business of producing diesel engines for a variety of uses. Today, and still owned by the Hatz family, the company builds around 60,000 such engines a year, in a range of 1.5 to 80hp. But its tractor days are over.

HSCS

Hofherr-Schrantz-Clayton-Shuttleworth was formed in 1900, a combination of Hungarian interests and the English steam traction engine concern Clayton & Shuttleworth, which had a strong presence in eastern Europe. HSCS was wholly Hungarian-owned from 1912 and built its first tractor, a single-cylinder gasoline machine, in 1923.

The company was bought by Lanz of Germany in 1938, when HSCS concentrated on building the famous Lanz Bulldog tractor under licence. The Bulldog was very popular in Europe, and was also built in Spain, Poland and France as well as Australia. Its popularity stemmed from its simple semi-diesel two-stroke engine, a robust unit that could run on almost any type of fuel, including waste oil. (Landini of Italy built semi-diesel singles as well.) The basic Lanz design saw HSCS right through to the 1950s. In 1951 the concern was renamed Red Star Tractors, to suit the new political regime, and began using the DUTRA brand name in 1960.

By the 1960s HSCS had left its semi-diesel period far behind. Instead, it began to build far more sophisticated four-wheel-drive machines bearing the DUTRA badge. The DUTRA 2500, for example, was launched in 1967 with a twin-cylinder Csepel diesel engine producing 34hp. In 1973, HCSC/DUTRA merged with another Hungarian tractor maker, RABA, which built Steiger machines under licence.

Well named 'Le Robuste': HSCS tractors were designed to be strong and reliable, which they undoubtedly were.

The Huber 18/36, with transverse four-cylinder motor and longitudinal radiator. In this picture it is possible to clearly see the moving fanbelt and the PTO.

HUBER

Edward Huber was another true pioneer of farm tractors and actually built a batch of machines as early as 1898. They were powered by Van Duzen single-cylinder engines (Van Duzen had powered John Froelich's pioneering tractor of 1892), but suffered from unreliable ignition. Huber abandoned the project and did not return to tractors for over a decade.

Huber, like so many early tractor manufacturers, was a self-made man. Originally apprenticed to a blacksmith, he later invented a successful hay rake, set up a company to manufacture it, and later added threshers and steam engines. He was a prolific inventor and was awarded over 100 different patents.

In 1911, he made another attempt at a practical gasoline tractor; the Farmer's Tractor was more successful,with a twin-cylinder opposed engine of 311ci (5.1 litres). It was followed in 1912 by the slightly larger 13/22, still with a horizontally-opposed twin but rather more sophisticated, with a Pickering governor and full enclosure, apart from the chain final drive. That same year Huber's first big tractor, the four-cylinder 30/60, was unveiled. This was on a much larger scale: 1,230ci (20.2 litres), 8-ft (2.4-m) drive

It may look like a steam traction engine, but all Hubers were internal combustion-engined. Note the exposed steering gear and drive wheels.

Hurlimann built compact, technically advanced tractors that were appropriate for their native Swiss terrain.

wheels and 65-gallon (295-litre) fuel capacity.

But Huber didn't really make a success of its tractors until the advent of the little Light Four of 1917. From then on the company became wedded to four-cylinder engines. The trend in the 1910s was for tractors to be lighter, cheaper and easier to use than the monster pioneers: the Light Four weighed only 5,200lb (2359kg), while delivering a useful 12hp at the drawbar, 25 at the belt. It remained a part of the Huber line-up until 1928. Alongside it, Huber offered a bigger 15/30 engine in the same chassis, and the completely different 25/50 Master Four.

Unit construction arrived in 1926 with the Super Four 18/36, powered by an overhead-valve Stearns engine (four cylinders, of course) with force-feed lubrication. It was soon joined by the similar 20/40 Super Four, though this was found to be unusually modest in its power claims. Tested at Nebraska, it produced 32hp at the drawbar, 45 at the belt. The same thing happened in 1927 with the new 25/50 Super Four, which turned out an impressive 50/70hp, and was rapidly re-rated as a (still conservative) 40/62. (Many manufacturers were not as self-effacing as Huber in their power claims.)

The Modern Farmer-series was launched in 1931, in an attempt to capture a slice of the lucrative row-crop market, starting with a three-plough 30-hp model. It was replaced in 1937 by the Modern Farmer LC (tricycle row-crop) and L (standard-tread). There was also a smaller Model B in the late 1930s, another row-crop machine, this one with modern streamlined styling, electric starting and lighting.

Like so many other tractor makers, Huber had to cease production during the Second World War and failed to make a comeback afterwards, though it did survive as a maker of construction equipment.

HURLIMANN

Switzerland, despite its small size and mountainous terrain, has produced several tractor manufacturers, all of which produced small, low-profile, often four-wheel-drive machines that were suited to their environment. Buhrer, for example, began making tractors in the 1930s and was an early user of both diesel (1941), multi-range transmissions (1954) and powershift (15-speed Tractospeed, 1964). Vevey also started out in the 1930s, offering five-speed transmissions from the word go, and the choice of CLM two-stroke or Saurer four-stroke diesels.

Hurlimann pre-dated both these rivals by a few years, producing its first tractor in 1929. Like them, it was at the forefront of technical development, and in 1939 claimed to have built the world's first direct-injection four-cylinder diesel tractor. This was reintroduced as the D100 in 1945, with five-speed transmission, PTO, two-speed belt pulley and differential lock. It also produced a respectable 45hp (powerful in its day) and had a low centre of gravity, due to relatively small rear wheels. (The latter feature was important to Swiss farmers, who often had to work on steep slopes.)

In the 1960s, the company was one of the first European manufacturers to offer high-horsepower tractors, notably a 155-hp model using the company's own six-cylinder diesel. But the backbone of its range still consisted of compact four-cylinder tractors like the D-310 of 1975 and 5200 of four years later. The latter featured new squared-off styling; in fact, early 1970s Hurlimanns looked very similar to their predecessors of 20 years earlier. That same year, Hurlimann, which was already using its components, was taken over by SAME of Italy.

Hurlimann's current range includes the Prince compact tractors (25–42hp), mid-range XE (50–76hp) and the big XB.

INTERNATIONAL HARVESTER

International Harvester, for so long the biggest of the American tractor giants, was the result of a merger in which the McCormick Harvesting Company, the Deering Harvester Company, plus three smaller concerns, sought to acquire strength under a larger umbrella. Ironically, however, the company was often troubled by internecine rivalry between its fiercely loyal dealerships, many of which considered themselves to be part of the Deering camp, or the McCormick, but never both. But the new International Harvester Company was saved by its tractors, notably the little Mogul, the Titan, and the all-conquering Farmall. It is all the more unfortunate then, that the 1960s, '70s and '80s saw a steady decline until International Harvester was taken over by Tenneco, the parent company of Case, in 1984.

Cyrus Hall McCormick had patented his improved reaper a century and a half earlier, but it was 13 years before he began producing it in Chicago. McCormick was a native of Virginia, but like many other tractor pioneers had moved West, attracted by the developing farmland of the prairies. Cyrus died in 1865, but his son, Cyrus Jr., carried on to confront

The tractor that made International Harvester's fortune: the Farmall.

TITAN
MFD BY
INTERNATIONAL HARVESTER COMPANY
CHICAGO, U.S.A.
IHC
PATENTS
PENDING
T.V. 12400

their biggest rival, the Deering company. William Deering, a businessman who had invested in the Marsh Harvester company, began to engage in a sales war with the Deering Harvester Company's most bitter rival – McCormick. But even Deering could see that this was leading nowhere and conceived the idea of selling his company to McCormick in 1897. This came to nothing, but merger terms were finally agreed in 1902, when the companies joined to form International Harvester.

Both companies had already built stationary gasoline engines, but International Harvester didn't produce its first tractors until 1906. Even these were built for International Harvester by Ohio Manufacturing, primitive single-speed machines using Famous stationary engines of 10, 12, or 15hp. Improved tractors with gear drive followed in 1908, and International Harvester was sufficiently enthused to bring its tractor-building in-house. By 1910 it was selling big machines of 20, 25 and 45hp under the Reliance brand name, which was soon changed to Titan.

The mid-1910s saw a turning-point for International. Until then it had made a wide range of big, heavy tractors weighing up to 22,000lb (9979kg). Every model was made in small numbers, no more than a few hundred at most, but two new tractors – the 8/16 Mogul and 10/20 Titan – changed all this. They were small and light (the Titan weighed 5,700lb/2586kg, the Mogul 4,900lb/2223kg) and cheap enough to be affordable by many more farmers; moreover, they were far easier to handle than the 10,000-lb (4536-kg) behemoths previously on offer. They were instant hits; the little Mogul sold 5,000 in one year alone, surpassing International's entire production up to that point. So successful were the new babies, that International Harvester ceased production of all its old monster tractors to concentrate on just these two.

The reason two new tractors were produced was to satisfy those McCormick and Deering dealers, who, more than a decade after the merger, still insisted on having different tractors to sell, so that's what they got. The 8/16 Mogul was for the McCormick dealers, a simple twin-cylinder tractor that nevertheless was quite advanced for its time. The Titan was a twin as well, laid out like the Mogul, with its cylinders horizontal. It was much bigger, at 490ci (8.0 litres), and was provided with water injection to dampen down pre-ignition (pinking). Like many early tractors, the 20-hp Titan started on gasoline but ran on kerosene once the engine had warmed up. The big tank at the front of the tractor wasn't to hold kerosene, but water; instead of a radiator, the engine was cooled by radiated heat from this 35-gallon (159-litre) container.

The year 1917 was another turning-point for International. The United States Justice Dept. ordered that it consolidate its separate McCormick and Deering dealerships as it was breaking the anti-trust laws by owning so many outlets. From then on, each sales territory could have only one dealer to sell one brand of tractor: the International.

So the new 8/16 of that year became the first International. It was far in advance of the Mogul 8/16, reflecting just how fast tractor development was proceeding. Instead of two cylinders, it had four, running at a heady 1,000rpm. It had more efficient radiator cooling instead of a simple tank. There was a three-speed transmission, and at 3,660lb (1660kg) this 8/16 was 25 per cent lighter than the old one. Not only that, but the engine was covered by a hood and the new International boasted the first power take-off on an American production tractor. However, the 8/16 wasn't without its flaws, notably the riveted chassis and exposed chain drive, but it consolidated International's position as a major manufacturer.

International's big problem (as was every other U.S. tractor maker's of the time) was Henry Ford. First, the Fordson F was cheap, so cheap that International had to offer a free plough with every new machine merely to keep pace. Second, the Fordson was a genuine miniature of a full-scale tractor, with four-cylinder engine and completely enclosed transmission. It was therefore vital that International provide something similar.

In 1921, it did. The International 15/30 (soon rebadged as a McCormick-Deering, thanks to continuing dealer problems) was as up to date as a tractor could be for its time. The transmission was by gear-drive in an oil bath. Its four-cylinder engine had pressure lubrication and overhead valves, and the crankshaft had a lifetime guarantee. If the cylinder liners wore out, one simply removed them and fitted new ones. The chassis was of one-piece cast iron, more rigid than a riveted frame, to keep all those drive gears in alignment. It was relatively light, too (at

OPPOSITE
The lightweight 10/20 Titan (as well as the 8/16 Mogul) confirmed International Harvester's position as a major tractor manufacturer, with production now numbered in the thousands rather than the hundreds.

OPPOSITE
There was only a primitive cab for this early International Harvester; in fact, driver comfort was barely considered during the first 30 years of tractor design.

5,750lb/2608kg one-third less than the old Titan 15/30), and could easily pull a three-bottom plough. Best of all, it cost $1,250 – not exactly in the Fordson league, but cheap enough for many farmers. Over 128,000 were sold in eight years.

Two years after the impressive new 15/30, a two-plough 10/20 version was announced. This was really a 15/30 in miniature, with all the same advanced features. Instead of big brother's 381-ci (6.2-litre) engine, the 10/20's power unit was of 284ci (4.6 litres), still enough for 20-belt-hp. It was even longer lived than the 15/30, in production right up to 1942, by which time International had built 216,000.

These two tractors did International a great deal of good but better was to come. The Farmall of 1924 was the answer to a crying need. Until then, tractors had fallen into one of two categories. They were heavy and powerful for belt work or for pulling large implements, or light and nimble for cultivating row crops without damaging the plants. Few farmers could afford to buy two tractors, so the one they owned tended to be restricted to one type of task, leaving the others to be done by horsepower or by hand.

But the Farmall, as its name suggests, could do both. With 20-belt-horsepower it was meaty enough to drive a thresher or shredder, while 13hp at the drawbar was sufficent for a two-bottom plough. It also had a power take-off to drive binders and mowers. However, the Farmall could also tiptoe its way between delicate crops, thanks to high clearance, and had a wide rear-wheel spacing to straddle two rows, so both could be cultivated in one pass. At the headland, it could turn in its own length, with turning brakes and small, narrow front wheels. In short, this was the tractor that could square the circle – the Farmall really could do it all.

The farmers loved it, the press loved it, but there was just one problem. International Harvester management decided to hold production down, fearing that the new Farmall would damage sales of the standard-tread 10/20, which had about the same power and cost around the same to buy. In fact, International Harvester allowed only 200 Farmalls to trickle out of the works in its first year, and would only market it in areas where the 10/20 wasn't doing too well. Fortunately, the Farmall's enthusiastic reception persuaded them that it would be an even bigger success than the 10/20. And it was: over 4,000 were sold in 1926, and ten times that amount in 1930. They needn't have worried about the 10/20 either, because it went on selling as well as ever.

The Farmall had also established a new class of tractor, the general-purpose or row-crop. These were defined by adjustable wheel treads (the width between the wheels), high clearance, and nimble steering. Other tractors were 'standard-treads' with non-adjustable treads. So successful was the concept that other U.S. tractor manufacturers all rushed to build their own Farmall types: John Deere, Allis-Chalmers, Case, Oliver and Minneapolis-Moline soon had more powerful row-crops ready to roll, prompting an International Harvester advertisement of 1934: 'If it isn't a McCormick-Deering, it isn't a Farmall.' This underlined just how strong the Farmall brand was, universally recognized by farmers as a tough and useful machine. International would carry on using the name right into the early 1970s.

It had taken International Harvester seven years of experimentation to come up with the Farmall. And it took it another seven to offer a more powerful version, the F-30. Maybe there was more excuse this time; the company had been kept busy supplying the demand for the 10/20, Farmall and 15/30, which was upgraded to 22-drawbar-horsepower, 36 at the belt. There was another reason for the delay. The F-30 was quite new, much more than a Farmall Regular (as it was now called), with a larger engine slotted in. It did have a bigger motor, of course; in fact an extra half-inch on the bore gave a capacity of 284ci (4.6 litres) and despite a lower rated speed of 1,150rpm, the F-30 produced 20hp at the drawbar and 30 at the PTO. It was well-equipped, too, with a belt pulley, solid rim wheels (pneumatic rubber tyres later became an option on all the Farmalls), an adjustable radiator shutter, and regular or narrow tread. So far so good: but the F-30 turned out to be less popular than the Regular, for the reason that many small farmers didn't want a bigger Farmall at all, but a smaller, cheaper one.

The following year they finally got it. The Farmall F-12 was on a much smaller scale than the original, let alone the F-30. At 113ci (1.8 litres), its little four-cylinder engine was less than half the size of the first Farmall. International Harvester didn't make an engine small enough, so for the first couple of years a Waukesha unit was bought in until the company's own engine was ready. The F-12

201

MOGUL

was a featherweight 2,700lb (1225kg), 30 per cent less, but with the concept unchanged. The baby Farmall could pull a one-bottom plough and be adjusted to cultivate two rows at a time. One new feature that soon made its way onto the other Farmalls – in fact, all other row-crop tractors, come to that – was that the rear wheels were mounted on splines. Now the rear tread was adjustable by sliding the wheels in or out to allow for different crop spacings, making it a truly adaptable tractor.

The same year that the F-12 was announced, the Farmall Regular was renamed the F-20 and received slightly more power and better steering. But International hadn't forgotten its standard-tread tractors, the market for which was still sizeable. In 1932, the now elderly 15/30 was modernized by fitting the Farmall F-30's engine to produce the W-30. Slightly less powerful than its predecessor, with 20-PTO-hp, 31 at the belt, it was nevertheless cheaper to make. It also heralded a whole new range of W-series standard-tread machines. The W-12 was a

OPPOSITE
The little 8/16 Mogul was a huge success, with over 5,000 sold in one year alone

LEFT
The Farmall evolved and developed into many different models, with a major update in 1939. This is the mid-range, high-clearance HV.

standard-tread version of the F-12 Farmall, with a slightly more powerful engine.

There were bigger standard treads as well. Even the W-30 wasn't powerful enough for the big wheat producers of the Midwest, so in 1935 International Harvester announced the W-40 series. John Deere is often given credit for producing America's first wheeled diesel tractor, but International was there a decade earlier, though, in truth, the WD-40 wasn't a true diesel.

It was a hybrid that started on gasoline and switched over to diesel when warmed up, but diesel nevertheless, equipped with carburettor, spark plugs and a diesel injection pump. It was a big four-cylinder of 355ci (5.8 litres) producing 37hp at the drawbar, 52 at the PTO, which made it one of the most powerful tractors available. It was efficient too, at 14.69hp/hr per gallon. There was a pure gasoline equivalent, the WK-40, with a smaller six-cylinder motor of 298ci (4.9 litres), but that could only manage 9.88hp/hr per gallon, according to the Nebraska tests.

These were big machines: the WD-40 carried 31 gallons (141 litres) of fuel and 14 gallons (62 litres) of coolant. It weighed in at 7,550lb (3425kg). After a decade and a half of Fordson influence, when two- and three-plough tractors dominated the U.S. market, it looked as though the big wheat-processing tractor was back.

It is interesting to note that these standard-tread tractors – the W-12, -30 and -40 – were badged as McCormick-Deerings, while after the Second World War the Farmall was branded a McCormick Farmall: International hardly got a look in! The same

OPPOSITE
The big F-30 Farmall supplanted the original F-20 in 1931, and was soon joined by the smaller F-12.

LEFT
Alongside the row-crop Farmalls, International Harvester offered a whole range of standard-tread tractors, the W-series. These sold in smaller numbers than the hugely successful Farmalls, but had their own niche market. Some, like this WD-40, were powered by a unique diesel/gasoline hybrid engine.

The McCormick-Deering W-30: the International Harvester standard-tread tractors were still badged McCormick-Deering, while the Farmall name was reserved for the row-crop machines.

was true of the company's range of crawlers, which flourished in the 1930s to compete with Caterpillar. These were based around the power units of the 20-, 30- and 40-hp wheeled tractors, and carried the brand name TracTracTor. The smallest T20 was the most popular, being small and affordable enough for modest farmers, while the big TD40 used the WD-40's hybrid diesel/gasoline engine.

Meanwhile, the Farmalls got their first major facelift in 1939, though work had begun three years earlier, when industrial designer Raymond Loewy was brought in to give them a cleaner, more modern look. Many U.S. tractor manufacturers were doing the same thing at this time. Loewy certainly transformed the Farmall, enclosing the fuel tank, steering bolster and radiator in a single smooth housing unit. Even the wheels were restyled, and an orthopedic surgeon was hired to reshape the driver's seat. Farmall A was the first of the new generation, replacing the little F-14 (itself an update on the F-12) and adding adjustment for both front and rear axles. With 13hp, it was a one-plough tractor designed for single-row working, though there was a two-row B-model as well.

Later the same year, the new Farmall H replaced the F-20, with 19-drawbar-hp and 24 at the belt. It continued the Farmall tradition, but was more comfortable and roomy than the tractor it replaced. Finally, the M (33-belt-hp) did the same job for the F-30, but belied its size in being more nimble and easier to use than the old F-12. But the big seller, like the F-20 before it, was the mid-range H. Lighter and more comfortable than its predecessor, it was ideally suited to the thousands of 250-

Just like Dad's! But the Farmall Cub was no plaything; it was a genuine miniature Farmall that sold in large numbers. 'A Cub in size, but a BEAR for work,' as the advertisement said.

Eventually, the International badge replaced that of McCormick-Deering.

acre (100-hectare) American farms which then prevailed. And as tractor historian P.W. Ertel points out, it came along just as 200,000 original Farmalls were reaching the end of their working lives. As it turned out, nearly twice as many Hs were sold up to 1953, so there must have been a few conquest sales as well.

International Harvester's standard-tread tractors received the Raymond Loewy treatment as well, and were updated the year after the Farmalls. They sold in far smaller numbers than the phenomenally successful Farmalls, but still satisfied a market worth serving. So W-4 was the standard-tread Farmall H, and W-6 did the same for the M. For the first time there was a diesel option on the W-6, though the WD-6 didn't use a diesel/gas hybrid like the WD-40, but a straight diesel conversion of International Harvester's 248-ci (4.0-litre) four. It was 420lb (190kg) heavier and (more to the point for most farmers) cost 30 per cent more to buy. The real diesel takeover was still over a decade away.

There were few changes during the Second World War, but in 1947 International introduced a Farmall aimed at those for whom even the little A was too much tractor. The Cub was built along the same lines as all the other Farmalls, but with a tiny four-cylinder engine displacing just 60ci (978cc), and producing 7hp at the drawbar, eight at the belt. Far from being too small to be useful, the Farmall Cub proved to be what many farmers were looking for, and was soon outselling the A. Meanwhile, the A itself became Super A with an hydraulic lift replacing the pneumatic one, while the B was given more rear-tread adjustment and tricycle front end and renamed the C. A couple of years later a power boost to 16/21hp made it the Super C, while H and M took the same route in 1952, acquiring more power and the 'Super' tag. By this time, International's new factory at Doncaster, England was up and running, and would build thousands of smaller tractors right up to the 1985 takeover by J.I. Case.

Most of the major U.S. tractor manufacturers could point to one major technical milestone they could call their own: the three-point-hitch (Ford-Ferguson); pneumatic tyres (Allis-Chalmers); one-piece chassis (J.I. Case). International's was the powershift. Now, almost every tractor on the market has this feature, but in the early 1950s

The T20 TracTracTor was International's most popular crawler in the 1930s, small enough for farm and orchard work as well as construction.

OPPOSITE
The McCormick-Deering W-12 was produced from 1934 to '38, when it was replaced by the W-14.

BELOW
The Farmall name survived on row-crop tractors right up to the 1970s. This is a 1957 450, International's second biggest tractor that year.

tractors were restricted to simple car-type gearboxes, with between four and six forward gears. If a sticky patch was encountered when ploughing, it was necessary to stop the tractor to change down before attempting a restart.

International Harvester changed all that with the Torque Amplifier, a two-speed epicyclic gear mounted ahead of the standard gearbox. This had two big advantages: it gave a two-range transmission, doubling the number of ratios available, and shifting between ranges could be achieved without stopping or declutching. So successful was the TA system that within a few years all the major manufacturers had come up with their own versions. International Harvester fitted it first to the Farmall MTA, later extending it to the Super W-6 and Farmall H. The same year, 1953, it unveiled Fast Hitch, an alternative to the Ferguson three-point-hitch, with fast, easy mounting of implements. But like Case's Eagle Hitch, International Harvester was to learn that a three-point-hitch was the standard for which to aim.

But 1955 brought reorganization. International Harvester's entire line-up was renamed or numbered. The Super A was now the 100, B was 200, Super H became 300 and Super MTA 400, while the 600 was the big WD-9 standard-tread tractor. There were technical changes to justify the new numbers. All the Farmalls got power increases, with an ultra-low transmission called Hydra-Creeper available on the 200. The 300 got new streamlined styling, Torque Amplifier, a bigger 169-ci (2.8-litre) engine, Fast Hitch, and live PTO. Both it and the 400 also benefited from a new hydraulic system called Touch Control, with easier, more ergonomic operation.

An interesting new model, and a sign of the times, was the International 300 Utility (row-crop tractors were badged Farmalls, all the others were Internationals). Designed to compete with the Ford and Ferguson small tractors, this was mechanically identical to the Farmall 300, but with a lower profile and seating that made it ideal for front loaders and for entering low-roofed barns which the taller Farmall was not able to manage. In time, 'utility' tractors like this would become just as popular as row-crops, and later still the distinction between the two would become meaningless. As it was, even in 1955/56 the Utility 300 marginally outsold its Farmall equivalent. A Utility, incidentally, happened to be International Harvester's three-millionth tractor, built in April 1955.

Around this time, International promoted

McCORMICK-DEERING
W-12

The two-plough 10/20 was the most successful International prior to the Farmall. In a 19-year run, over 200,000 were made.

the Electrall as a safer alternative to belt or shaft drive off the PTO. A substantial 37.5-amp electrical generator was mounted where the PTO would have been, able to drive an electric motor on a baler, combine, or any number of other machines. Electrical wires were certainly safer than exposed spinning shafts or belts, but farmers didn't seem to appreciate this, and the Electrall option was dropped. In 1957, the entire line-up was mildly updated, the smaller tractors being renamed 130 and 230, the bigger ones 350, 450 and 650. Most were available as gasoline, diesel or LPG, reflecting the demands of the time.

Meanwhile, farmers demanded more power, and International Harvester responded in 1958 with six-cylinder engines for the new 460, 560 and 660 tractors. The 460 and 560 both used variations of the 263-ci (4.3-litre) six used until then by the TD-9 crawler, and which here came in diesel, gas or LPG form. It certainly had power (62hp in the 560) but this proved too much for the 560's final drive, which had remained basically unchanged since the 1938 Farmall M, and which only had half the power. Once out in the field, they began to fail, and International Harvester had to spend $100,000 redesigning the final drive and replacing damaged ones.

The Farmall's reputation had been damaged as well, which was a pity as the latest generation had other advances like integrated hydraulics, three-point-hitch and greater driver comfort. All this was to no avail; for the first time ever, John Deere sales surpassed those of International Harvester. In fact, according to P.W. Ertel, the failure of the 560 had been something of a turning point: it was '... the beginning of a progressive downward slide in International's fortunes that eventually culminated in the failure of the company in the 1980s.'

The 1960s was the horsepower decade, and International showed its determination not to be left behind with the 4300 four-wheel-drive machine. Designed to compete with the likes of Steiger and Wagner, it boasted over 180-drawbar-horsepower from an 817-ci (13.4-litre) turbocharged six-cylinder diesel, which was built in-house. It was a monster weighing nearly 15 tons that could pull a ten-

McCormick, International or Farmall? This D-430 appears to be all three. At least Deering has been dropped.

For 1976, the Pro Ag 86-series renewed the whole range of two-wheel-drive Internationals. The two-door Control Center cab was the greatest innovation, with acres of tinted glass, double-walled doors, and a high-tech ventilation system.

bottom plough with ease; but some said it was too big for most farms and only about 44 were made, most going to industrial users.

Perhaps a more crucial job for International Harvester in the early 1960s was to recover from the 560 debacle and win back the Farmall reputation for cast-iron reliability. As well as advances in its new mid-range tractors, the 404 and 504 (dry replaceable air filter element, and three-point-hitch with draft control), the company proceeded with an all-new range of big tractors to replace the 560/660. The new generation, unveiled in the summer of 1963, ranged from the 54-hp 606 Utility (six-cylinder gas or diesel) via the 72-hp 706 (which replaced the 560) to the 94-hp 806, which was International Harvester's most powerful row-crop tractor yet. The latter used a new 361-ci (5.9-litre) six-cylinder diesel that was rugged and long-lived. The transmission offered up to 16 forward speeds (four-speed gearbox, two ranges plus optional two-speed TA) and the driver now sat ahead of the rear axle on a well-upholstered seat. Front-wheel-assist was an option for the first time as well as (from 1965) a cab, which soon added an air-conditioning option.

The 94-hp 806 was impressive enough, but 100hp plus had already been achieved by rivals, so International Harvester had no choice but to follow suit. The 1206 of August 1965 used a turbocharged version of the 806's six-cylinder diesel, which punched out 113hp at the PTO, 98 at the drawbar. So powerful was the 1206, that an all-new transmission had to be designed for it, with specially hardened gears, heavier pinions, and final-drive gears. International Harvester engineers had evidently learned their 560 lesson well!

Perhaps it was memories of that troublesome final drive that led International Harvester to experiment with hydrostatic drive. It had been seen on the gas turbine HT-340 prototype; now the turbine had proved far too noisy and thirsty for tractor use, but its hydrostatic drive worked well. The principle is simple. The engine drives an hydraulic pump which sends oil at high pressure to hydraulic motors in each driven wheel. Fully automatic, it allows the driver to control both speed and direction with a single lever. Although less efficient than gear drive, it did give an infinite variation of speeds. International Harvester introduced the system in the 656 tractor in 1967, and so successful was it that hydro drive was extended to the 54-hp 544, 84-hp 826 and 112-hp 1026.

But International Harvester wasn't about to abandon conventional gear-drive tractors. The same year the 656 was launched, these were updated as the 56-series, ranging from a gear- drive 656 to the 1256, now with larger 407-ci (6.7-litre) turbo-diesel. The 1256 would be uprated again in 1969 as the 1456 with 132hp at the PTO; once again, the transmission was beefed up. Most of these tractors were still available in both Farmall row-crop and International utility formats. There were more driver features, such as two-post ROPS, a tilting steering wheel, and high-back seat with hydraulic suspension. A cab was still optional, but it was greatly improved in 1970 as the two-door Deluxe cab with optional heater or air conditioning.

International hadn't forgotten small utility tractors, and unveiled a new line in 1971, built at its Doncaster factory. The 32-hp 354, 40-hp 454 and 52-hp 574 were 'world tractors', designed to be sold in any market with only minor changes. All had the choice of gasoline or diesel power, three-point-hitches with draft control, and disc brakes. An eight-speed synchronized transmission and two-speed PTO underlined that these were not cut-price tractors, but simply big ones writ small.

Meanwhile, the U.S. end of the company hadn't been idle, and the same year saw the unveiling of the new 66-series. The same gear drive or hydrostatic drive choices were unchanged, but with longer-life clutch on the former and a new rubber-mounted cab with 40sq ft (3.7m²) of glass – not to mention a choice of radios and eight-track tape players. But more exciting than any of this was an all-new range of diesel engines designed for use in both trucks and tractors. The six-cylinder family ranged from an 85-hp 360-ci (5.9-litre) to a 133-hp 436-ci (7.1-litre) turbo. But even the latter was no longer enough to win the power race, especially when International Harvester heard that Massey-Ferguson was planning a V8 row-crop tractor. The company was fortunate in having a range of ready-made engines in its truck division, and for the International 1468 chose a 550-ci (9.0-litre) V8 that produced 145hp at the PTO. It was also remarkably economical at 15.6hp/hr per gallon, due partly to an injection system that switched it to four-cylinder operation when idling or with light loads. Under heavy load, all eight would operate.

Not that this was the most powerful

OPPOSITE
The 7488, the last big four-wheel-drive International, was affectionately known as 'Super Snoopy', owing to its large front overhang.

tractor to wear an International badge at the time. (The Farmall badge, incidentally, was finally dropped in 1973, after almost half a century.) Rather than build its own four-wheel-drive super-tractor in the 1970s, International Harvester bought a 28 per cent share in Steiger and acquired theirs instead. Actually, the 4366 did use some International Harvester components, notably the engine and final drive from a 1466, but it was assembled by Steiger, a four-wheel-drive articulated machine in the classic mould. A V8 was added in 1975 to produce the 4568; again the motor was International Harvester's own (a turbocharged V8 of 800ci/13 litres) but the tractor was built by Steiger. The arrangement worked well, giving International Harvester a 28 per cent share of the U.S. four-wheel-drive market in the mid-1970s.

The whole range of two-wheel-drive tractors was renewed in 1976 with the Pro Ag 86-series. Ranging from the 85-hp 886 to the 161-hp 1586, and including a 100-hp 186 Hydro, the Pro Ag's biggest innovation was its brand new cab: the Control Center. This still had two doors for easy access, but now with opening side and rear windows with 43.2sq ft (4m^2) of glass. The driver sat 18in (46cm) further forward than before, smoothing the ride, and there were double-wall doors and heavy rubber seals to keep out dust. A sophisticated ventilation system included a self-cleaning air filter. There were several other changes such as 85 gallons (386 litres) of fuel storage, while all the 86-series was covered by a two-year/1,500-hour warranty. The big four- wheel-drive tractors were restyled along 86-series lines, and became the 4386 and 4586.

That took care of the big and mid-range machines, but the small utility and row-crop tractors were renewed in 1978 with the 84-series. Still built at the Doncaster plant, but now with diesel engines from International Harvester's factory at Neuss in Germany, the 84s came in six basic models. Smallest were the 384 Utility with 36-PTO-hp and 484 with 42hp. There was a mid-range 584 (52hp) and 684 (62hp), plus a hydrostatic-drive Hydro 84, which was based on the 684. Finally, the 784, powered by a 246-ci (4.0-litre) four-cylinder diesel, offered 65-PTO-hp, but still in a fairly compact tractor. All of them used an eight-speed transmission (four speeds with a two-speed range), differential lock, and two-post ROPS. It said a lot for the 84 that it remained in production after the takeover by Case, well into the 1990s.

International's last major new model was the 2 + 2 line unveiled in 1979. Affectionately known as the Super Snoopy or Ant Eater, thanks to its protruding snout, the 2 + 2 claimed four-wheel-drive traction with two-wheel-drive manoevrability, thanks to full articulation. It married the standard rear half of a 86-series with a new front end-mounted engine ahead of the front axle, to aid weight distribution. Two models were offered, the 130-hp 3388 and 150-hp 3588, with a 170-hp 3788 added the following year. The 2 + 2 was certainly manoevrable, with a 15.6-ft (4.75-m) turning circle, tighter than many two-wheel-drive machines.

But International Harvester entered the 1980s in a weakened position. It was still second to John Deere in sales, even though a major strike in 1979 had lost it revenue, while a farming slump was about to hit the United States which had a disastrous effect on tractor sales. But the company remained bullish, investing millions of dollars in the new 50-series of high-powered row-crop tractors, not to mention the new 234, 244 and 254 compacts, an improved 2 + 2, and updated four-wheel-drives. The 50-series spanned the 135–185-hp range, and included an 18-speed fully synchronized transmission with new wet clutch. The new tractors could be easily identified by their massive, bright-red boxy looks, though engines were developments of the existing 400-series. So confident was International Harvester in its new tractor that the warranty was extended to three years/2,500 hours. A smaller 30-series, spanning 81–136hp, and with the same boxy styling as the 50s, was launched at the same time. The 2 + 2 was updated mildly as the 60-series and International Harvester contracted Mitsubishi of Japan to supply a range of compact tractors from 15–21hp. There were plans for an innovative transmission, too, combining both gear-drive and hydrostatics. The Vari-Torque, intended for the 50-series, promised to combine the efficiency of gear-drive with the variable speed of hydro.

But all this activity came to nothing. Despite selling its share in Steiger, International Harvester had run out of money, and in 1984 the agricultural equipment division was sold to Tenneco, parent company of J.I. Case. The old Farmall factory was closed, and the last International tractor rolled off the line in May 1985. It was the end of an era.

7488

Not all 86s had that plush cab. This 1486 was one down from the top-range 161-hp 1586.

Iseki didn't just build mini-tractors. This is a Big-T 115 and there was a six-cylinder T 125 as well.

ISEKI

Japanese tractors reflect the requirements of their own market, being predominantly small, compact machines suitable for small farms. Small Japanese tractors they may be but, like many Japanese products, they are well-engineered and extremely reliable. North American tractor manufacturers were quick to realize this, and many, such as Ford, began to import Japanese compact machines from the 1970s onwards, selling them under their own badges and colours. International Harvester, to give another example, also sold Mitsubishi tractors under its own name. In fact, it was rare for Japanese machines to be marketed in any other way in the United States, Kubota being the exception.

White was a little more honest, though. The Isekis it sold through its dealers in the 1980s were badged as White Isekis, and started with the three-cylinder 2-30 and 2-35,

Another home-market Iseki, but the tractors were sold in the United States as Whites during the 1980s and early '90s.

both of which were marketed up to 1984. Both these compact tractors used Isuzu diesel engines, producing 28 and 33hp respectively; the bigger motor measured 108ci (1.8 litres) and both tractors came with an eight-speed transmission but no cab.

ISEKI
TK
あなたのための、
実用派トラクタ。
ISEKI TKシリーズ
新登場!!
低コスト営農を強力にバックアップする、
エコノミータイプのトラクタTKシリーズ。
基本性能を磨き抜いた実用派ながら、
充実した本格装備が魅力です。
水田から畑、ハウス、酪農まで、
幅広い作業を能率よく
こなします。
TK33
ISEKI
TK33キャビン仕様機（33PS）
TK25 (25PS)
TK29 (29PS)
TK33 (33PS)

Bigger Isekis soon followed, notably the 2-45 and 2-62, still Isuzu-powered, but with four-cylinder diesels of 169ci (2.8 litres) and 219ci (3.6 litres). Power outputs reflected the badging, with 44 and 61hp, while both tractors had 20-speed transmissions. The biggest Iseki offered by White was the 2-75, sold in North America between 1982 and 1988. This was powered by a 75-hp six-cylinder diesel (Isuzu, of course), which measured 329ci (5.4 litres). Like all the White Isekis, it came without a cab.

In 1988 these bigger Iseki tractors were dropped by White in favour of its own American 60 and 80, but the smaller compacts were offered right up into the early 1990s, when AGCO assumed control and put an end to White's Japanese imports. But Iseki is a well-established manufacturer, and the loss of White's business was not a major blow.

In 2002 it continued to offer a range of compact tractors such as the utility TK546. This is one of the company's bigger machines, powered by a 48-hp four-cylinder diesel of 135ci (2.2 litres), with a two-speed PTO and 16-speed transmission (four-speed gearbox with four ranges). Hydrostatic steering and an air-conditioned cab are other features. At the other end of the scale, the TM217 is a small compact tractor with 17hp available from its 62-ci (1-litre) indirect-injection diesel. This is enough for a lift capacity of nearly half a ton and a road speed of 12mph (19km/h).

IVEL

This is thought to be the world's first practical small tractor. Dan Albone patented his 'agricultural motor' in 1902, and took it into production the following year. Albone, a native of Biggleswade in Bedfordshire, England, was an inventive man, as well as a champion racing cyclist. He produced bicycles (including the first 'ladies' frame), tandems, and even motorcycles.

His three-wheeled tractor was powered by a twin-cylinder horizontally-opposed gasoline engine, producing 20hp at 850rpm. It was simple and lightweight, scaling only 3,638lb

The Ivel: probably the world's first practical small tractor.

OPPOSITE
A new name in tractors, and a new concept. Construction machinery maker JCB wowed the tractor world with the Fastrac in 1991.

BELOW
High-speed road haulage was the Fastrac's big strength.

(1650kg), though the patent included an early type of power take-off, something that would be universal in all tractors within a few years. Named after a river near to its inventor's home, the Ivel tractor was to remain in production until 1920. Some, moreover, were reportedly built in America as well.

But Ivel was not destined to be one of the great tractor dynasties. Albone died in 1906, and without his guiding hand Ivel Agricultural Motors drifted into eventual receivership by 1920. But Dan Albone's legacy is clear. Even if his gasoline tractor had not been the first in the world, it was certainly the first in Europe, and presaged a new generation of small lightweight machines.

JCB

It was never Joe Cyril Bamford's intention to be a tractor manufacturer; even though his roots lay in farming, the English firm that bore his initials was famous the world over for its bright-yellow backhoe 'diggers'. He began by famously acquiring an old welding set for £1 (this was 1945) and built his first farm trailer largely from scrap and an old Jeep axle. Operating out of a lock-up garage in Uttoxeter, Staffordshire, he soon progressed to hydraulic tipping trailers, then hydraulic front loaders, the first of these fitted to a Fordson Major. On a sales trip to Norway in 1953, Joe spotted an hydraulic backhoe. He bought one, brought it home, and soon built his own, again fitting it to a Fordson. Combining both backhoe and front loader on one machine was an obvious next step and the JCB digger was born, soon to become a familiar sight on construction sites everywhere. It was a huge success, and by the time the company celebrated its 50th birthday in 1995, 18,000 had been built, more than half of them for export.

In the meantime, however, JCB was returning to its roots in agricultural machinery. Research on European farmers showed that most tractor work – in fact, up to 70 per cent – wasn't in the field, but on haulage or road work between jobs. The Fastrac was JCB's answer. Launched in 1991 (though the first prototype had been tested four years earlier), it was the first genuine high-speed tractor for many years and the first ever to be commercially successful. The key to its success wasn't just a 40-mph (64-km/h) capability on the road but all-round suspension and external disc brakes to keep this in check. The rear suspension was hydraulic and self-levelling, both longitudinally, to cope with the weight of rear

N665 GEH
JCB
SPLENDIMO
LELY
LELY OPTIMO 280 C

JCB
FASTRAC

JCB
JCB
FASTRAC 135
AND 155
• Proven draught work and PTO capabilities • 75kph (45mph) roadspeeds for haulage work
• New higher torque Perkins 6 litre, 6 cylinder engines offering either 135 or 150hp
• JCB Selectronic option allows pre-selection of gear range/direction • On and off road dual purpose tyres
• JCB Powersplit gearbox for instant 22% upspeed • Meets full legislation for on and off road use
S P E C I F I C A T I O N

implements, and from side to side for traversing steep slopes. The rear load deck could also take a 2.5-ton load, and power came from the Perkins 1000-series six-cylinder turbo-diesel, ranging from 115–170hp.

But at the same time, the Fastrac was a fully capable field tractor, able to pull a five-bottom plough, plus nearly 3 tons on the front linkage. There were front and rear PTOs, and of course four-wheel-drive was standard, with JCB's Quadtronic (which automatically switched between two- and four-wheel-drive, depending on need) appearing in 1996. Since the Fastrac was first unveiled, other manufacturers have produced their own high-speed tractors, imitation, as everyone knows, being the sincerest form of flattery.

JOHN DEERE

The story of John Deere is an extraordinary one. Alone among U.S. tractor manufacturers it survived a turbulent 20th century without merger, takeover or bankruptcy and remains one of the oldest companies in America. Moreover, for the first 50 years of its tractor production, it accomplished this with an apparently outdated twin-cylinder design when every major rival was progressing to fours and sixes. In 1960, however, it swept that half-century of tradition away with an entirely new line of four- and six-cylinder tractors, a bold move that could have ended in disaster. John Deere had the same interest in 19th-century farm machinery as International, Case and Massey-Harris, yet it was smaller than any of them, in spite of which, it grew to be the U.S. market leader, a position it held for

LEFT
The Fastrac was a huge success, capable of field work as well as road haulage. Its rationale stemmed from research that showed how tractors in Europe were used on tarmac for up to 70 per cent of their working day.

OPPOSITE
The Fastrac 1135 was a later variation on a theme.

OPPOSITE
The Waterloo Boy gave John Deere its entrance ticket to the tractor market.

BELOW
How it all started. John Froelich's machine was the world's first internal combustion-engined tractor.

decades. But at odds with this huge success as a tractor maker is the fact that Deere was a late, almost reluctant, entrant to the business.

John Deere, a blacksmith, was born in 1804 in Rutland, Vermont, the son of William Ryland Deere, an English immigrant tailor. By his late 20s the young Deere was married and specializing in tool-making, his shovels and hoes already renowned for their quality. But an economic slump left him in debt and John Deere, as so many before him, decided to head West in search of opportunity. He found it in Grand Detour, Illinois, setting up shop once again and sending for his wife and five children to join him. Many of the farmers there had originated in the east, and were finding the rich, heavy soil of Illinois difficult to work. It had a tendency to stick like glue to the cast-iron ploughs of the time, making it necessary to stop every few yards to turn the plough on its side and scrape off the glutinous mass.

John Deere discovered a solution. He designed a smooth steel ploughshare, suitably shaped, that would be self-cleaning, and built one out of a piece of broken saw blade. It worked, and was so successful that by 1847 Deere was making 1,000 ploughs a year. The following year, he built a new factory in Moline, on the Mississippi, better placed for supplies of steel and coal, which in 1853 churned out 4,000 steel ploughs. Three years later, the figure was 15,000 and John Deere was the undisputed 'Napoleon Plough Maker'. But he was getting older, too, and soon his eldest son Charles took over the day-to-day running, leaving his father to experiment in the workshop and farm his own land. In fact, members of the Deere family, either by blood or marriage, retained control of the company right through to 1982.

Despite this long-term stability, John Deere was not an industrial giant in the early 1900s. J.I. Case, International and Massey-Harris all made a huge range of farm implements, whereas Deere offered just five. There is little evidence that the company was tempted by epoch-making tractors either, probably because, unlike its bigger rivals, it had never built steam traction engines. It wasn't until 1912 that the company commissioned C.H. Melvin to build it an experimental gasoline tractor. The three-wheeled machine he designed was bi-directional, but was unreliable and lacked traction and the project was dropped. Joseph Dain (a member of the Deere board of directors) thought he could do better, and came up with a three-wheel, three-wheel-drive tractor using a four-cylinder Waukesha engine. However, the board was unenthusiastic and production was delayed until 1917. By then Dain had died, and without his support only a few Dain-Deeres were actually made. It eventually cost over $1,200, far more than the new Fordson, or for that matter, the twin-cylinder Waterloo Boy.

The Waterloo Boy was a descendant of the world's first internal combustion-engined tractor, designed by John Froelich in 1892. And it was to be John Deere's introduction to the tractor business. Froelich's tractor was crude but worked well, and a group of investors formed a company to build it. Unfortunately, the production machines (only two of which were actually delivered to customers) didn't work well at all and the young company switched to making stationary engines instead. The Waterloo Gasoline Engine Co. prospered, and in 1911 was joined by a man called Parkhurst, who brought with him three twin-cylinder tractors of his own design.

By 1914, this had developed into the famous Waterloo Boy, which would remain in production for ten years. It was always a simple machine, with its twin-cylinder horizontal engine, exposed gears, and rear-wheel-drive. The first Model R had just one

KEROSENE
WATERLOO BOY

OVERTIME

forward ratio, one reverse, and its engine measured 333ci (5.5 litres), producing 25hp at the belt, 12 at the drawbar. It was this mechanical layout, a twin-cylinder horizontal engine driving the rear wheels, that John Deere would adopt for half a century.

Meanwhile, the company needed to get into the tractor business. International Harvester was a giant by this time, the largest tractor manufacturer in the world, and also offered almost every type of agricultural machine one could imagine. There was a danger that if John Deere didn't expand as well, it would be swallowed up by International Harvester. So from 1911 the company began to diversify, buying up firms that made elevators, spreaders and hay-makers. Its own line of harvesters was launched soon after and it was clear that tractors would have to be next.

Waterloo was the obvious choice. Its tractors were well-established and successful: better still, the company was up for sale. So in 1918, John Deere bought it. By then, the Waterloo Boy had been updated as the Model N with a two-speed gear. No one could deny that there were lighter, more modern alternatives, but for $850 the Boy wasn't much more expensive than a Fordson. It was also selling well overseas. Britain, embroiled in the First World War, and prevented from importing grain by a German blockade, was crying out for tractors to boost home production of food. The Fordson was playing a key role, but Britain also bought over 4,000 Waterloo Boys, sold under the Overtime brand name. 'Overtime' had all the right connotations, suggesting hard work that suited a simple, reliable machine like the Waterloo Boy down to the ground. (An interesting aside is that the Irish distributor of Overtime tractors was an unknown engineer by the name of Harry Ferguson.)

As a means of getting John Deere into the tractor business, the Waterloo Boy had served its purpose, but its basic design stretched back over ten years at a time when tractor development was forging ahead by leaps and bounds. Compared with a Fordson, or any other small modern tractor, it was heavy and unwieldy. Fortunately, the Waterloo engineers already had a replacement on the drawing board which was brought into production as the Model D in 1923, just in time to take advantage of the recovery in tractor sales after the disastrous agricultural slump of 1921; Deere had planned to make 40 Waterloo Boys a day in the second half of that year, but ended up selling just 79 over the whole 12 months.

OPPOSITE
Waterloo Boys were exported to Britain and Ireland as Overtimes, sold for a while by Harry Ferguson.

BELOW
A non-starter: John Deere's own three-wheel-drive four-cylinder tractor of 1917 barely got off the ground.

RIGHT
The first true John Deere? Perhaps not: the first Model D had been designed by the engineers of the Waterloo Boy.

OPPOSITE
In response to the International Farmall, John Deere tackled the row-crop market, first with the GP (General-Purpose), then with Models A and B.

Like the Waterloo Boy, the Model D was powered by a twin-cylinder, slow-revving horizontal motor, but there the resemblance ended. The D was built around a modern unit frame, its two-speed transmission was fully enclosed, and the radiator was up-front, car-style. Like many early tractors, it started on gasoline, switching over to kerosene once it had warmed up or when the radiator was 'too hot to hold your hand on', according to the manual. Its 465-ci (7.6-litre) motor produced a useful 27hp at the belt and around 1,000 were sold in its first year. These were hardly Fordson-type mass-production figures, but enough to establish Deere as a serious tractor maker. In fact, the Model D was to be a huge success, for over a stunning 30-year production run (the longest yet for any tractor), 161,000 were built.

However, John Deere could not afford to rest on its laurels. Just as the Model D was getting established, International launched its Farmall, the tractor that could do both row-crop and haulage work: as the name suggested, it really could do it all. The Farmall made such an impact, and filled such an obvious need, that it became crystal-clear

JOHN DEERE
GENERAL PURPOSE

Like many tractor manufacturers, John Deere produced crawler versions of its wheeled models. This MC used the same twin-cylinder motor as the John Deere 'Johnny Popper'.

Left-side view of "MC" with turned-down orchard-type muffler.
JOHN DEERE
The "LITTLE GIANT" of the Track-Types
Low in first cost . . . Low in operating cost . . . Low in maintenance cost
The "MC" carries on, in full measure, the John Deere Tractor reputation for maximum all-around economy.
Osco Woodie of Scottsville, North Carolina writes: "On my farm, the "MC" pulled a heavy disk harrow 13 hours using only 11 gallons of gasoline."
H. T. Duncan of Concord, California, writes: "My 'MC' Tractor is really better than I originally expected because it develops so much power and my gas consumption is just half of what I used on my former tractor of similar size."
This is the saving the "MC" makes *on the job.* It does not include the lower maintenance costs which owners of John Deere 2-cylinder tractors enjoy.
Right side view of "MC." Regular track shoes are 12-inch. 10- or 14-inch shoes are available as extra; also 12-inch snow track shoes.

that every tractor maker would need to emulate it.

John Deere's version was the GP, which arrived in 1928: it actually started out as the Model C, but there was apparent confusion between 'C' and 'D' when dealers phoned their orders through! Mechanically, it was very similar to the D, though the 311-ci (5.1-litre) side-valve engine was significantly smaller, producing 10-drawbar-hp, 20 belt. It still had twin horizontal cylinders, of course. Its innovation lay in its wide, high-arched front axle, which enabled the GP to straddle a row of crops. This meant it only left two wheel tracks in the field (the Farmall left three) and could cultivate three rows at a time against Farmall's two. It also featured a mechanical power lift, by which implements could be raised or lowered by pressing a foot pedal using engine power. So popular was the option that it soon became standard. All the GP lacked, compared with a Farmall, was power and ground clearance. The first problem was partially answered by upsizing the twin to 339ci (5.5 litres), while the GP WT (wide tread) introduced a 76-inch (193-cm) rear tread and three-speed transmission. Now it could cultivate two rows or four, and the sheet metal was changed to improve visibility. Buyers also had a choice of wide front or twin-wheel tricycle front ends.

The GP could never hope to match the Farmall in terms of numbers sold, but 30,000 over its eight-year production run was quite respectable enough. Enough for John Deere to have joined the big league of agricultural machinery makers by 1929. With 21 per cent of the market it was second only to the mighty International Harvester.

But the company could have been forgiven for giving up in the few years that followed. The financial slump of 1929 had far-reaching consequences in that industrial output was halved in 1933. Wages and prices fell, and the numbers of the unemployed went through the roof. Inevitably, all of this filtered through to farming, and crop prices plummeted along with everything else. As if that was not enough, there were fierce droughts in 1930 and '34, while in Kansas and Oklahama strong winds blew away the top soil, creating the notorious dust bowls. Every tractor manufacturer cut back production and laid off workers. Production of the entire industry slumped to a low of 20,000, one-tenth the amount it had been just a couple of years earlier. Deere was especially hard hit, having recently begun to sell machinery to farmers on credit, many of whom were now growing barely enough to feed themselves; in fact, prices were so low that it just wasn't worth the effort to try to produce a commercial crop.

In the midst of all this, Deere boss Charles Deere Wiman (grandson of the first John Deere) ordered the rapid development of two new general-purpose tractors. It was a courageous decision which involved halting research on non-powered machinery, but it underlined the company's commitment to the tractor business. As it turned out, he could

At 410ci (6.7 litres), the three-plough Model G of 1939 was the biggest John Deere yet. In fact, it was the largest row-crop tractor available at the time.

JOHN DEERE

hardly have timed this better because by 1934/35, when the Models A and B were launched, a farming recovery was in full swing, largely due to the effect of President Roosevelt's New Deal.

All this had the effect of enhancing the growing reputation of John Deere tractors. By the mid-1930s, most rivals were using higher-revving four-cylinder engines or even smooth-running sixes. Deere stuck with 'Johnny Popper', the low-revving slogger. It might have been simple, but the John Deere twin had already endeared itself to thousands of American farmers: it was rugged and reliable, with the sort of low-rev lugging ability particularly suited to field work. Moreover, it invariably used less fuel than a higher-revving four.

So for the Model A, research chief Theo Brown and his team came up with an updated version of the same thing. Now with overhead valves, it produced almost as much power as the early GP, but with a slightly smaller 309-ci (5.0-litre) engine. It had 24-belt-hp, 16 at the drawbar, though it was still a very simple kerosene-burning engine, with cooling by a thermosyphon rather than a water pump. Not that the A (and the B) was outdated. Quite the reverse. In fact, John Deere's secret was to build several advanced features into a simple, reliable tractor: farmers trusted the simplicity but appreciated the new features, such as an adjustable rear tread, with the wheels able to move in or out on a splined axle. There was a hydraulic implement lift as well, another industry first, though not to be confused with the Ferguson three-point-hitch; the Deere version could only move implements up or

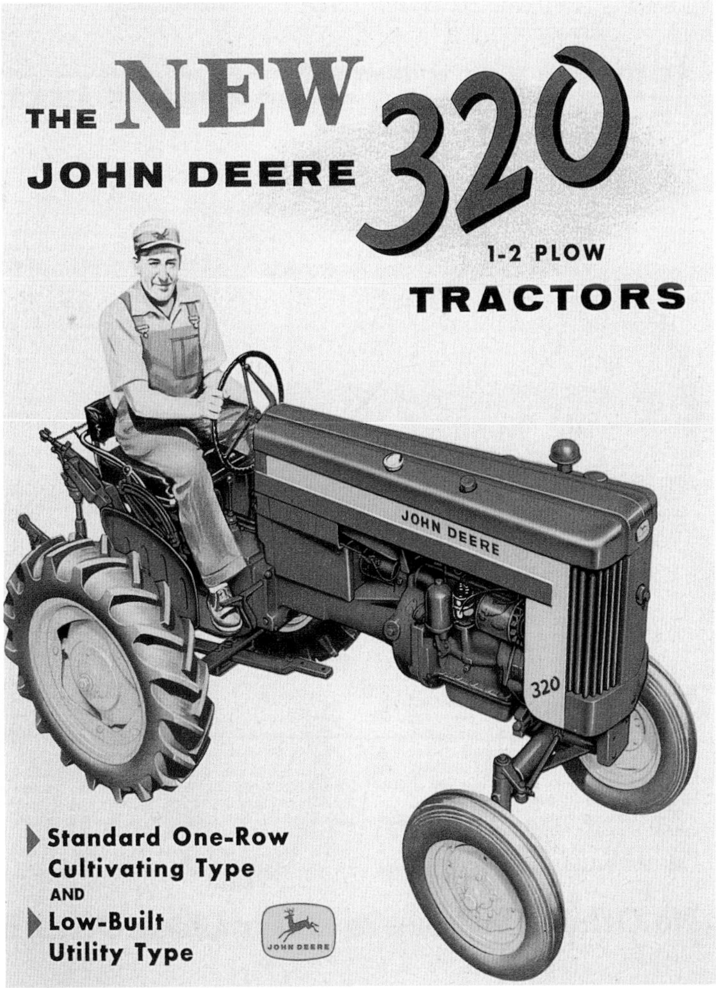

OPPOSITE
A marathon slogger. The original Model D was in production for 30 years.

LEFT
Post-war, all John Deere tractors abandoned letters for numbers: this little 320 was a new utility machine added in 1955.

down, and had no automatic draft control or sophisticated geometry. Meanwhile, the new rear axle gave extra crop clearance and allowed the inclusion of a centre-line-hitch and PTO.

The A was billed as a six-horse tractor, but there was still plenty of room for a smaller version equivalent to four horses. This was the Model B, launched the year after its big brother. It was a miniaturized version of the A, pure and simple, with all the same advanced features but with smaller dimensions and a 149-ci (2.4-litre) version of the new twin; it gave 14hp at the PTO, just under 10 at the drawbar. It was successful because over 50 per cent of American farms still consisted of 100 acres (40 hectares) or less, and tractors of this size

John Deere's first diesel, the big R, and its successor, the 80, were for years the most fuel-efficient tractors working in the United States.

made perfect sense in the circumstances.

Both A and B were general-purpose row-crop tractors, now the biggest selling category, though both came in a wide variety of guises. The B came as a BW wide front-end model, as a BO orchard tractor or BNH/BWH high-clearance machine. As was usual, there was an industrial version, the BI, and Lindeman Power & Equipment produced a crawler conversion, the BO Lindeman, that could also be had with pneumatic tyres, which the A soon offered as well.

As time went on, both A and B were treated to engine upgrades: the B went to 175-ci (2.9-litre), then 190-ci (3.1-litre), while the A was boosted to 321ci (5.3 litres). Both also received a six-speed transmission in 1941, while other conveniences such as electric starting were eventually taken on board. But a far more obvious change was the Henry

ABOVE
The Johnny Popper laid bare. The simplicity of these sturdy twin-cylinder John Deeres is easy to see, but their days were numbered.

LEFT
The 420 was an update of the 1952 40, which in turn was a development of the small Model M.

JOHN DEERE
830
DIESEL

There's a new John Deere 30 Series Tractor
FOR EVERY FARM—CROP—PURPOSE

Dreyfuss styling from 1938. Most tractor manufacturers were renovating their machines at this time – a trend begun in Oliver's sleek 70 in 1935, which itself was following a wider 1930s trend to make utilitarian objects such as trucks and refrigerators look part of the modern age.

Dreyfuss did his job well, clothing the John Deere A and B in smoothly squared-off sheet metal that looked both attractive and functional. It suited the twin-cylinder Deere down to the ground where swooping streamlining just wouldn't have been right. And it didn't just look good. The slimmer hood improved visibility, while a substantial front grille prevented the radiator from collecting debris. Dreyfuss's styling only spread slowly across the Deere range, due partly to the onset of the Second World War. In any case, the company was also busy making preparations to launch two more new tractors, the large Model G and smaller H. Both followed the same lines as the Models D, A and B, but on different scales. The G was a three-plough tractor, with about the same power as the recently uprated D (34/26hp) but weighing about half a ton less. At the time, it was the largest row-crop machine available; the familiar twin came in 410-ci (6.7-litre) form, the biggest yet. The little H, on the other hand, used the smallest-yet John Deere twin, at just under 100ci (1.6 litres) to give 15/13hp.

During the Second World War, the company was occupied with military work, making items as varied as tail-wheel assemblies for planes, mobile laundry units, and munitions. This had the effect of restricting tractor production, but John Deere emerged from the war with a brand new factory at Dubuque on the Mississippi. In fact, Dubuque (John Deere's peace dividend) was to produce

OPPOSITE
The 830 was the last of the John Deere big twins.

FAR LEFT
The 30-series: the final incarnation of the twin-cylinder John Deeres.

LEFT
Big row-crop tractors like this 4250 did much to see John Deere through the troubled 1980s.

JOHN DEERE
4320
DIESEL

its first new tractor after the war, the little Model M. Replacing the H, the Model M was a departure for John Deere in more ways than one. First, its twin-cylinder engine was mounted vertically rather than horizontally, and drove the rear axle via a shaft, rather than directly through gears. Second, it was a utility tractor designed to meet the Ford 9N head-on. As such, it was low and compact with adjustable axles – a cross between the traditional row-crop and standard-tread tractors.

John Deere's other new tractor of the late 1940s was another departure. The Model R of 1949 was the company's first-ever diesel and also the largest tractor it had ever built. The R was a genuine five-plough machine. Its engine was an upsized 416-ci (6.8-litre) dieselized version of the classic Deere twin, producing an impressive 51hp at the PTO, 46 at the drawbar. Not only was it one of the most powerful tractors available, it was by far the most fuel-efficient as well, setting a new record for fuel economy at Nebraska with 17.35hp/hr per gallon. Even by the standards of the 1980s and '90s, this was a very good figure indeed. Little wonder that over 20,000 Rs were sold between 1949 and '51.

Through the 1950s, the faithful twin-cylinder range was gradually updated. In 1952, all were renamed using a two-number system. The little Model M became the Model 40; B became 50, A 60, G70 and (a little later) the R became Model 80. Gasoline versions now had more power, thanks to a duplex carburettor; three-point-hitches with draft control became the norm, as did live hydraulics and PTO; there was power steering; and at last, the twin-cylinder engine acquired a water pump. A new 70 Diesel used a little V4 gasoline donkey engine to start it. More renumbering in 1955 saw '20' added: 40 became 420, and so on, while a small 320 utility tractor was added to the bottom of the range. Finally, two years later, the 30-series arrived, with minor convenience changes for the driver. The year 1959 saw the 435, powered by a twin-cylinder General Motors two-stroke supercharged diesel.

For all its attachment to the twin-cylinder format, and a fiercely loyal band of owners, John Deere knew that change was inevitable. In the 1950s, the horsepower war had been gathering pace, but farmers didn't only want more power – they also wanted better transmissions, more adaptable hydraulics and greater comfort. Sadly, two cylinders weren't enough any more – the scope for more power was limited – and their big torque pulses needed a heavy-duty powertrain.

A four-cylinder mock-up had been built at the Waterloo factory as early as 1950, but it was another three years before the official go-ahead was given to the start of work on a new generation of tractors. They would be almost completely new, modern enough to leapfrog ahead of the opposition and ready for launch in 1960. Above all, it was imperative that no one should know what was going on at John Deere.

And no one did. The design team was moved into an old grocery store in Waterloo, well away from the factory. The drawings that were made were sent out to job shops

OPPOSITE
In the late 1960s, the 20-series was the first major update on the ground-breaking four- and six-cylinder 10-series. As well as this 4320, there was the 122-hp 4520, John Deere's first turbocharged tractor.

LEFT
Much smaller, and much later, came the four-wheel-drive 2040S, but still in the same green-and-yellow livery as the original Waterloo Boy.

over a wide area, so that no one could put two and two together; they weren't even identified as coming from the John Deere tractor department! When the prototypes were finally ready for testing, a 684-acre (274-hectare) farm was bought a few miles south-west of Waterloo, well away from prying eyes. Even when the first production tractors were ready to be shipped out on trucks and rail wagons, they were concealed within large cardboard cartons. Consequently, the seven years of research, development and testing remained secret; when the New Generation was launched in August 1960, the assembled dealers were astonished to see an all-new line-up of tractors that resembled nothing that John Deere had ever produced before.

There were four of them. The 36-hp 1010 came with a four-cylinder diesel or gasoline engine and a five-speed transmission, and was available in a wide variety of forms. The 47-hp 2010 was similar, apart from its eight-speed Syncro-Range transmission, which allowed shifting between high and low ranges without stopping. The largest four-cylinder machine was the 59-hp 3010, which incorporated John Deere's new hydraulic system. This used one large pump to provide hydraulic power for the implement lift, power steering, power brakes and three remote

The company began to make its own four-wheel-drive super-tractors in 1970. This 7520 was an update of the original 145-hp 7020.

Throughout the 1970s and '80s, super-tractors were growing in size, power and sophistication. Expensive to buy and run, they nevertheless made savings on big farms in that they were able to work faster than conventional two-wheel-drive machines.

hydraulic circuits. But the big 4010 was expected to be the best-seller, at least in America, where the power race was proceeding apace. With a six-cylinder gas, diesel or LPG engine, 50 per cent more power was offered than the old 730 but cost only 18 per cent more to buy. A 121-hp 5010 joined the line-up the following year, the industry's first two-wheel-drive tractor with over 100hp. There was also the four-wheel-drive 8010, a 215-hp super-tractor that Deere had offered from 1959, bought in from Wagner, though this was less successful. The drive train simply wasn't tough enough, and both clutch and transmission regularly failed in service; all but one of the 50 8010s sold were recalled under warranty. Even rebadged as 8020s, it is thought to have taken seven years to get rid of the unwanted stock.

There were no such problems with the new in-house tractors. Despite a range on which 95 per cent of the parts were brand new, there were no recalls or redesigns. Only the two smaller tractors disappointed, though they were soon upgraded with more of the 3010/4010 features. They were also supplemented by new tractors from Deere's Mannheim, Germany factory. (John Deere had bought the Lanz plant in 1956 and like most of the major U.S. firms, was turning itself

RIGHT
John Deere's 3000-series covered the 55–85-hp lower-powered range. The 1990s dropped-nose look is now in evidence.

OPPOSITE
Specialist yard loaders were a new market in the 1990s, though John Deere's first offering, the 3400, was built for it by Matbro.

into a global business. It could now make tractors not only in France, Argentina, Mexico, Spain and South Africa, but also in Germany and North America.)

Meanwhile, there were regular updates across the range, such as an eight-speed powershift in 1963, allowing clutchless on-the-move shifting through all eight ratios. In 1968, the 4520 was John Deere's first turbocharged tractor, with 122hp from its 404-ci (6.6-litre) six-cylinder diesel. It was as powerful as the 5010's 531-ci (8.7-litre) non-turbo diesel engine. In order to put that power to the ground, it also had hydrostatic front-wheel-assist, a feature that later became optional on the smaller 3020 and 4020.

At the time, Deere was still working on a prototype two-wheel-drive tractor with 200hp: the X60, as it was designated, never reached production. The company also shied away from a full hydrostatic transmission (unlike International, which offered this feature from 1967), though it did make a prototype automatic transmission which combined infinitely variable speeds of up to 16mph (26km/h) with a three-speed manual shift. But although the 200-hp X60 had come to nothing, John Deere did launch its own large super-tractors in 1970, with four-wheel-drive and articulated steering.The 145-hp 7020 shared many parts with the standard machines.

The 1960s were good years for John Deere. Not only had the New Generation replaced the old without a hitch, but the company had also finally overtaken International Harvester as the largest U.S. maker of farm and light industrial equipment. The 1960 New Generation needed replacing, but to keep the momentum going, the company somehow had to recreate something with the same impact as the original. Some say it managed it in 1972 with Generation II, thanks largely to the Sound Gard cab.

Awareness of the need for safe, comfortable cabs had grown only slowly among tractor manufacturers. John Deere had pioneered roll-over protective structures (ROPS), offering them as an option from 1966, and making the patent freely available to all its competitors. Meanwhile, aftermarket cabs had become generally available during the 1960s; these kept the rain off, but tended to be noisy dust boxes the rest of the time. The Sound Gard cab was rubber-mounted to the tractor and had four-post ROPS built in. Quiet and comfortable, it was permanently pressurized to keep dust out, while a heater or air conditioning was optional. All-round tinted glass ensured absence of glare as well as good visibility, and underslung pedals, a seat belt, and adjustable steering wheel added up to a revolution in cab design. Despite its extra cost, three-quarters of buyers of the best-selling 4430 were willing to pay extra for Sound Gard.

It was an option on all the new 30-series tractors, which covered the 80-hp 4030, 100-hp 4230, 125-hp 4330 and 150-hp 4630. The latter three all used the same 404-ci (6.6-litre) six-cylinder diesel, in naturally aspirated turbo and turbo-intercooled forms

JOHN DEERE
3400

The compact 4500 was really a Japanese-made Yanmar, sold in North America wearing John Deere colours.

All mod cons. A 21st-century tractor interior would have been unrecognizable to the pioneers of 100 years ago.

Who'd have thought it? Only a few years after American-made small tractors seemed an impossibility, John Deere announced the U.S.-built 5000-series.

respectively. They all had the eight-speed Syncro-Range as standard, with a new long-life clutch and the wet-type hydraulically-operated Perma-Clutch. There were two tranmissions options: a straightforward powershift or a new 16-speed Quad-Range, which added a two-speed range to the Syncro-Range. As for the smaller tractors, these were increasingly composed of a mixture of Mannheim and Dubuque products.

In 1973, the 35-hp 830, 45-hp 1530 and 70-hp 2630 were added to bracket the 2030, using three- and four-cylinder diesels. These in turn were replaced a couple of years later by 40-series equivalents: 2040 and 2240 from Mannheim, 2440 and 2640 from Dubuque. The range of tractors sold only in the United States (let alone those produced for other markets) had by now become so complex that a year-by-year listing would constitute a volume in itself. Suffice to say that the 40-series covered the 40–70-hp class and were joined by an 80-hp 2840 in 1976.

At this time, John Deere was working on a high-powered gas turbine tractor. A 250-hp motor was actually built, but its problems of low torque rise, high fuel consumption, and cost of manufacture were never resolved and the 1973 oil crisis put paid to it once and for all. Instead, the company concentrated on conventional diesel power for the rest of the 1970s, and the big 40-series tractors of 1977 gave plenty of that. Now with larger 466-ci (7.6-litre) six-cylinder motors, they spanned the 90–180-hp range, with non-turbo, turbo and turbo-intercooling. Remember the big four-wheel-drives launched in 1970? These

LEFT and BELOW LEFT
The original 1992 5000s (this is a top-range 5510, added later, as well as a 10-series update) all came with three-cylinder diesel engines, nine-speed transmissions, and power steering. The 5510 is shown here in both high-clearance and cabbed forms.

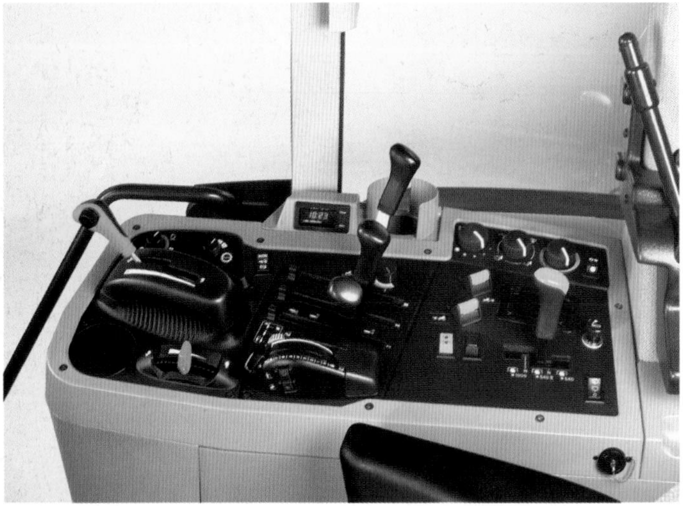

ABOVE
As tractors grow more complex, so do the controls to operate them.

RIGHT
More than ever before, ergonomics was playing a part in tractor design. Note the passenger seat in this John Deere tractor.

OPPOSITE
The 6420S was a development of the new 6000-series John Deeres, which were built in Mannheim, Germany from 1993.

had been gradually updated alongside the 4 x 2s, but in 1981 two new 50-series super-tractors were unveiled. The 8450 (225hp) and 8650 (290hp) were named the Belt Tightners. They were joined by the all-new 8850, powered by John Deere's own V8 turbo-diesel, and which pushed out 370hp at the crankshaft, 300hp at the PTO.

John Deere was fortunate to be in a strong position in the early 1980s, having invested in new plant, facilities and tractors. Nevertheless, the company did suffer during the decade when a sustained slump hit tractor sales in the United States, not to mention the rest of the world, as never before. The company lost money in 1986 and '87, while the workforce was cut by nearly half, which meant that over 27,000 people lost their jobs.

6000s were not only used for farm work; this 6620 also has an optional front loader.

But John Deere survived, and in better shape than many of its rivals. International was taken over by Case, while Allis-Chalmers closed down altogether. Deere, by contrast, ended the 1980s in control of over half the U.S. tractor market.

Slump or not, John Deere introduced the 50-series in 1982, the big row-crop tractors (each with 10hp more than before) starting with the 100-hp 4050, then 140-hp 4450, 165-hp 4650 and 190-hp 4850, the latter a new tractor rather than an update. There were several new features, such as castor-action mechanical front-wheel drive. Deere had offered hydrostatic front-wheel-assist since 1968, but a mechanical system offered more traction, combined with a tight turning circle in this latest guise. The big 4850 was also given a 15-speed powershift, optional on the smaller tractors, which were fitted with 16-speed Quad Range as standard. Sound Gard became quieter still, while Investigator II was an electronic system that warned of faults in any of the tractors' systems.

To match these big row-crop machines, an updated set of mid-range 50-series machines (the Efficiency Experts) covered the 45–85-hp range, from the three-cylinder 2150 to the six-cylinder 2950. These were all Mannheim-built tractors, but to fill the 40-hp class, John Deere imported a Yanmar machine in corporate colours and called it the 1250. Bigger Yanmars, a 50-hp 1450 and 60-hp 1650, were added in 1984. The 1650 set another new economy record at Nebraska, which had been held by the John Deere 720 since 1956.

Another Japanese import was the 25-hp Model 900, designed for cultivating single rows of flowers or vegetables. In fact, several specialist tractors were added to the range during the mid-1980s, such as the high-clearance four-wheel-drive 2750 Mudder and a range of wide-tread tractors designed for wide-row crops like tobacco: the 2350, 2550, 2750 and 2950. There was a low-profile 2750 aimed at orchard work, and the 95-hp 3150, whose mechanical front-wheel-drive engaged automatically when it was required.

The Mannheim machines were updated again in 1987, as the 55-series. There was no more power, but yet more specialists joined the range, such as the 2355N orchard/vineyard models. The transmission choice was bewilderingly wide, offering collar shift, TSS (top shaft synchronization), TSS with Hi-Lo

Originally a four-cylinder tractor, the 6000 was later supplanted by a six-cylinder 6900. This is the updated 6920.

The six-cylinder 7000s, built at John Deere's long-established factory at Waterloo, also came in for updates, in this case as a 7810.

For 1993, the new 7000-series became John Deere's upper-mid-range row-crop tractors, offering up to 170hp. Not that this set any records: the prototype 200-hp X60 had been built 25 years earlier.

(16-speed), TSS creeper (12-speed) or 8-speed collar shift with hydraulic direction reverser. The Waterloo-built 55-series, the big row-crops, didn't appear until 1989, described by author Don McMillan as 'the largest new product announcement in the history of John Deere'. There were six of them, all powered by a redesigned 464-ci (7.6-litre) six-cylinder diesel. For the first time, they offered a choice of wheelbase – 106- or 118-inch (269 or 300-cm) – from the 105-hp 4055 to the 200-hp 4955. The latter was Deere's first row-crop tractor to break the 200-hp barrier. In the John Deere tradition, it set a new record for fuel efficiency at Nebraska. It also had the 15-speed powershift as standard, while the smaller 55s all made do with the faithful 16-speed Quad Range and an electrohydraulic hitch control. Alongside the big 55s, the four-wheel-drive super-tractors were updated as well. Now tagged 60-series, they had a new longer wheelbase chassis and the choice of three new transmissions: 12-speed Synchro, 24-speed PowerSync with built-in Hi-Lo, and a 12-speed powershift. Power ranged from 200hp for the 8560 to 370hp for the Cummins-engined 8960. It is hardly surprising that triple wheels were optional.

John Deere made few model changes in the early 1990s; perhaps it was taking stock after having survived the toughest economic decade for tractor makers since the 1920s. But the '90s brought its own changes, one in particular that was quite unexpected. From the late-1970s onwards, building small and even mid-range tractors in the United States was becoming increasingly uneconomic. Every major manufacturer imported cheaper machines from abroad, rebadged them, and sold them as their own. John Deere, which owned a whole selection of worldwide plants, was able to take its pick. Apart from a brave but short-lived attempt by White to build 60- and 80-hp machines in the United States, it looked like the end of the sub-100-hp American-made tractor.

Except that it wasn't. During the 1990s, John Deere would start making smaller tractors on home soil again, gradually replacing the German imports, though Yanmar of Japan continued to build Deere's line of compact tractors. The 5000-series was launched in 1992, an all-new line-up built at a new factory in Atlanta, Georgia. The 40-hp 5200, 50-hp 5300 and 60-hp 5400 all had three-cylinder diesel engines, nine-speed transmissions and power steering. For the following year, the mid-range row-crop tractors, the 55-series, were replaced by the 6000/7000-series. Like the 5000s, these were almost all-new, though nine components were actually carried over. The four-cylinder 6000s came from Mannheim, the six-cylinder 7000s from Waterloo, covering a huge range, and kicked off with the 75-hp 6100, ending with the 140-hp 7800 – eight tractors in all – with Deere's own new range of diesels. All were topped by a new Comfort Gard cab, claimed to be the quietest in the world at 72dB(A). It also had 40 per cent more space inside than the old Sound Gard, and a 29 per cent greater area of glass. Transmission (including a 19-

The biggest row-crop John Deeres were renamed 8000 in the late-1990s, while the super-tractors became the 9000-series.

speed powershift and later the 20-speed PowrQuad), hydraulics, PTO and electro-hydraulic hitch were all new too.

But there was to be no rest for the Deere engineers. Next up for renewal were the big row-crop tractors, the 4000s. These became 8000s, with more power and a new 16-speed powershift transmission across the range. The 8100, 8200 and 8300 (160–200-hp) used the same diesel engine in different forms, and were topped by a new 225-hp 8400, powered by a new 496-ci (8.1-litre) engine. It also had front-wheel-assist as standard (an option on the others) and Field Cruise control could be specified as well. In 1996, the company diversified into telescopic handlers, unveiling the 4400. These specialized yard machines were increasingly taking over from general-purpose utility tractors for yard work, equally happy stacking bales as shovelling corn. The 4400 was actually built for John Deere by Matbro of Britain, a specialist in this type of machine. That same year, a six-cylinder variant of the 6000 was introduced, the 6605, with a range-topping 6900 following on later.

Deere had also noted the success of Caterpillar with its revolutionary rubber-tracked crawlers. In 1999, therefore, it offered a rubber-track option on the big 8000-series row-crops. So successful was this that it was soon extended to the articulated super-tractors which by now were labelled 9000s.

Meanwhile, the 6000 and 7000s received a new fully-automatic electronically-controlled transmission. Against all the odds, John Deere had survived a turbulent century independently, and had made it to the top of the pile. It could confidently face the 21st century with equanimity.

LEFT
Rubber tracks were among the options on the 21st-century 8000. However, this owner has stuck with conventional wheels and tyres.

BELOW
'Save fuel, increase traction, reduce compaction': this was the Holy Grail as far tractor owners were concerned.

SAVE FUEL, INCREASE TRACTION, AND REDUCE COMPACTION
Optimize your 9000 Series Tractor to tread lightly, and pull like a locomotive
It's easy. 1) Choose the right size dual or triple radial tires. 2) Add the correct amount of weight and balance it properly. 3) Inflate your radial tires to the new lower-pressure recommendations. With exclusive John Deere weight packages and tire options, it's a cinch. Studies conducted by Ohio State University and University of California, Davis, have proven conclusively that properly equipped tractors with correctly inflated tires will reduce compaction, increase productivity, and save fuel. Summaries of their findings are shown on the next page.
JOHN DEERE
9300

Keck Gonnerman, like John Deere, could divide its history into two- and four-cylinder eras. This tractor is from the latter.

KECK GONNERMAN

'Kay Gee' was based in Mt. Vernon, Indiana, where the Keck brothers, John and Louis, teamed up with Louis Gonnerman in 1873 to build steam engines, threshers and sawmills, diversifying into gasoline tractors by 1917.

They did not make the massive prairie tractors typical of the time, but offered a relatively small 12/24 instead. Similar in appearance to the contemporary Aultman-Taylor, this used a twin-cylinder engine of 531ci (8.7 litres) and cost $1,250. A slightly larger version, with a 7.25-in (184-mm) bore instead of the 12/24's 6.5-inch, gave 15/30hp, though it cost $400 more than the original. Like other tractor manufacturers of the time, Keck Gonnerman was forced to cut its prices to combat falling sales and the threat of the Fordson (by 1923, the 15/30 cost just $1,075 and should you require a canopy it would be an extra $25).

But the 15/30 was looking very outdated compared with the new generation of lightweight tractors. So in 1928 Keck Gonnerman announced a completely new range of modern four-cylinder machines. There was no attempt (which was probably wise) to compete with the Fordson end of the market, and the smallest of the new Keck Gonnermans was the 18/35, using a 382-ci (6.3-litre) Buda engine up to the 1935, and a larger Waukesha thereafter. Electric lighting and starting were optional.

Shorter-lived was the 22/45, which was soon re-rated as a 25/50. At 9,800lb (4445kg) it weighed nearly twice as much as its smaller brother, and the price was close to $3,000. Many of the major components were bought in, such as the Le Roi 606-ci (9.9-litre) four-cylinder motor, Ensign carburettor and Eisemann magneto. Finally, the biggest new Keck Gonnerman was the 27/55, which like the 22/45 was soon relabelled, this time as a 30/60. Maybe Keck Gonnerman was like Huber, inclined to be excessively modest in its power claims? Whatever the case, the 30/60 was a powerful machine, popular with sawmill operators. Production ended in 1937. According to historian Charles Wendel, Keck Gonnerman made little effort to promote its tractor line from then on, though the 18/35 ZW was produced up to the Second World War, when production was suspended and thereafter never resumed.

RACING.
THOROUGHBREDS
WITH A
SOFT TREAD.
190
Lamborghini

LAMBORGHINI

Ferruccio Lamborghini was building tractors long before he achieved fame with luxury sports cars. The story goes that he only went into the car business after an altercation with Enzo Ferrari. Lamborghini had complained that his Ferrari had a noisy gearbox, to which the great man riposted that Lamborghini should stick to making tractors! Lamborghini responded with his own line of luxury sports cars to rival Ferrari's, but his main business was still tractors, as it had been since the late 1940s.

Lamborghini came from a farming background but had also studied engineering at Bologna, and these two aspects came together after the Second War War. From 1947, in a swords into ploughshares operation, he used surplus ex-military hardware, of which there was to be an abundance in post-war Italy, to build tractors. Lamborghini managed to buy 1,000 Morris truck gasoline engines as power units, though some of these were converted to diesel using Lamborghini's own patented hot-bulb ignition.

Gradually, the ex-military percentage reduced, and the L33 tractor of 1949 assumed more Lamborghini content than ever before; the company soon began building its own transmissions as well. When the supply of ex-army Morris engines dried up, Lamborghini turned to German MWM and English Perkins diesels, before developing his own range of air-cooled engines in 1954.

But Lamborghini's ambitions lay beyond tractors, and by the early 1960s the company was also producing oil burners and ventilators – plus, of course, following Ferrari's put-down,

Ferruccio Lamborghini built tractors long before he turned his attention to luxury sports cars, but sold up to SAME in the late 1960s.

sports cars. Meanwhile, the tractor business was flourishing, with output up to 1,500 per year. But Lamborghini's confidence was shattered when a massive order from Bolivia for 5,000 machines fell through in the 1960s. Consequently, he sold up to SAME, the well-established Italian concern that had been making tractors since the 1920s.

Such takeovers often mean closure, but under the SAME wing, Lamborghini tractors enjoyed a new period of prosperity. Production of both wheeled and crawler tractors, with two-, three-, four- and six-cylinder air-cooled engines soon reached 5,000 a year and 10,000 by 1980. A new generation of thoroughly

There were narrow tyres and full spraying equipment for this Lamborghini 674.

modern Lamborghinis followed, and the respected badge now seems secure as part of the SAME/Deutz group.

LANDINI

Giovanni Landini never saw the tractors that bore his name. He had started out as a blacksmith's apprentice before setting up his own machine shop in 1884. The young Landini concentrated on making agricultural machinery at first, progressing to steam engines in 1911 and portable internal combustion engines six years later. He died in 1924.

But his sons carried on the business, and only a year after their father's death launched the first Landini tractor, a 30-hp machine using a *testa-calda* (hot-bulb) single-cylinder engine. Hot-bulb engines are often described as semi-diesels because they have no electric ignition system. But unlike full diesels, the fuel is ignited by a hot chamber in the cylinder head (the hot bulb), and not by engine compression. Hot-bulb engines ran on the two-stroke principle, and were fairly crude devices, though they could run on almost any combustible fuel and had the great benefits of simplicity and cheapness.

The Landini became the leading Italian tractor of this type, and power was gradually increased until the Super L of the mid-1930s offered '40hp normal or 48hp maximum'. The huge single-cylinder engine measured 744ci (12.2 litres) and was rated at 620rpm. By 1934, Landini was making 900 big singles a year, and employing 250 people.

Production resumed after the Second World War, but like other European manufacturers of big single-cylinder diesel-

Landini offered crawlers, such as this front-loader C135, as well as wheeled tractors.

type machines, Landini soon succumbed to pressure. The new generation of multi-cylinder diesel tractors was smoother and more powerful than any single. One by one, the European manufacturers threw in the towel: Lanz of Germany was taken over by John Deere; Marshall of England abandoned the tractor market altogether to concentrate on crawlers; and Landini would probably have perished but for Dr. Flavio Fadda.

Fadda negotiated a licensing deal with Perkins, and in the late 1950s quickly introduced a new range of Landinis, all powered by modern Perkins diesels built under licence by Landini itself. But the company still couldn't survive on its own and was taken over in 1960 by Massey-Ferguson, which found Landini attractive because it produced a range of crawlers which the Canadian-based company didn't have.

Landini bloomed under new ownership, now finding a ready market for its crawlers (a new range of which was launched in 1962) as well as its specialist tractors. Given its Italian origins, Landini was strong on vineyard tractors where Massey-Ferguson, with its U.S./North European focus, was weak. The company was slower to diversify into bigger tractors, but unveiled its first six-cylinder machine in 1977, which was also the first 100-hp-plus Landini. These had been predated by the 1973 6/7/8500-series, with 12-speed (plus four reverse) transmission.

There were more new launches in 1982 and 1985 with orchard and vineyard tractors, while 1988 saw the mid-range wheeled machines updated as the 60/70/80-series. Another update four years later resulted in

landini
blizzard 95
• power-flow Transmission
• landtronic Electronic Lift + Electro - Hydraulic Diff Lock
• Q - Cab
• Gearbox lateral levers

OPPOSITE
The Landini 9880. The company concentrated on single-cylinder tractors until the late 1950s, when it was saved by a new range of Perkins-powered machines.

FAR LEFT
Later Landinis, such as this Blizzard 95, still used licence-built Perkins engines.

LEFT
Landini's top tractor for the 1990s was the Legend, which came in 115-, 130- and 145-hp forms.

tractors such as the Blizzard 95, still with a licence-built Perkins diesel, a 4.236-litre non-turbo producing 80hp. Landini's high-power range through the 1990s was the Legend, offering 115, 130 and 145hp. All were powered by a six-cylinder Perkins of 385ci (6.3 litres) and all had four-wheel-drive.

Typical of Landini's mid-range in 2002 was the Mythos DT100, with a 243-ci (4.0-litre) four-cylinder Perkins turbo-diesel and a 30-speed transmission (five speeds, three ranges and two-speed powershift). By that time, Landini had a new owner, which in 2001 announced that it had bought the ex-Case-International Harvester plant in Doncaster, England to produce a range of tractors under the reborn McCormick brand. It looked as though the McCormick red and the Landini blue were set to form a new European partnership.

LANZ

It could be said that Heinrich Lanz of Mannheim, Germany, had been building the definitive European tractor for over 30 years. The semi-diesel, single-cylinder Bulldog was produced in huge numbers; in fact, over 200,000 had emerged by the time production ceased in 1956, built under licence in Austria, Spain, Poland, France and Australia.

The company had been making steam traction engines before it turned its attention to large multi-cylinder motor cultivators in 1911. However, it would be another ten years before the famous Bulldog appeared. With its crude but reliable hot-bulb two-stroke engine, the Bulldog was intended mainly for stationary work; its forte wasn't agility in the field, but simplicity, cheapness and reliability. The hot-bulb engine had been invented in England by Herbert Akroyd Stuart, and was

LANZ
15/30 HP
CRUDE OIL TRACTOR
TYPE HR 5
LANZ
UNRIVALLED
for economy and efficiency
SIMPLICITY
of design and handling
DEPENDABILITY
in service
ADAPTABILITY
to all kinds of work
PDE 1663 e

OPPOSITE

LEFT: The four-wheel-drive Landini 10000S.

RIGHT: A 1941 French advertisement for a Lanz Bulldog.

FAR LEFT

An advertisement for a Lanz Bulldog EIL HR9. The Bulldog was a popular choice for road haulage as well as field work

LEFT

The 15/30 used the same single-cylinder layout as the Bulldog.

BELOW

A Lanz HR8, showing the massive size of the semi-diesel single.

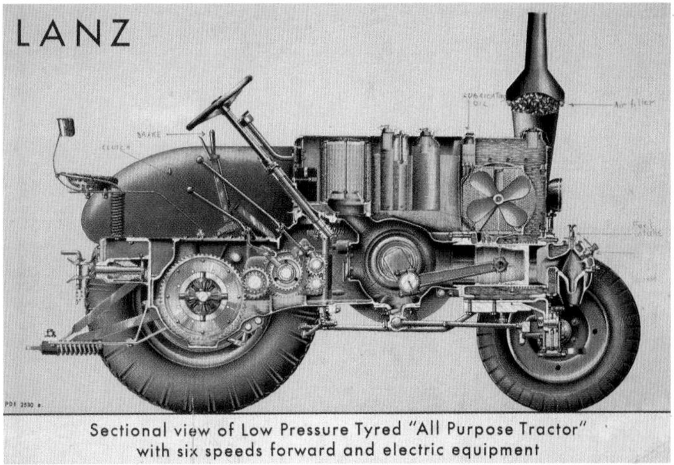

Sectional view of Low Pressure Tyred "All Purpose Tractor"
with six speeds forward and electric equipment

The Lanz Bulldog was built in France, Spain and several other countries, all under licence.

used in heavyweight tractors by fellow Englishman Richard Hornsby. But it was Lanz which popularized the form, whose other main advantage was that it could run on almost any combustible liquid fuel. It was started by playing a blow lamp over the hot bulb (the cylinder-head hot spot that ignited the vaporized fuel), then vigorously turning the starting handle which doubled up as the tractor's steering wheel, and which could be attached to a flywheel or steering column as required.

There were several different models of Bulldog using engines of between 380ci and 862ci (6.2 and 14.1 litres). An articulated four-

Lanz later built more conventional tractors, such as the one pictured here.

wheel-drive version, the Acker-Bulldog, was produced for three years from 1923; in 1926 the 19/24-hp Gross Bulldog was launched, which allowed a plough speed of 2–5mph (3–8km/h), or up to 9mph (14.5km/h) on the road. Radiator cooling was a great advance in 1929 with the 28-hp HR5 and 32-hp HR6, built up to 1935. After the Second World War, the final Bulldogs, built up to 1954, were semi-diesels, started on gasoline with a unique rocking-action electric starter.

Lanz was taken over by John Deere in 1955, which spelled the end of the Bulldog. Instead, the Mannheim factory began to produce conventional multi-cylinder diesel tractors, starting with the four-cylinder 300 (26hp) and 500 (31hp). The colour changed from Lanz pale blue to John Deere green-and-yellow; a twin-cylinder 200 and 10-speed 43-hp 700 appeared in 1960. The Lanz name was soon dropped, apart from its use in the home market, but the Mannheim factory thrives today, building tractors both for Europe and for export to North America.

The French Latil was primarily used for haulage, but with four-wheel-drive was also capable of field work.

Latil later abandoned tractors in favour of forestry machines, but it was long after this advertisement appeared.

LATIL

Although it could not be regarded as a household name, even among tractor enthusiasts, Latil of France was building four-wheel-drive tractors as early as 1914, and continued to do so right into the 1950s. With their truck-like bonnets and smallish, equal-sized wheels, Latils bore more of a resemblance to road vehicles than field tractors, which reflected their use, as Latil machines were as popular for road hauling and forestry work as they were for farming.

Georges Latil invented a portable engine pack in 1898 as a direct replacement for horsepower, which could fit between the shafts of carts or implements. His first four-wheel-drive tractor appeared in 1914, complete with four-wheel-steering. It was produced into the 1920s, and was put to a variety of uses, including agricultural conversions. Developments of the Latil, still with four-wheel-drive, were built in Belgium and England in the 1930s. In fact, England was still building Latils under licence into the late 1950s.

A typical 1930s Latil was the JTL, powered by a 183-ci (3.0-litre) gasoline engine with six-speed transmission. Like its predecessor, this looked more like a truncated truck chassis than a tractor, but with four-wheel-drive and various wheel options was a genuine five-plough machine. By the 1950s it had grown into the H14 TL, with a 342-ci (5.6-litre) diesel producing 45hp. There was four-wheel-drive and four-wheel-steering, of course, plus an eight-speed transmission. New features were two-way controls and two driving seats, so that the Navette, as it was called, could be conveniently operated in either direction. The company also made a reversible plough; at the headland, one disconnected, then moved the tractor to the other end of the plough and hitched up again for the return run.

Sadly, Latil failed to survive the 1950s independently, and was taken over by truck maker SAVIEM. It then lost interest in the agricultural tractor market and began to concentrate increasingly on forestry machines.

LEADER

There was more than one maker of Leader tractors in North America, but it is an odd fact that no machine was ever tested at Nebraska. The first company was based in Grand Rapids, Michigan. The Leader Gas Engine Co. was set up in 1913 as the result of a takeover of Sinz-Wallin of Grand Rapids and Midland Tractors of Detroit. The resulting Leader tractor didn't last long, however; it weighed 5,000lb (2268kg), and was powered by a horizontally-opposed twin-cylinder motor giving 12hp at the drawbar.

Next up was the Leader Tractor Manufacturing Co. of Des Moines, Iowa. Established in 1918, this had no connection with the previous Leader, and announced itself to be the successor to the Ohio Tractor Mfg. Co. By 1920, it was selling the 12/25-hp Rex tractor which bore a resmblance to the Huber Light Four. It was powered by a four-cylinder Waukesha engine of 326ci (5.3 litres) and weighed 5,600lb (2540kg); in 1920, one of these would have cost $1,800 ready to begin work.

Another Leader Tractor Manufacturing Co.

Leader, of Chagrin Falls, Ohio, offered this little Model D in 1950, powered by a 133-ci (2.2-litre) Hercules engine.

popped up 30 years later, this time in Chagrin Falls, Ohio, though it was also listed with a Cleveland address. This incarnation sold the little two-plough Model D, which weighed just 2,500lb (1134kg). Powered by a 133-ci (2.2-litre) Hercules four-cylinder engine, it was able to pull two 12-inch (30-cm) ploughs. A belt pulley and power take-off shaft were standard, but this attractive little tractor was never tested at Nebraska.

MAN

A quarter-century before it ever built tractors MAN (Maschinenfabrik Augsburg-Nurnberg, to give its full title) was the first company in the world to pioneer a diesel engine. How? Because it collaborated with Rudolf Diesel himself to build the first diesel in 1897. MAN went on to make trucks from 1915, and it was inevitable that the company should turn to diesel power, its first diesel trucks appearing in 1924.

That same year, MAN introduced a range of tractors, using similar four-cylinder diesel engines to those in the trucks. The company was no stranger to the agricultural market, having built motor ploughs in the early 1920s. But there was little demand for either these or the new tractors, and MAN abandoned the farm market after only a few years.

It made another attempt in 1938, this time with a tractor that was big and powerful for its time, the 50-hp AS250, though this had only been available for a short while before war intervened. MAN returned to trucks and military work, and also ran the Latil tractor plant in France as part of its contribution to the German war effort.

MAN did not start series tractor production until after the Second World War.

The MAN Ackerdiesel. Tractors were never a large part of the company's output; it sold these interests to Porsche in 1958.

After the war, it took MAN another five years to re-enter the tractor market, but it did so with machines that were more sophisticated and complex than the single-cylinder Lanz or Hanomag. The new generation of MANs had the option of two- or four-wheel-drive, which was most unusual at the time. It was soon being offered across the 1950s range of 25–45-hp machines. Bigger tractors followed, such as the 50-hp four-cylinder 4S2 (with four-wheel-drive, of course) on which a cab was optional.

But tractors were still a small part of the MAN concern, which concentrated on truck production. The company was looking for a way out of its tractor sideline, and in 1958 linked that part of its business to Porsche tractors. Four years later, Mannesmann, then owner of Porsche tractors, built the last MAN-badged tractor, 40,000 of which had been made since 1924.

MARSHALL

The Marshall tractor was Britain's contribution to the European tradition of simple machines powered by huge single-cylinder diesels. Marshall had been a successful maker of steam engines, and built it first gas tractor in 1908. Inspired by the German Lanz machine, in 1929 the company launched a new single-cylinder two-stroke diesel, the 15/30. Unlike the Lanz (or for that matter the Landini or HSCS diesels), the Marshall was a full diesel which ran on engine compression rather than a hot spot, so cold starting didn't involve playing a blow torch on the cylinder head. Instead, a lighted wick was used, followed by crank starting, and later cartridge or even electric starting.

Proudly advertised as 'All-British', the Marshall soon became a favourite of British farmers, and the chug-chug of its low-revving power unit (rated at 750rpm) was a familiar sound in the 1930s. A smaller 12/20 was also built, and in 1945 the original was restyled as the Series I. It looked more up to date, but under the skin this latest Marshall was almost identical to its pre-war cousin. As the 1950s progressed, Marshall (like Lanz, Landini and HSCS) would find its single-cylinder diesel increasingly outclassed by the smoother, more powerful four-cylinder opposition.

Marshall was almost as much a British institution as the Canadian-owned Massey-Ferguson.

OPPOSITE and BELOW Marshall persevered with the single-cylinder diesel layout in a vain attempt to keep up with the multi-cylinder opposition, but this was not to be. Updates, such as an hydraulic lift and electric start, weren't enough to save it.

But in the meantime it received regular updates. The Series II of 1947 boasted better brakes, new bearings and improved cooling, as well as larger rear tyres. But it still suffered from occasional transmission failures, despite bigger bearings. This was finally solved with the Series III, which had a substantially beefed up and redesigned final drive. Despite more changes to the engine (cooling system, lubrication, piston and fuel pump), the Series III still had trouble maintaining its rated 40hp for long periods. Finally, the Series IIIa of 1952 addressed the problem with a pressurized cooling system and other changes. An electric start was offered, as well as an Adriolic hydraulic lift and three-point-hitch. But the opposition was now cheaper as well as more powerful, and the truth was that the venerable Field Marshall was out of date. Supercharging was considered and rejected, but Marshall did build the bigger, more expensive 70-hp MP6 from 1954, powered by a Leyland six-cylinder diesel. But even this couldn't prevent the company from abandoning the tractor market altogether in 1957 to concentrate on crawlers. However, that wasn't quite the end of Marshall tractors; in the 1980s it bought the Leyland tractor business, rebadging the Leylands as Marshalls, and building them up to 1991.

There was a crawler version of the Marshall, based on the same mechanical layout.

A quarter of a century after it had ceased production, Marshall returned by buying up the Leyland tractor operation. This venture lasted for several years, and a range of two- and four-wheel-drive machines was produced.

MASSEY-FERGUSON

Massey-Ferguson, one of the best known names in tractors, was the result of a 1953 merger between Massey-Harris of Canada and Harry Ferguson Inc. The mercurial Ferguson had been in close contact with Massey-Harris for some time; with his agreement with Ford in tatters, he needed a new business partner to build his tractors for him, and this is where Massey-Harris came in. Famously, the Canadian management rejected the deal as too risky, but they soon realized that building a modern lightweight tractor with a three-point-hitch was not only risk-free, it was also essential for survival.

So when Ferguson returned in the early 1950s and suggested selling his Detroit factory to Massey-Harris, the Canadians went one better. They offered to merge Massey-Harris with the entire Ferguson operation which was now having tractors built in England as well as in America. In August 1953, the deal was done, and Massey-Harris-Ferguson (Massey-Ferguson as it was soon to be known) was born. But within a year, Harry had departed. The Canadians were unimpressed by the big Ferguson 60 under development in England, and saw Harry's role as president of the new company purely as symbolic when Ferguson was looking forward to real power. It was not the first time that Ferguson had fallen out with a partner; David Brown and Ford had both built tractors with him in the past, but both agreements had broken down. Harry Ferguson may well have been a genius, but he could also be irascible and domineering.

After buying out Ferguson's shareholding

One of the early models from the Massey-Ferguson regime: a high-clearance 65.

Actually a repainted Minneapolis-Moline, the 97 gave Massey-Ferguson a 100-hp tractor to sell until its own was ready.

for $15 million, the Canadian management found itself in charge of a potentially huge company, with plants on both sides of the Atlantic. Indeed, for a time, Massey-Ferguson really was the biggest tractor maker in the world. To underline the point: when Massey-Ferguson was taken over by AGCO in 1994, the U.S. giant found that its turnover had doubled.

However, this was the 1950s and all this was still in the future when the uppermost idea was to continue with both lines of Ferguson and Massey-Harris tractors built in Detroit, Canada and England. It was a bad move, as both companies specialized in small machines, though it has to be said that the advanced Fergusons were superior. There was a modicum of badge engineering, with some Massey-Harris tractors sold as Fergusons and vice versa, but no real rationalization. Worse still, Massey-Ferguson had no big tractor to offer; Ferguson's LTX five-plough 60 was a thoroughly tested prototype and an impressive performer, but the Canadians decided not to make it. The LTX had no row-crop tricycle version for the American wheat belt, and came with a specially designed Ferguson engine, though bought-in units from Perkins or Continental would have been cheaper.

But from 1957 things began to move forward. The range was rationalized, with the MF TO-30 (the old Ferguson TO-30) taking over at the bottom end of the range, while the MF 50 became an enlarged version of the Fergie 35. To complete the mid-range, a new MF 65 was announced, with a 50-hp Continental engine and six-speed transmission. It also offered a 12-speed

MASSEY-FERGUSON

powershift transmission called Multipower, which allowed on-the-go shifting between two ranges. And while the LTX may have been defunct, Massey-Ferguson had no intention of staying out of the big tractor market, so vital to sales in the United States and Canada. The fastest route was to buy in someone else's machine. Minneapolis-Moline supplied its beefy 75-hp Gvi in Massey-Ferguson colours, sold as the MF 95 Super. (All of this post-1957 generation, incidentally, came in the new Massey-Ferguson corporate colours of red bodywork and grey chassis, combining the old Ferguson and Massey-Harris colour schemes.)

Meanwhile, the 95 Super was serving its purpose, establishing Massey-Ferguson firmly in the American wheat belt, thanks to its 425-ci (7-litre) six-cylinder diesel. To fill the gap between the 95 and its home-built 65, Massey-Ferguson also bought in the Oliver 990, a 60-hp machine rebadged as the Massey-Ferguson 98. But these were only stopgaps, and in 1959 the company unveiled its own big tractor, the 88, which came with 60-hp four-cylinder engines in gasoline or diesel forms. Reflecting the company's American focus, there was a row-crop version, the 85, with adjustable front axle or tricycle front end. The market demanded more power than these two could provide, however, so until its own 100-hp machines were ready, Massey-Ferguson bought another Minneapolis-Moline, selling it as the MF 97. A 68-hp 90 in 1962, built by Massey-Ferguson itself, completed the range. By then, Massey-Ferguson had also taken over diesel engine manufacturer Perkins, thus guaranteeing its own engine supply.

However, the smaller tractors were beginning to look dated, which was addressed with the new Red Giants of 1964. Just like Ford and other manufacturers of the time, Massey-Ferguson was now designing tractors for world markets, and the new range, which replaced the old 35, 50 and 65, fitted this category well. In fact, the 135 used the same power units (Continental gasoline or Perkins diesel) as the 35, but added new styling, Multipower transmission, and auxiliary hydraulics for operating equipment off the tractor. The 150 was very similar, though the 165 had a bigger 50-hp 203-ci (3.3-litre) Perkins and 176-ci (2.9-litre) Continental. With the U.S. market in mind, both 150 and

ABOVE
Four-wheel-drive was an option on the 97.

OPPOSITE
Gradually, MF began to build its own big tractors, such as this 68-hp 90 of 1962.

MASSEY-FERGUSON 35

165 had a row-crop-friendly front end.

These U.K.-built Red Giants had big U.S.-built brothers, too – the 90-hp 1100 and 120-hp 1130. Both were powered by the familiar Perkins 354-ci (5.8-litre) straight six, with or without turbocharging. Even these weren't big enough to keep up with the Stateside power race, however, and as the 1960s progressed Massey-Ferguson fought to keep up. In 1968 the MF 1150 was basically a powered-up 1130, with a 135-hp Perkins V8. Moreover, Massey-Ferguson was not ignoring the growing market for big four-wheel-drive super-tractors, and was building its own 1200 in Canada. Initially, this used the Perkins six, but it was soon followed by the Caterpillar V8-powered 1500 and 1800, offering up to 171hp. These would be replaced by the big 4000-series in 1975.

The 1970s was the era of the quiet, comfortable cab; John Deere and Allis-Chalmers, to name but two, had already travelled this route and Massey-Ferguson did not intend to get left behind. New, quieter cabs were fitted to the 80-hp-plus tractors from 1971, many of which also received small power boosts. To signify this, and not to mention new styling, the 1100 became 1105, the 1500 1505, and so on.

The smaller machines followed suit in 1973, acquiring the same styling and a power increase. The entry-level 200-series (really an update on the 100-series Red Giants) kicked off with the 34-hp 230 and ranged up to the 82-hp 285. All were made at the Banner Lane plant in Coventry, England, while mid-range tractors were built at the Massey-Ferguson factory at Beauvais, France, and in Detroit.

MASSEY-FERGUSON
35X
TRACTOR
More power for the world's best selling tractor

OPPOSITE and LEFT
While it was busy building up the high-powered end of its range, Massey-Ferguson also carried on with the 35, a direct descendant of the all-grey Ferguson.

RIGHT
To fill the mid-range, Massey-Ferguson enlarged the 35 into the new 50, and added a 65 into the bargain.

OPPOSITE
Another rebadged Minneapolis-Moline, the 95 Super was based on the 75-hp Gvi.

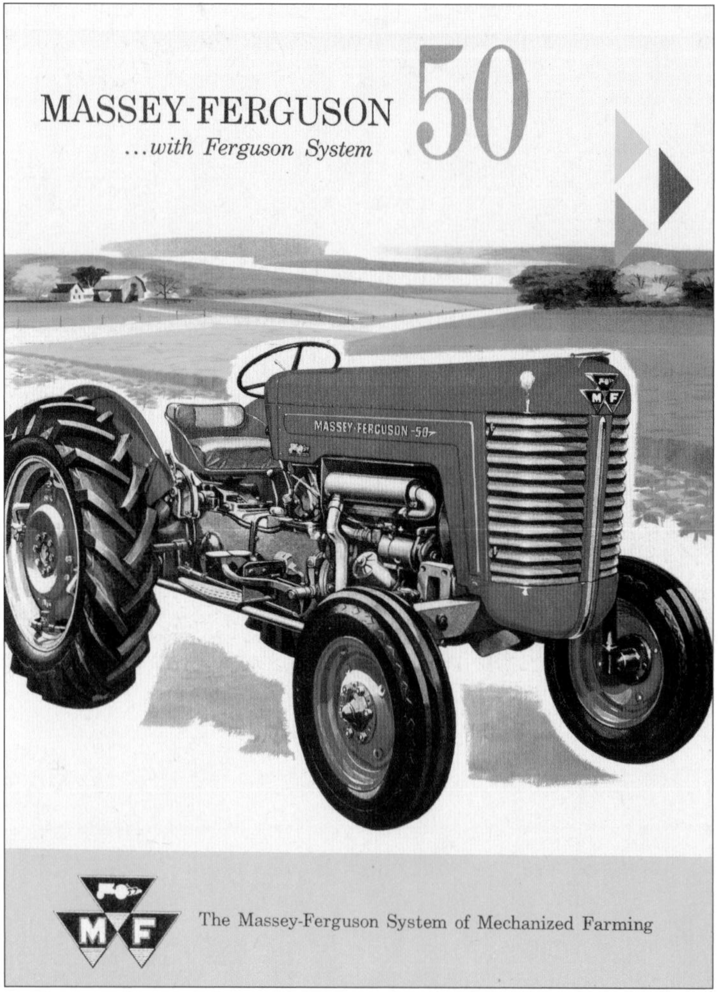
MASSEY-FERGUSON 50
...with Ferguson System
MASSEY-FERGUSON -50
The Massey-Ferguson System of Mechanized Farming

Landini tractors would soon be imported as well, while the biggest machines were still being made in Canada and the United States; Massey-Ferguson was a truly international company.

The Banner Lane-built 200-series was supplemented by the more modern 500-series in 1976 and covered the 47–88-hp range. This had an all-new cab on anti-vibration mountings with remote linkages. The hydraulics and Ferguson linkage were updated as well, and a two-speed PTO came as standard, as did hydrostatic power steering. Meanwhile, American farmers in particular continued to demand ever more powerful two-wheel-drive tractors, and Massey-Ferguson responded with the 160-hp 2770 and 190-hp 2800, soon upgraded to 166 and 195hp and renamed 2775 and 2805 respectively. Half a class down, the MF 2675, 2705 and 2745 replaced the old 1105, 1135 and 1155 in 1978.

But even the 195-hp 2805 wasn't powerful enough to compete with the biggest super-tractors, so for 1980 Massey-Ferguson abandoned Perkins in favour of a massive 903-ci (14.8-litre) Caterpillar V8 diesel. This gave 179hp in the new MF 4800, 211hp in the 4840 and 273hp in the range-topping 4880. A 324-hp 4900 soon followed, making Massey-Ferguson the horsepower market leader, at least for a while. Standard transmission on all of these was 12-speed, but an uprated version with three powershift ranges (18 speeds in all) was an option.

But these were not happy times for Massey-Ferguson which was hard hit by the early 1980s slump in U.S. tractor sales. It was obliged to close the factory at Detroit, the

MASSEY FERGUSON 95 SUPER

A pattern was developing in which the smaller and mid-sized Massey-Fergusons were built in England, while the big ones, like this 90-hp 1100, were produced in the United States, followed in 1968 by the 135-hp V8 1150.

plant that Harry Ferguson had built at record speed in 1948, after his quarrel with Ford.

But even in bad times, no manufacturer could afford to neglect the updating of its range, and Massey-Ferguson replaced the 1970s 500-series with the 600 in 1981. Although a joint English-French project, the 600 was built at Banner Lane and represented a move upmarket. It was launched as the 66-hp 675, 77-hp 690 and 88-hp 698 (there was no replacment for the lowest-powered 47- and 60-hp 500s). A 95-hp 699, powered by a six-cylinder Perkins diesel, joined the range at the other end. The cab was much improved, with better ventilation, was less noisy, and had the option of air conditioning, while there was a four-wheel-drive option right across the range.

All these high-tech luxury features may have given the impression that Massey-Ferguson was leaving its low-cost roots behind. After all, Harry Ferguson's dream had always been of a lightweight, simple, tractor, sold at the lowest possible cost. That role was now filled by the ageing but well-loved 200-series. It received some of the new 600-series features, and wasn't replaced until 1986 by the 300-series; but that too continued the tradition of simplicity and low price which was finding new appreciation in Third World markets. However, the range now extended up to the 104-hp 399 with the latest Perkins Quadram diesel, so maybe it wasn't quite so simple after all.

As well as helping to develop the 600-series, the French Beauvais factory was also designing tractors in its own right, its major contribution to the 1980s being the Topline 2000-series. Slotting in between the 600 and the bigger Canadian-built tractors, these offered from 110hp (as the 2640) to 147hp (2720), all using variations on six-cylinder Perkins diesels, with or without turbos or

Massey-Ferguson's 300-series of the late 1980s was a simpler, cheaper tractor than the more sophisticated 600. This is the top-of-range 399.

550
MF

intercoolers. All had a push-button-operated 16-speed transmission and four-wheel-drive, while electronic linkage control was added in 1985.

A lower-powered version, with many of the same high-tech features, soon followed, though it was confusingly named the 3000. All 3000s had electronic linkage control, from the 71-hp 3050 to the 107-hp 3090. A new feature was Autotronic, which offered some automatic control over the differential lock, four-wheel-drive, and PTO engagement. The optional Datatronic (if one could handle the modernist marketing hype) was a new driver information system, using electronics to digitally display a huge range of data in the cab.

Higher-powered versions followed in 1987 to replace the 2000-series. Power choices now went from 113 to 133hp (turbo) and 150hp (turbo-intercooler). But these only lasted three years before the entire 3000-range was replaced by the 3600. Perkins' latest six-cylinder diesel powered all but the top-model 3600, complete with Quadram system. This used a combustion chamber built into the piston crown, with four lobes to optimize fuel/air mixing. Perkins claimed that this would make for more rapid combustion and even out combustion pressure peaks, as well as boosting torque at low speeds. Actually, the highest-powered 3600 used a 180-hp Valmet engine; it was a rare occurrence for Massey-Ferguson to use a non-Perkins engine.

Meanwhile, transmission developments had been proceeding apace, and the 3600 needed more than its 18 speeds. It got them in 1992 with Dynashift. This mounted a four-speed epicyclic gearbox to the standard eight-

OPPOSITE
A Massey-Ferguson 550 doing duty as a boat trailer in France.

LEFT
Massey-Ferguson was unable to avoid the power race and responded with this 1150 in 1968, with Perkins V8 engine and 135hp. It was one of the last hot-rod two-wheel-drive machines.

The little MF135 came in a wide variety of formats, such as the narrow-tread vineyard model seen here.

speed transmission, giving 32 speeds in forward or reverse, 24 of which were shift-on-the-go. Moreover, there was no chance of the driver selecting low-range reverse at top speed on the road; if he did, the transmission electronics simply blocked it. Datatronic and Autotronic featured too, of course.

By this time, Massey-Ferguson was linked to AGCO. The new American giant, which only a few years previously had emerged from a management takeover of Deutz-Allis, bought Massey-Ferguson's North American arm in 1991. Three years later, it added more, and Massey-Ferguson has been one of the many AGCO brands ever since. But, as already noted, it was enough to double AGCO's turnover overnight.

Just as Massey-Harris had been forced to rationalize 40 years earlier, so also was AGCO. The plethora of tractors in the 85–180-hp class was replaced by just two

Slotting in beneath the 135 was this neat little 130.

PÖTTINGER
362

Through the 1980s the 300-series carried on as Massey-Ferguson's straightforward, no-nonsense machines. The 362 is pictured opposite, the 365 on the left.

In the late 1970s, no major manufacturer could afford to be without a four-wheel-drive super-tractor. This was Massey-Ferguson's offering, the Canadian-built 1250, powered by a Perkins six-cylinder diesel.

lines: the 6100- and 8100-series. The first covered the 86–111-hp range, with 16-speed Speedshift transmission as standard and the 32-speed Dynashift remaining an option. The 8100 carried on up to 180hp, taking over where the top 3600s had left off. Datatronic was updated as Datatronic II, now offering up to 22 functions, including four memories, a print-out, and cost analysis. Meanwhile, the big 4 x 4 super-tractors were dropped altogether; AGCO didn't like the idea of them competing with its existing big tractors. This didn't mean that Massey-Ferguson was barred from the 200-hp plus tractors, however; the 9240 of 1995 was a 215-hp machine with four-wheel-drive and a Cummins diesel engine.

The smaller tractors had to wait until 1997 to be renewed, but when this happened the 4200-series marked a distinctive break with the older Banner Lane-built tractors. Massey-Ferguson claimed that 70 per cent was new or redesigned over the 300-series, and the new tractor certainly looked different,

Made in Beauvais, France, the 3000-series was launched in 1986 as a lower-powered version of the high-tech 2000.

MF
MASSEY - FERGUSON
3090
datatronic

OPPOSITE
Massey-Ferguson's 3090 was the top model of the original 3000 range, with a 107-hp power unit and Autotronic, which gave some automatic control of the differential lock, four-wheel-drive, and PTO engagement.

LEFT
The 4300-series is the last tractor range to be built at Massey-Ferguson's Coventry plant before it is due to close in 2003.

RIGHT and OPPOSITE
In 2003, 4300 production is due to be transferred to Massey-Ferguson's Beauvais plant. In 4365 guise, it is powered by a four-cylinder Perkins engine of 245ci (4.0 litres) and 95hp. Transmission is 24-speed with two-speed powershift and powershuttle.

4365
MASSEY FERGUSON

MASSEY FERGUSON
4240

with its big glassy cab and 1990s sloping nose. There was an extensive range, from the 52-hp three-cylinder 4215 to the 75-hp four-cylinder 4235 and 110-hp six-cylinder 4270. All were Perkins-powered, while transmission options included a basic eight-speed shuttle set-up on the sub-85-hp models and a 12-speed shuttle or 18-speed Speedshift on the bigger ones. Four years later, the 4200 was updated as the 4300, now covering the 50–120-hp range. It still used a three- four- and six-cylinder Perkins engine, though now with extra torque and able to meet the new generation of tough emissions legislation. There were new controls for the

OPPOSITE and LEFT Massey-Ferguson's 4200-series preceded the 4300, and in the 1990s offered a huge range of 52–110-hp and three-, four- or six-cylinder Perkins diesels. Pictured here is the export 4240 (opposite) and the U.K.-market 4325 (left).

RIGHT and OPPOSITE
Post-AGCO takeover, the bigger Massey-Fergusons were represented by the 6100- and 8100-series, covering 86hp upwards. This is an updated 6270 with four-wheel-drive.

6270
MASSEY FERGUSON
AMAZONE

RIGHT
Some of the last Massey-Fergusons to await completion at Banner Lane, Coventry.

OPPOSITE
LEFT: Much of the 4200-series tractors was aimed specifically at haulage duties.

RIGHT: Meanwhile, the bigger 6280 could easily cope with implements at both ends.

transmission and electronic linkage control, plus a Supercreep transmission allowing speeds as low as 1mph (2km/h).

But sadly, it looked as though the 2002 4300-series would be the last new tractors to be built at Massey-Ferguson's Banner Lane plant in Coventry. Tractors bearing the Ferguson badge had been produced by this factory for over half a century, but AGCO was adamant that Britain had become too expensive a base for manufacturing. Nor was it part of the European Community common currency, another factor which persuaded AGCO to concentrate its European production in Beauvais in France. The intensely patriotic Harry Ferguson would have been far from pleased.

RIGHT and OPPOSITE
The 8260 (right) and 8240 (opposite) were late 1990s updates of the 8100, Massey-Ferguson's replacement for the high-tech 3600. As well as Autotronic, it featured Datatronic II, which allowed electronic monitoring of 20 different functions, with four memories to cope with different drivers. There was a new wet clutch, new front axle and a chassis reinforcement frame.

8240

RIGHT
The transmission of the 8100 (later 8270 shown here) was an electronically-controlled 32-speed forward or reverse, with four-speed powershift.

OPPOSITE
The 240-hp 9240 was launched in 1995, the first fruit of Massey-Ferguson's takeover by AGCO. It was based on AGCO's own White range, but with a Cummins aftercooled diesel and rear axle made by David Brown.

MASSEY FERGUSON
9240

MFG. BY M.D. PRESS CO.
1 MI. SO. YENROUGIS BELTWAY
SIGOURNEY, IA. 52591
STROBEL BROS. GMC
45-90
BULL PULL
45-90

MASSEY-HARRIS

Canada's best known and most successful tractor manufacturer, Massey-Harris came about as the result of a merger. Daniel Massey and Alanson Harris were close rivals, building mowers and binders in the mid-19th century for the huge Canadian market. However, they made the sensible decision to merge in 1891, and Massey-Harris was born. Unlike some other mergers in the tractor industry, this one seems to have been relatively painless, and the two companies integrated smoothly to create the largest machinery manufactory in Canada.

Although the intention was to produce a full range of agricultural products, it was 20 years before Massey-Harris built its first range of gasoline engines.

There was still no sign of a tractor, however, and when in 1915 the company finally launched one, it was bought in from outside. The Bull Tractor Company of Minneapolis produced the Big Bull, an unusual three-wheeler with one large drive wheel, front steerer, and small outrigger wheel. The Big Bull, which was light by contemporary standards at 4,500lb (2041kg), and could claim an impressive 24hp at the belt, was marketed by Massey-Harris in Canada. Unfortunately, it failed to live up to its claims and was a flop and Bull tractors soon went out of business.

Massey-Harris tried again in 1918 with the Parrett tractors. These had been designed by Dent Parrett of Illinois who was no manufacturer, but had had the machine built for him by Independent Harvester of Plane, Illinois. Massey-Harris agreed to have the

OPPOSITE and LEFT
The Bull Pull 45-90, part-restored, with massive four-cylinder engine and imposing appearance. Massey-Harris distributed this tractor from 1915 but it was not a success.

MASSEY-HARRIS

OPPOSITE
The Massey-Harris No.2, a 12/22 tractor with enclosed gear drive.

LEFT
The Massey-Harris No.3 was larger, rated at 15/28hp from its 397-ci (6.5-litre) Buda four-cylinder engine. Both tractors were soon outdated and too expensive and Massey-Harris dropped them in 1923.

MASSEY-HARRIS
Pacemaker

OPPOSITE
The Pacemaker, an update of the same U-frame concept that Massey-Harris had used since 1928.

LEFT
The Massey-Harris four-wheel-drive GP was advanced but flawed: it had excellent traction, but a clumsy turning circle and non-adjustable tread widths.

tractor made in Canada as well and agreed to take care of the distribution, while the Parrett would carry the Massey-Harris badge.

Parrett's design was far more conventional than the Big Bull. Again, it was a lightweight, but had four wheels and a four-cylinder engine with two-speed transmission. Initially, it came as the 12/25-hp No.1, later updated as the 12/22-hp No.2, with enclosed rear-wheel gears. Either would run on gasoline or kerosene. There was also a bigger No.3, rated at 15/28hp due to its 397-ci (6.5-litre) Buda four-cylinder engine. So far so good, but Parrett's original design dated back to pre-1914, and at this time tractor development was forging ahead, with the result that the Parrett/Massey-Harris was beginning to look extremely dated when compared with younger, cheaper rivals. Sales were disappointing and Massey-Harris was obliged to drop the Parrett in 1923.

But it would be third time lucky: while all this was going on, the machine that would finally give Massey-Harris its successful entrée into the tractor market was already on sale. The Wallis Tractor Co. of Racine, Wisconsin, was building an advanced little machine called the Wallis Cub, with a steel U-frame forming a light and rigid unit-construction chassis. After three years without

Challenger

OPPOSITE
The Challenger was a great success, a conventional row-crop machine that used the same U-frame construction that Massey-Harris had acquired along with the Wallis Cub in 1928.

LEFT
The sleek six-cylinder 101 was an all-new tractor in 1938, replacing the Wallis-type U-frame with a cast-iron chassis.

a tractor, Massey-Harris negotiated to market the Wallis in Canada. The arrangement worked so well that Massey-Harris took over the entire Wallis concern in 1928, and within a year all Wallis tractors were badged as Massey-Harris products and selling well.

There was now no stopping Massey-Harris, and it launched its first in-house design in 1930. It was audacious, clever, but flawed, and with hindsight, over-ambitious. This was the era of the general-purpose tractor, machines that were small and agile enough for row-crop work but with enough power for useful drawbar duties as well. International had pioneered this concept with the Farmall, and every rival had followed suit. But where these were all conventional high-clearance machines with two-wheel-drive, Massey-Harris's General Purpose could hardly have been more different. It had four-wheel-drive (not a new idea, incidentally, as 4 x 4 tractors had been tried 20 years before) through equal-sized wheels, and the rear axle was able to tilt independently to follow undulations. Powered by a 226-ci (3.7-litre) Hercules engine with high crop clearance and a choice of tread widths, the GP seemed to be an innovative variation on the general-purpose theme.

Unfortunately, it was nothing of the sort. Tractors in the Farmall mould required agility above all else, and this the Massey didn't have; its driven front axle made for an

One of Massey Harris's smaller post-Second World War tractors was the 22 of 1948. It was a larger-engined update of the 124-ci (2.0-litre) 20.

What every happy farmer and his dog needs: a Massey-Harris 44.

unwieldy turning circle, and although it was possible to specify tread widths between 48 and 76 inches (122 and 193cm) to suit different crops, these weren't adjustable, so that whatever adjustment a new GP left the factory with could not be altered. The GP did prove useful for specific jobs, such as forestry, where its four-wheel-drive paid dividends, but as a rival to the Farmall it was a non-starter.

Not that Massey-Harris need have worried. Its range of Wallis-based tractors was proving a great success. It initially came in two sizes – 12/20 and 20/30 – and the latter was updated as the Model 25 in 1932, with more power. Four years later, Massey-Harris

RIGHT
The 44 was a huge success for Massey-Harris, with a 260-ci (4.3-litre) engine that was available as gasoline, distillate, LPG or diesel, and a five-speed transmission.

OPPOSITE
The Massey-Harris 33 replaced the 30 in 1952, filling a gap in the range as a heavy three-plough tractor. It included a diesel option.

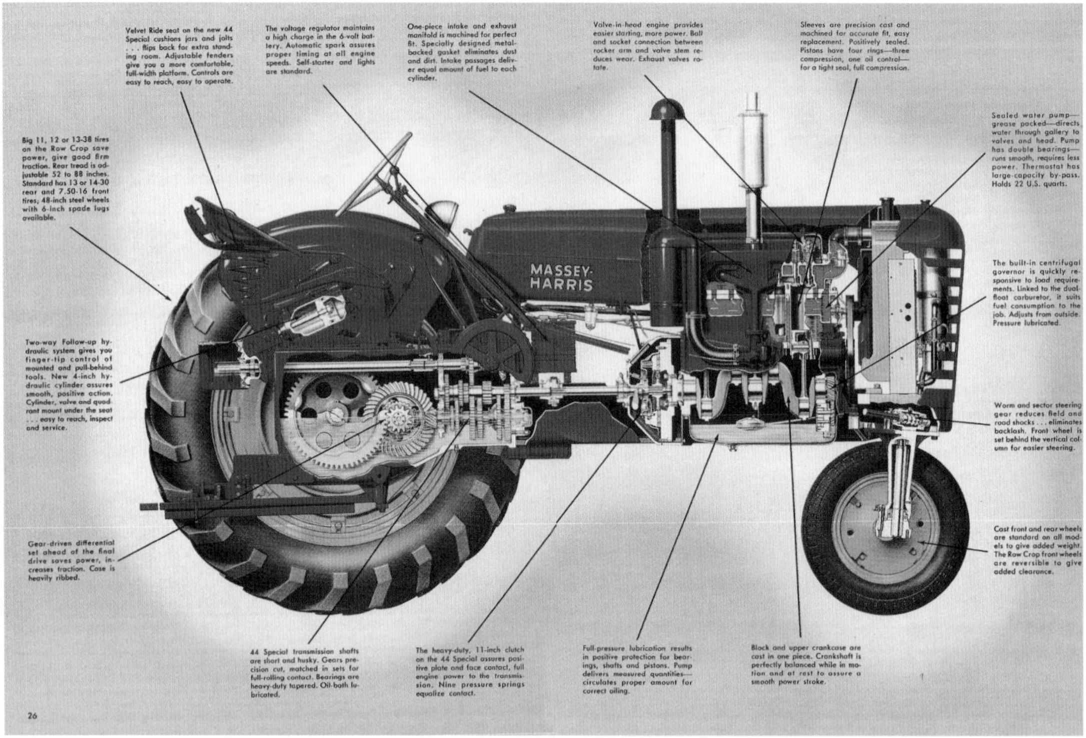

updated the concept for its second attempt at a row-crop machine. The Challenger of 1936 fitted the bill: it used the 12/20's 248-ci (4.0-litre) engine and U-frame chassis, but had narrow front wheels and an adjustable rear track. With a useful 24/32hp and weighing a modest 3,700lb (1678kg), the Challenger proved a good performer. It was updated in 1937 as the Twin Power Challenger, with two-speed PTO (1,200 or 1,400rpm) and there was a standard-tread version, the Pacemaker.

With the Big Bull and Parrett now distant memories, Massey-Harris tractors developed fast. For 1938, the completely new 101 was unveiled. This did away with the old Wallis U-frame, substituting a heavy cast-iron chassis instead, though the transmission and rear axle were still an integral feature. The exciting part was a smooth six-cylinder Chrysler motor of 201ci (3.3 litres), giving 31hp at the belt (36hp with the higher of the Twin Power speeds engaged) and 24 at the drawbar. There was a four-speed transmission and modern streamlined styling, and the 101 came in both row-crop and standard forms. The following year it was joined by the smaller 101 Junior, with a 124-ci (2.0-litre)

MASSEY HARRIS
33
MASSEY HARRIS

RIGHT
One of the last of the Massey-Harris-badged tractors, the 555 was a mild update of the big 55. Alongside it, 44 became 444, with a two-range, ten-speed transmission.

OPPOSITE
Another view of the Massey-Harris 44, which was also available as the six-cylinder 44-6, powered by a 226-ci (3.7-litre) Continental unit.

MASSEY-HARRIS
miracle-powered 555
gives big jobs the full power treatment

four-cylinder Continental and 16/24hp. The year after, with the Second World War making material supply increasingly difficult, the big Model 25 was replaced by the 201, with 57-hp 242-ci (4-0-litre) Chrysler engine, 202 (60-hp Chrysler) and 203 (64-hp diesel). That same year, the 101 received a power boost as the 101 Super, and the little 81 was launched as a lighter, cheaper version of the 101 Junior.

Once peacetime had returned, Massey-Harris continued with updated versions of its pre-war tractors. So the new Model 20 was based on the 81, and the 20/30-hp Model 30 replaced the 101 Junior, with 162-ci (2.7-litre) Continental and five-speed transmission for the bigger two-plough class. Meanwhile, the 101 was replaced by another Massey-Harris success story: the 44. A three/four-plough machine, the 44 utilized a five-speed transmission and offered a choice of four- or six-cylinder engines (of about the same power), first as gasoline or distillate, with diesel and LPG options following on. Like its predecessor, it came in row-crop or standard form. There was also a bigger 55, continuing the Model 25 tradition and aimed at the wheat belt of North America. In 1947, a new baby tractor joined the range in the form of the little Pony. With just 8hp at the drawbar, 10 at the belt, this was a single-plough machine that weighed only 1,520lb (689kg). By now Massey-Harris had strong links with Europe and the Pony was also assembled in France with SIMCA or Hanomag diesel engines.

Despite their frequent updates and power boosts, however, the Massey-Harris tractors were beginning to look increasingly outdated. Crucially, they lacked the hydraulic three-point-

MASSEY
HARRIS
44
MASSEY HARRIS

hitch with which Harry Ferguson and Henry Ford had revolutionized tractor design from the late 1930s. Neither did they have live power take-off or live hydraulics, which Massey-Harris's compatriot Cockshutt had pioneered. Oddly, Massey-Harris management had turned down the chance to build Ferguson's advanced little TO-20 for him in the late 1940s, which must have been all the more galling as more and more rival tractors followed the Ferguson/Ford path.

Fortunately, a second chance came when Harry Ferguson approached Massey-Harris again in 1952, offering his U.S. manufacturing arm for sale, to which the president of Massey-Harris responded by suggesting a full merger instead. Ferguson agreed, and in August 1953 the new Massey-Harris-Ferguson company was announced. Logically, this should have meant dropping the outdated smaller Massey-

Harris tractors, replacing them with the Ferguson, but the intention was clearly to carry on with two separate lines, with some rebadging here and there to fill the gaps in each range. Massey-Harris, after all, had only the year before produced a new three-plough tractor, the 33. So Massey-Harris red-and-yellow tractors continued to roll off the production line, with extra power for the renamed 44 Special in 1953, and dual-range transmission making it the 444 in 1955. The 33 got the new transmission as well (becoming 333) and the big 55 became 555.

But it was soon clear that the dual-line strategy wasn't working. In fact, the newly merged company was in such dire straits that it decided to approach John Deere to ask for a takeover. Deere declined. But against the odds, Massey-Harris survived, but only after its restructuring into Massey-Ferguson in 1957. The old red-and-yellow tractors were dropped, and a new line-up in red-and-grey Massey-Ferguson colours, with Ferguson technology dominating, was launched. This turned the company round; as part of Massey-Ferguson, Massey-Harris was effectively heading one of the biggest tractor manufacturers in the world.

OPPOSITE
LEFT: My little Pony. Massey-Harris launched the 8/10-hp Pony in 1947 to compete with other small tractors. It was not a great success.

RIGHT: The Pacer was in the same mould as the Pony, but was no more successful.

LEFT
Massey-Harris tried again with the Mustang, but none of these small tractors had an hydraulic three-point hitch with draft control, which by the early 1950s was essential in order to be competitive.

744PD.
MASSEY-
HARRIS
HAM 7

OPPOSITE and LEFT
Massey-Harris made tractors in Britain as well as Canada and France. The 744PD (opposite) and 745 (left) were at first built in Manchester, later at Kilmarnock in Scotland. The 744 used a six-cylinder Perkins, the 745 a four.

The Matbro was a specialized yard shunter and loader that left conventional tractors free for other work.

MATBRO

In an era of big, capital-intensive farms, some farmers could afford to buy an expensive piece of equipment and keep it for just one task. In the 1990s a new type of tractor, the specialized yard shunter, came to the fore, of which the Matbro was a good example; it would never see field work, but it excelled at yard duties, which included shovelling grain and lifting straw bales.

The specification reflected this. The front loader could lift over 2.5 tons on the TR250 version, and the transmission was literally geared towards yard work. For this type of job, quick shifting between forward and reverse is essential, so the Matbro used a Clark powershift system with four forward speeds and three reverse, plus a torque converter. This was quite unlike a field tractor, which needs a multiplicity of ratios over a very wide speed range. The Matbro was made in the English Cotswolds, and was also produced in John Deere colours for a while, giving the U.S. manufacturer a contender for this growing market. Whatever the badge, it was powered by a choice of Perkins four-cylinder diesel engines, with or without turbos: 75, 96, 106 and 114hp. Just as important, a yard tractor has to be ultra manoeuvrable, so the Matbro was articulated to keep the turning circle to a minimum.

Matbro was taken over by the American Terex Coporation in 2001 and production of the TM200R and 250R (now rebadged as Terex) was moved to Manchester in northern England. Most major tractor manufacturers now offer a dedicated yard tractor of some sort.

McCORMICK

These days, brand new tractor marques are rare, but McCormick is exactly that. Although an old name from the pioneering days (it was one of the four companies that merged to form International Harvester) it was reborn in 2001, producing a range of three modern tractors.

McCormick came about when Case-IH

Old name, new marque. The McCormick MTX125 was a slightly updated Case, built in the ex-Case-International Harvester factory at Doncaster.

merged with New Holland to form CNH Global in 2000; the European authorities would only permit the merger to go through if Case-IH's Doncaster factory was sold off. Otherwise, it was feared that the new giant corporation would exert too much power in the marketplace.

In the event, the factory was bought by Landini of Italy, part of the deal being that Doncaster would carry on building Case CX, MC-X and Maxxum tractors under the new brand. These would still be sold through Case dealers, as McCormicks in Europe and as Cases elsewhere. This arrangement would last two years, so that in the long term McCormick would need to look for other designs to build, or produce its own.

The first McCormick, a Perkins-powered CX90, rolled off the Doncaster production line in January 2001, just over 50 years after the plant had been built by International. In 2002, McCormick announced its own version of the Maxxum, the MTX. But this was no badge engineering job: instead of Cummins power as in the Maxxum, the MTX used a Perkins six-cylinder engine, and added the option of Speed Sequencer, a multi-function control that replaced the more familiar gear lever and powershift lever. There was a range of five MTX McCormicks, ranging from the 118-bhp 110 to the 175-bhp 175, all with the same 16-forward, 12-reverse transmission. A 32-speed creeper transmission was optional, as was front axle suspension.

As a new tractor marque, McCormick faces the 21st century with confidence, with a bright red-and-silver colour scheme that gives a nod to its International past.

OPPOSITE and LEFT
Part of the McCormick resurrection deal was that the new marque would make and sell Case designs for two years. The C70 is pictured opposite and the MC100 is on the left.

McCORMICK
PEGORARO

OPPOSITE
A McCormick V80 crawler.

LEFT
One of the McCormick four-cylinder T-series, with grass tyres. The hope in 2003 is that, under new ownership, McCormick will provide an invigorated lease of life for the Doncaster factory.

OPPOSITE
The Minneapolis Threshing Machine Co. was a partner in the Minneapolis-Moline merger, but built tractors well before that time. This is the 22/40.

BELOW
The Mercedes-Benz MB-Trac 1300, a brilliant concept which pioneered the systems tractor, using implements at both ends.

MERCEDES-BENZ
Well before Mercedes, there had been Daimler and Benz, both pioneers of the gasoline engine. They merged in 1925 to form Daimler-Benz, which later became Mercedes-Benz when both were already well-established in tractors. Daimler had built a gasoline machine as early as 1912, and Benz produced massive Land Traktors of 40hp and 80hp from 1919, popular for forestry work.

But the real milestone came in 1922, when Benz built the world's first production diesel tractor. The twin-cylinder 30-hp S7 was initially a three-wheeler, with two outrigger wheels for stability, but was later replaced by the four-wheel BK. Mercedes-Benz carried on producing diesel tractors into the 1930s, when the Depression forced it to cut back.

The company didn't return to the tractor market until 1950, and even then it was with a far from conventional machine. The Unimog was a multi-use farm vehicle, half-truck, half-tractor, that had already been produced by Boeringer for several years. Under the Mercedes-Benz wing, it became an institution and was produced for over 40 years. The beauty of the Unimog was its sheer adaptability. With four-wheel-drive, PTO and three-point-hitch, it could do useful work in the field, but it also had an impressive hauling capacity and could reach 30mph (48km/h) on the road. Being so adaptable, it of course found many uses far beyond farming.

Meanwhile, its maker showed no inclination to try its hand at a conventional tractor, though in 1973 it did come up with the innovative MB-Trac. This was a systems tractor (like the Deutz Intrac, announced the same year) with three-point-hitches at both ends. This enabled it to carry two implements at once, and execute two field operations at a single pass, saving a great deal of time. Other significant features were the central cab, four-wheel-drive through equal-sized wheels, and even weight distribution. There was also a load platform to carry fertilizer or a spray tank.

The MB-Trac was a great success and 10,000 were built by 1980 when Mercedes-Benz sold the design to Schluter. Other systems tractors followed, such as the Fendt and JCB Fastrac. The MB-Trac finally ceased production in 1991, but the Doppstadt Trac 200, announced in 2002, was designed to be its spiritual successor.

MINNEAPOLIS-MOLINE
Three companies made up Minneapolis-Moline: Minneapolis Steel and Machinery, the Minneapolis Threshing Machine Company and the Moline Plow Company. Merged in 1929, the company formed was famed for its bright-yellow Prairie Gold tractors and

M T M Co
M T M Co
MINNEAPOLIS FARM MOTOR
BUILT BY
THE MINNEAPOLIS
THRESHING MACHINE CO.

The Minneapolis Threshing Machine Co. may have been an established tractor manufacturer, but in the new regime, Minneapolis Steel & Machinery was the dominant partner.

technical innovations such as four valves per cylinder, five-speed transmissions, and the first well-equipped cab, not to mention the world's first high-speed tractor. And despite being a group of three, they meshed together well, Minneapolis Steel concentrating on tractors, and its two partners on threshers and ploughs respectively.

Minneapolis Steel had been an early player in the tractor industry, building machines under licence for Case and Bull. But it launched its own line of machines under the Twin City brand name, used because the company had plants both in Minneapolis itself as well as St. Paul. The first Twin City tractors were conventional enough, giants of the wheat belt that were built on the same dimensions as the big steam traction engines with which they competed. One early Twin City was powered by an engine of 1,486ci (24.3 litres) producing 40hp at the drawbar and 65 at the belt. But even that was eclipsed by the giant six-cylinder 60/90, with 2,230ci (36.5 litres), 90hp at the belt, and weighing in at 28,000lb (12700kg). The company also made smaller machines, but these giants were its bread and butter, and the 60/90 was actually listed up to 1920.

So far, so conventional. But in 1917 came the first inkling that Minneapolis Steel was not afraid of innovation. Until then, most tractors were tall, ungainly objects that perched the driver aloft. The new Twin City 16/30 stood only 4-ft (1.2-m) high, with the engine completely enclosed by sheet metal. Seated low behind the long hood, the driver was further protected by large mudguards. Powered by a 588-ci (9.6-litre) four-cylinder engine, the 16/30 pioneered the modern tractor layout, and could even be ordered with an electric starter and lights. It was not a success, however, and only about 700 were ever made.

Not that this mattered, for two years later Minneapolis Steel launched the tractor whose basic design would see it right through the 1920s and early '30s. The little 12/20 was most advanced for its time. Its transmission was fully enclosed and together with the engine formed the major part of the frame; in other words, it was unit-constructed, like the new Fordson, which made it strong and relatively lightweight. The power unit itself had pressurized lubrication and, most unusual for a tractor, four valves per cylinder. Soon uprated as the 17/28, it produced nearly 23hp at the drawbar and 31 at the belt – not bad for 340ci (5.6 litres). The 12/20 may have cost

They didn't come much bigger than the six-cylinder 60-90 Minneapolis Twin City, with its 2,230-ci (36.5-litre) engine. The wide rear wheels were an attempt to prevent this 28,000-lb (12700-kg) giant from sinking into the mud.

twice as much as a Fordson, but farmers were impressed by its advanced specification and obvious strength. Over 3,000 were sold in the first year, and 14 years later it was claimed that its successor was selling at the same rate. It also claimed three extra years of life for these tough tractors, and buyers seemed to believe it. A larger 20/35 was built alongside the 12/20, which was uprated as the 27/44. Finally, 1926 saw the launch of the 21/32, which plugged the gap between these two, even though it came out of the same mould.

The 21/32 was actually the last new tractor designed by Minneapolis Steel before the 1929 merger. Minneapolis Threshing had a tractor of its own, the 27/42, but Steel's 27/44 equivalent was evidently superior, as the Threshing tractor was quickly dropped. So the Twin City tractor range continued unaffected by merger until 1932, when the Minneapolis-Moline corporate name was taken on, and the big chunky 'MM' logo appeared.

The first new Minneapolis-Moline tractor had actually been under development before the merger; the KT was a throughly modern row-crop machine, designed to compete with the bigger Farmalls and the John Deere GP.

TWIN CITY
21-32

It was designed to straddle one row and was able to cultivate three rows at once. At that time, there was some doubt as to whether three- or four-row cultivation would become the norm, so the KT was soon followed by the MT, which was mechanically identical apart from its tricycle front-end, and which allowed it to straddle two rows and cultivate four. In 1932, the 21/32 was updated as the FT, but the big 27/44 carried on unchanged.

But Minneapolis-Moline had no small tractor to compete with the Farmall F20 or John Deere A (the MT was actually thought to be too big for most row-crop farmers). In 1934, the gap was plugged with the all-new JT, another tricycle row-crop tractor, but much smaller than the MT and powered by a 196-ci (3.2-litre) four-cylinder engine producing 14hp at the drawbar, 22 at the belt.

It also came in standard-tread and orchard forms and, significantly, had a five-speed transmission. This allowed a road speed of 18mph (29km/h), and was destined to become a Minneapolis-Moline trademark when most rivals made do with three or four speeds. Meanwhile, the KT/MT were upgraded to produce 19/30hp and renamed KTA/MTZ, while the FT received a bigger 403-ci (6.6-litre) engine to become the FTA.

Only two years later, the JT was replaced by the Z, with a smaller 185-ci (3.0-litre) engine, but with more power (25/35hp). Interestingly, the all-new engine had its valves mounted horizontally, controlled by long rocker arms to make clearance adjustment as easy as possible. And following the mood of the times, the little Z acquired sleek, streamlined styling, while the old Twin City grey was replaced with the bright new Prairie Gold, another Minneapolis-Moline trademark. As with the JT, there were variations on the theme; ZTU was the row-crop, ZTS the standard-tread.

In 1938, Minneapolis-Moline's next new tractor was the much bigger U-series, a 5,000-lb (2268-kg) 38-hp machine that could pull a four-bottom plough: the UTU was actually the largest row-crop available at the time. Pneumatic rubber tyres were a new option, and all U-series variants were powered

OPPOSITE
The 21/32, the last tractor to wear the Twin City badge before the Minneapolis-Moline name was born in 1929.

LEFT
The Second World War-specification Minneapolis-Moline ZTX, used for haulage duties.

The big four-cylinder Minneapolis-Moline began life as the GT in 1938, uprated as the GTA four years later. It remained Minneapolis-Moline's top tractor well into the 1950s.

by the same 283-ci (4.6-litre) four-cylinder engine, available to run on gasoline, kerosene or distillate. (Minneapolis-Moline would soon become a pioneer of different fuels, offering LPG and diesel as well.)

But the U-series isn't remarkable for any of this. It is remembered for the UDLX, probably the world's first tractor to come with a steel cab. And it wasn't just the cab that made the UDLX special. Inside, there was a heater and radio, full instrumentation and windscreen wipers, even a passenger seat. With a special high-ratio version of Minneapolis-Moline's five-speed transmission, the Comfortractor could also top 40mph (64km/h) on the road. Here was a tractor, if you believed Minneapolis-Moline's publicity, that could double as a private car: one could plough all day, then drive into town at night in comfort. Of course, none of this lavish specification came cheap, and the UDLX was listed at an astronomical $2,150, which was possibly why only 150 were sold. But although a failure in terms of sales, the UDLX was well ahead of its time when one considers that nowadays most tractor drivers take a cab, heater and comfortable seat for granted.

Of more immediate relevance to many American farmers was the GT-series which was announced the same year. More power was being demanded, and the late 1930s saw the tentative power race that would gather pace in the 1950s and reach its zenith in the '60s. The GT was powered by the same engine that had started life in the 21/32, now in 403-ci (6.6-litre) form and producing 36hp at the drawbar, 49 at the belt. In 1942 it was

industrial as well as the usual row-crop. During the Second World War, a special military-specification version of the Z, the ZTX, was produced, intended for tarmac hauling and characterized by a steel cab, heavy front protective grille, and front tow-hitch.

Minneapolis-Moline ended the 1930s with a modern line-up of tractors that covered every market slot apart from the small single-plough class. But the decade following the Second World War saw the company rapidly falling behind, making little effort to update its existing machines; the attempt to sell a small tractor was short-lived, then abandoned. This lack of focus on the existing tractors was partly due to the

LEFT
The Minneapolis-Moline Model U was a conventional row-crop or standard-tread tractor, apart from the UDLX Comfortractor, of course.

BELOW
The R was Minneapolis-Moline's smallest tractor of the late 1930s, a miniaturized version of the Z, with 165-ci (2.7-litre) engine and a four- (rather than five-) speed transmission.

uprated further to produce 39/56hp in the GTA (denoted by its Prairie yellow grille, as opposed to the red grille of the GT). It was a long-lived tractor, still the big flagship of the range well into the 1950s. An LPG-fuelled GTC was added in 1951, and a 56-hp diesel GTB-D from 1953.

At the other end of the range, Minneapolis-Moline unveiled another small tractor in 1939, this one designed to slot in beneath the Z. The new R was really a smaller version of the Z, its 165-ci (2.7-litre) engine having the same horizontal valve arrangement and producing 18/24hp, though there was only a four-speed transmission to keep costs down. It was possible to have a steel cab, though, indicating that the UDLX had left its mark after all. Like its big brother, the Z, the two-plough R came in a range of variants – standard-tread and

OPPOSITE
The Minneapolis-Moline V began life as an Avery, but was unsuccessful as the smallest post-war Minneapolis-Moline .

BELOW
The Uni-Tractor was a brave attempt to produce a powered chassis that would free conventional tractors for other work; but the need for specific implements killed sales.

Uni-Tractor, a simple powered chassis to which harvesting equipment could be mounted direct. It was a good concept, which aimed to cut the cost of self-propelled equipment and release conventional tractors for other work. Unfortunately, it also needed specific implements which had to be bought as well, which severely restricted its sale.

In 1950 Minneapolis-Moline did finally secure a small tractor to sell, though perhaps more by luck than judgement. B.F. Avery, based in Louisville, Kentucky, came up for sale and offered the prospect of a stronger dealer network in the south (where Minneapolis-Moline was weak) and two ready-made small tractors, the single-plough V and the light two-plough BF. With the Model R powered up to make a space, these at last gave Minneapolis-Moline the full line-up it needed. The little 65-ci (1-litre) V was already popular with vegetable and tobacco farmers, while the 19/27-hp BF provided a lighter, cheaper alternative to the R. But neither lasted long. The V was dropped after two years, the BF shortly afterwards, followed by the R. Once again, Minneapolis-Moline was left with no small tractor.

Finally, 1955 saw the unveiling by Minneapolis-Moline of two genuinely new, up-to-date machines. The 335 followed the new utility format popularized by the Ford-Fergusons and combined a low profile with adjustable treads for row-crop work. Perhaps even more significant was the dual-range Ampli-Torc transmission, a two-speed planetary gearset that doubled the standard five-speed gearbox into ten speeds. Thanks to these, shifting between the two ranges was possible without stopping or declutching. This was fast becoming the industry standard in the 1950s, and at least Minneapolis-Moline was keeping up with the times.

Alongside the 24/30-hp 335, Minneapolis-Moline launched the 31/38-hp 445, with all the same features – Ampli-Torc, three-point-hitch and live PTO – though the 445 was available as a pure row-crop tractor as well as a utility. It also had LPG and diesel options not available on the 335.

The U-series was now nearly 20 years old, though the 5-Star that replaced it in 1957 persevered with the same 283-ci (4.6-litre) engine in gasoline or LPG form. As a diesel, it received a capacity boost to 336ci (5.5 litres). All the new features of the smaller tractors were offered, plus new styling and a different seating position that placed the driver astride the transmission, and which was more comfortable than the traditional high perch. The big GT-series was updated in 1959 as the Gvi, with more power and modern styling on the old GB chassis. It was also bought by

MINNEAPOLIS-MOLINE

Minneapolis-Moline launched itself into the new utility market with the 335 in 1955. Ampli-Torc allowed a ten-speed transmission, and front and rear treads were adjustable.

The Minneapolis-Moline 4-Star Super replaced the 445 in 1957, with a new colour scheme but the same Ampli-Torc transmission.

Massey-Ferguson and sold as the MF 95.

Meanwhile, the smaller tractors were subjected to a bewildering succession of renamings. The 335 became Jet Star and the 445 the 4-Star, but the 5-Star was now the M5. Later, both Jet Star and 4-Star were replaced by the Jet Star 3. None of this involved any serious updates, as Minneapolis-Moline appeared to be concentrating on its larger tractors. In fact, there would be no more brand new small tractors from Minneapolis-Moline before the company's demise in the mid-1970s.

The company was particularly keen on four-wheel-drives, and in 1962 announced the industry's first sub-100-hp 4 x 4 tractor, the M504. This was simply an M5 with mechanically-driven front axle. A four-wheel-drive Gvi, the G704, was added the following year. The ageing Gvi was replaced by the G705 and four-wheel-drive G706, though still with the same 504-ci (8.2-litre) six-cylinder engine in LPG or diesel form (101hp and 102hp respectively). There was also new

Now part of White, Minneapolis-Moline's independence was slowly slipping away, though it still built its own big tractors in the late 1960s. This G900 was powered by the company's own 425-ci (7-litre) gasoline or diesel engine.

rounded-off styling, echoed by the updated M602 and M604, which took the place of the M5/M504 in 1963.

The year after that, the new corporate styling appeared again on the U302, which was an updated Jet Star 3. It is interesting that this 56-hp three-plough tractor was now the smallest Minneapolis-Moline available; the company seemed to have abandoned a large section of the tractor market once and for all, possibly influenced in this by White Motors, which had taken over the previous year. White already owned Oliver and Cockshutt, and through the 1960s made great use of mix 'n' match badge engineering.

With Cockshutt strong on small machines, Minneapolis-Moline was left as the big tractor specialist. The M5 did get a final update as the M670 in 1964, now with the larger 336-ci (5.5-litre) engine across the range of gasoline, LPG or diesel. This engine, incidentally, was an upsized version of the original four-cylinder unit launched in the U-series in 1938, so no one could accuse Minneapolis-Moline of change for its own sake! But M670 apart, Minneapolis-Moline's last years were spent exclusively on big tractors. The G705/706 became the G1000 row-crop in 1965, with the same 504-ci (8.2-litre) six-cylinder engine and the now-familiar five-speed, plus Ampli-Torc transmission. From 1967, a slightly smaller G900 was run alongside, with a 425-ci (7-litre) version of the same motor. Unusually, these big machines still came with a gasoline option. The G1000 Vista (also on sale from 1967) offered a higher driving position.

But these were to be the last 'pure' Minneapolis-Moline tractors as White pursued its course of rationalization. Consequently, the first Minneapolis-Moline super-tractor, the A4T of 1969, used the Minneapolis-Moline 504-ci diesel engine and ten-speed transmission, but was built in White's own factory. It also persevered with LPG power, which of course the company had pioneered 30 years earlier. The powered-up A4T 1600 was the only articulated 4 x 4 on the market with an LPG option. And to satisfy three sets

The G1050 was Minneapolis-Moline's biggest tractor of the early 1970s, with a 504-ci (8.2-litre) version of the venerable six-cylinder motor. It was later boosted still further, to 585ci (9.6 litres) for the G1355.

The M670 was a final update of the M5 in 1964, with a bigger 336-ci (5.5-litre) four-cylinder power unit.

of dealers, it was also repainted and sold as the Oliver 2455 and (in Canada) the White Plainsman. Meanwhile, Minneapolis-Moline dealers were given imported FIAT tractors to sell, badged as the MM G350 and G450.

In fact, as far as the parent company was concerned, Minneapolis-Moline's greatest asset was its tough, durable six-cylinder engine, which was given a substantial capacity boost in 1972 to 585ci (10 litres) and 135hp. This would have been too much for the ageing Minneapolis-Moline drive train, so planetary final drives were added to the new G1350. The logical thing was to raid the White parts bin for a more modern transmission, so the G1355 (now with 143hp) used Oliver's younger 18-speed set-up. There was also a smaller G955 with a 451-ci (7.4-litre) version of the venerable six and a six- or 12-speed Oliver transmission.

But really, that engine was fast becoming the sole Minneapolis-Moline content in Minneapolis-Moline-badged tractors, and in 1974 White dropped the name altogether. The name may have died but the yellow-and-white colours were revived in 1989 for the White American 60 and 80 tractors, which also came in Oliver green, Cockshutt red and White silver. But even that was short-lived, and after its long, slow decline, which arguably began shortly after the Second World War, Minneapolis-Moline was finally dead and buried.

NEW HOLLAND

Today, New Holland forms part of one of the biggest tractor conglomerates in the world: CNH Global. But until 1986, its name had never appeared on a tractor. The story began a long time ago in 1895, however, when the company was set up in New Holland, Pennsylvania to build a corn mill. It branched into non-powered farm implements and a healthy business developed. In 1940, when New Holland produced one of the first successful automatic hay balers, it found itself under a new proprietor; another change of ownership came seven years later when the Sperry Corporation bought New Holland. Sperry was determined to make the transition into powered implements, and in 1964 bought a controlling interest in Claas, the German combine harvester manufacturer.

New Holland might still have only been associated with implements to this day but for the fact that its history changed course in

New Holland, Ford or Versatile? The Versatile name was used on Ford's super-tractors for some years, but in the 1990s the New Holland badge gradually replaced both.

1986, when it was bought by Ford. Ford's original intention was to add the New Holland implement line to its own tractors, giving it the full line-up of products to compete with specialists such as John Deere and Case-International. As part of that strategy, the super-tractor manufacturer Versatile came under the Ford-New Holland umbrella in 1987.

But the severe recession of the 1980s caused Ford to think again, and in 1990 it sold 80 per cent of its agricultural arm to FIAT of Italy. Part of the agreement was that the New Holland name would gradually replace Ford on tractors; the group's name was changed to plain New Holland in 1994, when Ford sold its remaining 20 per cent interest to FIAT. It was permitted to use the Ford name up to 2001, however.

This is a complicated story, which meant that some tractors of the 1990s badged as New Holland had Ford or Versatile ancestry, while later in the decade, as FIAT's ownership began to make itself felt, some Italian-built tractors carried the New Holland badge as well. Moreover, although they weren't Ford tractors any more, New Hollands carried on with the famous blue-and-black colour scheme.

One tractor with mixed heritage was the bi-directional Ford Versatile 9030. Designed by Versatile and re-engined by Ford, it was later badged as a New Holland. Versatile had

RIGHT
The bi-directional TV140 had its roots in the Versatile-designed 9030, though by the late 1990s the New Holland name was becoming increasingly well established.

OPPOSITE
After the merger with FIAT, then with Case to form CNH Global, New Holland tractors would come from a wide variety of sources.

actually pioneered the modern bi-directional tractor as early as 1977, with controls that could swivel through 180 degrees to make it equally adept at working in either direction. But New Holland's mass sales in the 1990s came from mid-range tractors like the 40-series, built at Basildon, in England. The 7740 was typical, with a 95-hp four-cylinder turbo-diesel; in fact, the 75,000th 40-series rolled out of Basildon in 1996. It was also sold as a FIAT S-series in some markets.

Top of the sub-Versatile range was the 70-series, announced as one of many changes in 1994. Badged as Ford-New Holland for some markets, the FIAT G-series for others, the 70 was an up-to-the-minute modern tractor. There were four models, the 8670, 8770, 8870 and 8970, producing 145, 160, 180 and 210hp respectively. All used the same 456-ci (7.5-litre) six-cylinder turbo-diesel engine in different forms, plus a 16-speed electronic powershift transmission.

Two years later, two new tractors, the 65–95-hp 35-series and 100–160-hp 60-series, were unveiled. Built in Italy, the smaller machine was sold as both a blue New Holland 35 and red FIAT L-series. It shared a modern low-nosed 1990s look with the bigger 60, and engines were four-cylinder diesels (from non-turbo 3.6-litre 65hp to turbo 3.9-litre 95hp) from Iveco, another Ford/FIAT co-operative venture. Its bigger brother came from Basildon, again as a blue New Holland 60 or red FIAT M-series, though in both cases the New Holland badge was prominent. All 60s were powered by a 463-ci (7.6-litre) six-cylinder diesel, including the new Gemini, which was designed to meet the 1997 EPA regulations, with great attention paid to fuel/air mixing and swirl. The successful 40-series was replaced in 1998 by the TS, continuing the low-bonnet theme, and with a choice of 80-, 90- or 100-hp diesels. A six-cylinder TS115 was announced the followng year using New Holland's own 7.5-litre Powerstar diesel. Unlike the other TS tractors, this one had standard four-wheel-drive and a 24-speed Dual Command transmission was optional.

That same year, New Holland Geotech, as the FIAT/New Holland corporation was known, announced it was merging with Case-International Harvester to form a new giant, CNH Global; this was so big that the competition authorities ruled that it close or sell off some plants to avoid charges of excessive market domination. But the New Holland name lived on.

8560 NEW HOLLAND

RIGHT
Mid-range tractors, like this 8340, were built at the Basildon factory in England.

OPPOSITE
The New Holland 5635, a small, adaptable row-crop tractor, was a rebadged version of the FIAT L-series.

5635 NEW HOLLAND
LOTUS

NUFFIELD
MYC 813

NUFFIELD
William Morris could rightly claim to be Britain's Henry Ford. He may not have had Ford's farming background and love of tractors, but he did go on to build a tractor that bore the name of his giant car maker, the Nuffield company. Before the Second World War, the British tractor industry was dominated by the Dagenham-built Fordson, but in the late 1940s the Government encouraged other manufacturers to go into the tractor business; not only was the country's

OPPOSITE
After the Second World War, William Morris responded to the British Government's plea for a new home-grown tractor with the Nuffield DM4 Universal.

LEFT
Not all Nuffield diesel tractors were Perkins-powered. This one used a BMC unit.

RIGHT
Bautz of Germany also sold the orange Nuffield.

OPPOSITE
In Britain, the tractor market was becoming rapidly dominated by diesel power, and by the mid-1950s 95 per cent of Nuffields were so-equipped. The 38-hp Perkins (shown here) was offered from 1950.

stock of working tractors in urgent need of replacement, Britain was also bankrupt, after six years of war, and needed to earn money fast through exports.

Nuffield responded with alacrity, and its new tractor was actually completed by 1946, though steel shortages meant that it didn't go into production for another two years.

It was a simple, yet up-to-date machine, with an optional three-point-hitch, PTO and Morris' own four-cylinder side-valve engine running on TVO (tractor vaporizing oil; a cheap low-grade fuel for farmers). Both row-crop M3 and utility M4 repaid the basic specification by coming in at less than £500; the last thing Britain needed in a time of austerity was a complex and costly machine.

The Nuffield tractor was simple and hard-working and without flaws. Other engine options were gradually added, notably a 38-hp Perkins diesel from 1950, essential in the British market where 95 per cent of Nuffields were diesel-powered by the middle of the decade. It sold well abroad, too, and 80 per cent of those early Nuffields were exported: the British Government's dream had come true. In fact, so successful was the

NUFFIELD

NUFFIELD

Nuffield tractor line that it survived and blossomed through various company takeovers and mergers to become the blue Leyland tractor line of the 1960s and '70s, some of which were exported to North America. Leyland tractors were bought by Marshall in the 1980s.

OLIVER

The Oliver Chilled Plow Works did not enter the tractor business until 1930, by which time it had been building and selling tillage equipment for 80 years. It began experimenting with row-crop tractor designs from 1926, but still lacked the in-depth expertise to go into production. The solution arrived three years later, when Oliver merged with the American Seeding Machine Co., Nichols & Shephard, and Hart-Parr tractors.

As mergers go, it was a perfect fit: American Seeding made seeders and planters; Nichols & Shephard specialized in threshers and harvesters. Better still, Hart-Parr had plenty of tractor-building experience, but had an ageing line-up and no row-crop tractor at all. Oliver had a modern row-crop ready to go but needed somewhere to make it. Reflecting the dominant partner of the four, the newly merged company was dubbed the Oliver Corporation.

The first new tractor to emerge was the Oliver-Hart-Parr Row Crop, an 18/27-hp machine with a single front wheel and adjustable rear tread. The rear tread could be altered relatively easily by sliding the rear wheels in and out on the splined axle, which would be the standard form of adjustment until power-adjust rear wheels appeared in the

la TRATTRICE
NUFFIELD
UNIVERSAL
4DM.60
a 4 RUOTE MOTRICI
POTENZA
ADERENZA
ECONOMIA
BMC DIESEL
ORGANIZZAZIONE DI VENDITA PER L'ITALIA ED ESTERO
Rapido innesto e disinnesto asse anteriore
Aumento di potenza al gancio fino all'80% rispetto ai tipi con 2 ruote motrici
Motore da 50 HP completamente utilizzati
Stabilità perfetta su qualunque terreno
Aderenza totale
Peso in ordine di marcia circa Kg. 2550
G. DAMILANO
VITTORIO CANTATORE
CORSO SAVONA 20 - TEL. 64.16.44-45-46 - MONCALIERI (TORINO)

OPPOSITE
Nuffield tractors were such a success that they led to the blue Leyland tractor range of the 1960s and '70s.

LEFT
Power, traction and economy was the promise of this Italian four-wheel-drive conversion of the Nuffield.

RIGHT
This was the age of heavyweight tractors: the Rumely OilPull (left) and the Nichols & Shepard (right) were typical Hart-Parr rivals.

OPPOSITE
Post-merger, the first tractors were Oliver-designed but made by Hart-Parr, so both names feature on this tractor.

1950s. However, there was still demand for a standard-tread machine, and the Row Crop was soon followed by a standard-tread 18/28. At the same time, a bigger Model A was unveiled (soon renamed 28/44, after its power rating) with a 443-ci (7.2-litre) four-cylinder motor. Both this and the 18/28 were popular industrial tractors.

But Oliver's real impact on the tractor industry was felt in 1935 with the 70. Until then, most tractors had been powered by lumpy, low-revving motors with two or four

OLIVER
HART-PARR
OLIVER
28-44

RIGHT
The first fruit of the new partnership was this high-clearance and adjustable rear-axle Row Crop, a rival to the International Farmall.

OPPOSITE
Oliver's 60 was a smaller, four-cylinder version of the six-cylinder 70: this is the Row Crop version.

OLIVER
ROW CROP
60

RIGHT
A black-and-white advertisement for the Oliver-Hart-Parr Model A.

BELOW RIGHT
A 60-series Row Crop.

OPPOSITE
The Oliver 80 was an updated version of the old 18/27 (Row Crop) and 18/28 (Standard).

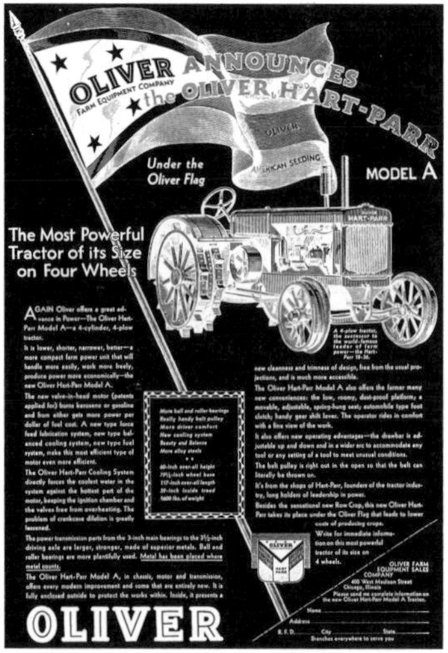

cylinders. They were of low compression to suit cheap, low-grade fuels. The 70 changed all that. Its six-cylinder Waukesha engine was smooth and relatively high-revving. It had a high compression ratio, by tractor standards, making it surprisingly powerful for its size (over 30hp at the belt, according to Nebraska) and just 212ci (3.5 litres). Of course, the high compression meant it also needed expensive high-octane gasoline (a first for any tractor), but a low-compression distillate version was available as well. To back up its glamorous engine, the 70 was a good-looker, sleek and streamlined, especially after Oliver introduced the Fleetline look in 1937. It was a great success, and around 65,000 Model 70s were built by the time production ended in 1948.

Meanwhile, the old four-cylinder machines continued, updated as the 80 (18/28) and 90 (28/44) in 1937. There was also a 99 high-compression version of the 90. In fact, Oliver was proving to be forward-thinking when it came to power units, despite the fact that it did not build engines itself; some 80s were fitted with Buda four-cylinder diesel engines in 1940.

The 60, a smaller four-cylinder version of the 70, was introduced that year. For the first time, it brought Oliver into competition with the smaller Farmalls and John Deeres, plus the new Ford-Ferguson tractor. It really was a miniaturized 70, with its 121-ci (2.0-litre) four-cylinder motor running at the same relatively high 1,500rpm. And like the 70 it was well-equipped, with a four-speed transmission and pneumatic rubber tyres, though an electric starter cost extra. It also shared the 70's sleek styling, which did it no harm at all.

After the Second World War, the big Olivers were beginning to look decidedly old-fashioned next to the 60 and 70, so in 1947 the 80 was replaced altogether by the 88. Now with six-cylinder Waukesha engines in gasoline, distillate or diesel form, with a six-speed transmission and electric start, it gave Oliver a thoroughly up-to-date big tractor. (The Hart-Parr name, incidentally, had been dropped before the war). Its modern six-cylinder motor gave nearly 38hp at the belt, and there was a live power take-off and live hydraulics, making the 88 an advanced tractor for its time. Naturally, it also assumed the 70's Fleetline styling. The big 90/99, however, was something of a Cinderella and retained four cylinders and the old boxy styling.

OLIVER
ROW CROP
OLIVER

RIGHT
Oliver's first utility tractor, the Super 55, had a diesel option and draft-controlled three-point-hitch.

BELOW
The six-cylinder 70 did much to enhance Oliver's reputation: this is the updated Fleetline 77.

OPPOSITE
Fleetline styling turned the 60 into the 66 in 1947, and a power boost made it the Super 66 seven years later.

It was inevitable that the 88's advanced features should trickle down to the smaller Olivers. The 66 and 77 replaced the 60 and 70 respectively, but shared many parts. The 66 now had a slightly larger engine, plus a diesel option for the first time, while the 77's six-cylinder motor was rejigged with a larger bore and shorter stroke to give a little more power. This too had a diesel option, with LPG on offer from 1952, replacing the old kerosene option. What they didn't have, though, was that Fleetline styling: the late 1940s look was clean and tidy, but not as sleek.

The big 99 hadn't been forgotten, though, and received an important update in 1952 with a Waukesha six-cylinder diesel engine of 302ci (4.9 litres). If that wasn't powerful

enough at 62hp, the Super 99 from 1955 was equipped with a three-cylinder two-stroke General Motors diesel. This high-revving supercharged engine produced 72-belt horsepower at a wailing 1,675rpm, making it the most powerful tractor available. This was no low-revving slogger like a two-cylinder John Deere, or even its own four-cylinder predecessor, and needed revving to produce that power. Overkill for a tractor? Maybe not, as Oliver offered the General Motors two-stroke option for many years.

Oliver's smaller tractors were updated throughout the 1950s as the Super 66, 77 and 88, with the company's own Hydra-Lectric hitch. There was also a new small utility tractor to compete with Ford – the Super 55 (34-hp gasoline or diesel, with three-point-hitch) – and a little 25-hp Super 44, a new single-row machine aimed at tobacco and flower growers. In the late 1950s, the entire line-up was renamed using three figures, as 440, 550 and so on, though the only actual advance was the two-speed Power Booster. This followed the industry trend of providing a shift-on-the-go two-range transmission in addition to the standard gearbox, and was fitted to the renamed 770 and 880. There was new squared-off styling, though, plus extra power for the 550 and supercharged 990 (now up to 84hp). One interesting variation was the 995 Lugmatic, a 990 with a torque converter to pull the tractor through sticky patches (it had an extra 5hp to cope with transmission losses).

But things were not going well for Oliver, as the fairly minimal changes of the late

SUPER 66
OLIVER

SUPER 99
OLIVER
DIESEL
OLIVER

1950s indicated, and in 1960 it was taken over by White Motors. P.W. Ertel acerbically remarks that 'White turned one of America's best known and most innovative tractor manufacturers into little more than a farm machinery marketing company'. Within a few years, Minneapolis-Moline and Cockshutt had also joined the White stable, and by the end of the decade all these names were interchangeable in a thorough-going badge-engineering regime.

White decided that if it was cheaper to import tractors than to build them in North America, then that's what it must do. Oliver's first imports were the Model 500 (32-hp utility) and 600 (40-hp utility), both built by David Brown of England. Painted Oliver green, they slotted in either side of the 550, which was still made in-house. However, the same year (1960) also saw two big home-grown tractors, the row-crop 1800 and wheatland 1900. The former came with 70- or 74-hp diesel or gasoline/LPG six-cylinder engines, the same 265-ci (4.3-litre) and 283-ci (4.6-litre) units as the 880 it replaced. Meanwhile, the 1900 continued the supercharged tradition, with a 92-hp four-cylinder two-stroke diesel, the GM 4-53. Both got slight power boosts as the Series B in 1963, and were joined by the 58-hp four-

OPPOSITE
Hot rod! The supercharged two-stroke Super 99 was one of the most powerful tractors on the market in 1952.

BELOW
There was bold new styling but few other changes for the 880 (88), apart from two-speed powershift transmission.

HG
OLIVER
OLIVER

Anytime is "HG" time
In any kind of weather, on any kind of going, the Oliver HG can go on working. Sand, mud or snow . . . hills, marsh or bottom land do not give you idle days when you have an HG.
The HG is a track tractor that is made for the farm—it will handle row crops! It comes in either 31, 42 or 68-inch tread widths, center-to-center, and has a full 20-inch clearance.
It's a great second tractor for the average two-tractor farm because it's an all-winter tractor. See your Oliver Dealer and ask him about the HG. The Oliver Corporation, 400 West Madison Street, Chicago 6, Illinois.
OLIVER Track-Tractor is an ideal "2nd tractor" on many farms. It can be fitted with a blade for erosion control, road maintenance or snow removal and with many other accessories.
OLIVER
"FINEST IN FARM MACHINERY"

plough 1600. They also had the two-range transmission, now known as Hydra-Shift, plus the option of Hydra-Power, which provided three powershift ranges. The latter gave 18 forward speeds when coupled with the standard six-speed gearbox.

But even though Oliver transmissions had been keeping up with the competition, by the mid/late-1960s its tractors were beginning to look outdated, though there were few major changes for the remainder of the decade. A boost in 1964 gave the 1650, 1850 and 1950 more power, the last one now up to 106hp at 2,400rpm, still General Motors diesel-powered. But what Oliver needed was a bigger engine to contest the growing 100-hp-plus market, rather than turning up the revs on General Motor's peaky two-stroke. It came in 1967 with a turbocharged version of the 1850's 301-ci (4.9-litre) six-cylinder diesel. The following year, White's big 478-ci (7.8-litre) six powered the new 2050 (119-hp) and 2150 (131-hp turbo) tractors. The 18-speed Hydra- Power was standard and front-wheel-assist was optional, as it was on the smaller Olivers.

This was good news, even though Oliver's identity was becoming gradually eroded. The imported David Browns were replaced by FIATs (beginning with the 1250 in 1965), which were badged as White-Olivers from 1969. But there were only minor changes to the home-built tractors: in 1970 slightly more power, new grilles, and the option of front-wheel-assist on the 1655 heralded the 55-series, from 1555 to 1955. Moreover, from 1971, many

OPPOSITE and LEFT
Oliver's acquisition of Cletrac introduced crawlers to the line-up. As an updated OC3, the HG was in production until 1957.

BELOW
The 52-bhp 600 and 32-hp 500 were repainted, rebadged David Browns.
BELOW

OVER / UNDER HYDRAUL SHIFT
OLIVER 1855

of the bigger tractors were simply repainted and rebadged Minneapolis-Molines: the Oliver 1865 was really a Minneapolis-Moline G950, the 141-hp 2155 a Minneapolis-Moline G1350, while the 2455 was a four-wheel-drive articulated machine, a mixture of Oliver and Minneapolis-Moline components.

Not that all big Olivers of the 1970s were thinly disguised Minneapolis-Molines. The 2255 was one of the last hot-rod two-wheel-drive tractors, powered by a Caterpillar V8 diesel of 473ci (7.7 litres) and 145hp. The end finally came in 1974 when the last Oliver, a 2255, rolled out of the Charles City, Iowa factory. White was determined to promote its own name as a tractor brand, which spelt the end for Cockshutt, Minneapolis-Moline and Oliver.

OPPOSITE
In the early 1970s, some Olivers were rebadged Minneapolis-Molines, but this 1855 was the genuine article, with 92-hp gasoline or 97-hp diesel engine.

LEFT
The 1955 was very similar, but with more power; the same six-cylinder diesel was uprated to 108hp. Front-wheel-assist was optional to help transfer all that power to the ground.

Platypus hoped to attract farmers with its modestly-sized crawlers.

PLATYPUS

Platypus crawlers were British, made somewhere between 1950 and 1957 in Basildon, Essex, where New Holland tractors are built to this day. Part of a company called Rotary Hoes Ltd., Platypus offered a small range of crawlers, mostly powered by Perkins diesel engines, though there was also a gasoline option on the smallest 28 and 30 models, which were offered throughout the whole of the above period.

'All you want in a crawler!' gushed the publicity. 'Compact power – rugged build – easy running – economical maintenance.'

The company made great play of the 30's easy maintenance steel tracks: 'On site repinning and bushing without special tools. Track pins and bushes are reversible to give extra life …Track disconnection at any link… Exceptionally cheap track replacements …Perfect sealing under all conditions, thanks to the bellows-type dirt seal, isolation chamber and axial oil seal to the sprocket drive shaft.'

Platypus was evidently keen to maximize its market, showing the 192-ci (3.1-litre) 34-hp 30 towing a plough and rotovator as well as with the bulldozer or bull-loader attachments. And there were several different track options: Narrow Gauge (31in/787mm) between track centres, 7- or 8-in/178- or 203-mm tracks); Wide Gauge (46-in/1168-mm width, 9- or 12-in/229- or 305-mm tracks); Extra Wide Gauge (54-in/1372-mm width, 9in or 12in tracks); Super Extra Wide Gauge (54-in width, 24-in/610-mm track). The latter, known as the Bogmaster, was designed for exceptionally soft ground, and Platypus claimed it exerted a ground pressure of less than 1.3 pounds per square inch. All of these variants used a six-speed transmission (three speeds over two ranges) offering 0.8 to 5.1mph (1.3 to 8.2km/h).

As if the 30 was not big enough, Platypus also built the PD4 from 1954, using a Perkins 51-hp L4 diesel or six-cylinder R6. Interestingly, it was stressed that the PD4 'costs considerably less than comparable performance tractors', so the agricultural market was obviously important to it. The Platypus 50, launched the following year, used the same Perkins L4 engine. Both these larger crawlers ceased production in 1956.

PORSCHE

Ferrari, Lamborghini and Porsche – all names to have graced not only tractors, but also exotic sports cars. However, Ferrari tractors actually had no connection with the bright-red Italian sportsters, though Ferruccio Lamborghini did once produce tractors before turning his attention to fast cars. But the Porsche tractor really was designed by Dr. Ferdinand Porsche himself, and even though the tractors kept his name for nearly 20 years, they were only built by the Porsche company for a short time.

Ferdinand Porsche was a prolific designer, and designed several tractors in his

The exotic name stuck, but Porsche tractors were only made for a few years by this producer of glamorous sports cars.

The single-cylinder Junior was the smallest Porsche on offer. This one is equipped for mowing.

career. During the First World War he developed big four-wheel-drive gun tractors for the Austro-Daimler company, as well as the prototype for a small farm tractor.

But it was in the late 1930s that the idea of the production Porsche tractor was born. While working on the Volkswagen 'People's Car', why not also produce a Volksschlepper, 'People's Tractor'? It actually entered production before the Second World War, though not many of them were built before war broke out. It was an unusual machine with a rear-mounted single-cylinder air-cooled engine and load space in the front.

But that wasn't the end of the Porsche tractor story. The company that would make Porsche sports cars – headed by Dr. Ferdinand's son Ferry – began work on a new Volksschlepper as early as 1945. When it was unveiled, the new Porsche tractor was more conventional than the original, with a front-mounted twin-cylinder air-cooled diesel engine. But within a few years, the production rights were bought by machine-tool maker Allgaier; it is probable that Porsche wished to concentrate on its burgeoning sports car business.

Allgaier was no stranger to tractors, having built some very basic single-cylinder machines (famously described as 'stationary engines on wheels') from 1946. It made a success of the Porsche, building about 25,000 tractors until 1957, when it sold the licence on to the Mannesmann engineering group. By this time the range had expanded to cover one-, two-, three- and four-cylinder machines of 14 to 50hp. Despite this wide range, the Junior, Standard, Super and Master shared 90 per cent of their parts. Typical was the Porsche Junior V, with a 14-hp single-cylinder air-cooled engine and six-speed transmission. The end came in 1964, when Mannesmann's tractor business was taken over by Renault.

RANSOME

Ransome of England built steam traction engines, and actually offered a gasoline tractor as early as 1902, though it owed far more to a converted motor car than a specifically designed farm tractor.

The first dedicated tractor was the MG2, a miniature crawler machine aimed at market gardeners – hence the 'MG', but nothing to do with the sports car of the same name. The MG was really a joint effort between Ransome, Ford and Roadless Traction, another English company, that did good business out of half- and full-track conversions of Fordson machines. The first MG2 was unveiled in 1936, powered by a small single-cylinder air-cooled gasoline engine, the twin rubber-jointed tracks controlled by twin levers. There was a directly mounted rear frame for attaching implements; the little MG was able to pull a single plough, and the engine (a 37-ci/600-cc) side-valve unit, was supplied by Sturmey-Archer, the cycle component and gearbox manufacturer.

The concept of the MG was such a success that after the Second World War Ransome was able to take up exactly where it had left off. Gradually, higher-powered MGs were introduced, but the basic concept of a small lightweight crawler remained unchanged. The MG6 of 1959 was powered by an 8-hp single-cylinder diesel, and the final MG40 was also diesel-powered. About 15,000 MGs were made before production ceased in 1966: more recently, the company has concentrated on lawn care machinery.

In 1997, Jacobsen, the American mower manufacturer, took over Ransome, and today

The Ransome crawler emerged with the help of Ford and Roadless Traction. About 15,000 were made.

The characteristic sloping nose may be long since gone, but there's no mistaking this 106-54 Renault.

the name remains on a whole range of mowers, sweepers and compact tractors. The latter range, from the 18-hp CT318 to the 45-hp CT445 are powered by three- or four-cylinder diesels. They come with four-wheel-drive, a choice of mechanical or hydrostatic drive, and a range of transmissions up to a 12 forward, four reverse.

RENAULT

France's foremost tractor manufacturer still survives today, having built its first farm tractor in 1918, when it had already been in

The Renault Herdsman, a lightweight four-wheel-drive tractor for the small farmer. It originally used an air-cooled Deutz diesel engine.

RENAULT
Renault
155.54
Turbo
TRACTONIC

OPPOSITE
Pre-Ares tractors like the 155-54 were Renault flagships.

LEFT
The wide range of Renault tractors extends far beyond agricultural use, typified by this front-loading 80-14.

RIGHT
The Ceres was Renault's flagship in the late 1990s.

BELOW
The vineyard market is an important one in France, hence the narrow-track Dionis 140.

business for 20 years. (Renault had been a pioneer car manufacturer from 1898 and actually began experimenting with tractors ten years later.) By the time the First World War broke out, the company was producing various four-wheel-drives and crawlers. During the war, Renault designed and built a

light tank for the French Army and the company's first tractor of 1918, the GP, was based on this design.

Naturally enough, it was a crawler, with a four-cylinder 30-hp gasoline engine and three-speed transmission. Unlike many European manufacturers, Renault steered clear of the single-cylinder semi-diesel layout, and stuck with spark ignition engines, though it would later build conventional full diesels. Indeed, it did further work on the feasibility of using methane and other gases as fuel, encouraged by the French Army and Academy of Agriculture.

A wheeled version of the GP, the HO, was launched in around 1920. Like the GP, it used a mid-mounted radiator, allowing for Renault's trademark sloping bonnet. This had two major advantages: improved visibility (a foretaste of the 1990s droop-snoop front-end), and a radiator which was less vulnerable to damage because it was tucked in safely between hood and fuel tank. Both HO and crawler H1 equivalent were replaced by the PE tractor in 1927.

Renault experimented with diesels from 1931, bringing its first into production two years later with the VY tractor. This relatively large machine was powered by a 266-ci (4.3-litre) four-cylinder diesel engine, and was the first French production diesel tractor.

From 1945, in an effort to build up French

The Renault Ceres 340X. Most Ceres machines left the factory equipped with Renault's Hydrostable TZ cab.

RIGHT, BELOW and OPPOSITE
The chunky Ares 500-series, with almost equal-sized wheels and plenty of high-tech innovation. But the three-point-hitch is still based on the principle laid down by Harry Ferguson 70 years ago.

agriculture damaged by six years of war, the newly nationalized Renault made tractors a priority, with 7,500 machines built from 1947–48. The 3040 was a major model for Renault, up-to-date and well-equipped, with a two-speed PTO, hydraulic lift, adjustable tread and a full electrical system. Another step forward was the D-series of 1956, which came with both air- and water-cooled diesels, as well as syncromesh gearbox and differential lock. The final Super D of 1965 added a three-point-hitch.

Four-wheel-drive and torque converters were added in the late 1960s, and in 1974 Renault unveiled a completely new

generation of tractors, covering the 30–115-hp range. There were two- or four-wheel-drives, plus the new feature of a forward/reverse shuttle transmission, which allowed rapid changes of direction.

In fact, Renault proved itself to be one of the most innovative European manufacturers in the years that followed, especially in cab

RENAULT
Ares

OPPOSITE
The Ares 600 would have found this load well within its limits.

LEFT
The TZ Hydrostable cab was a great advance when launched in 1987, giving the cab its own suspension system, which was independent of the tractor, and making life for the driver easier and more comfortable.

design. The new TX cab of 1981 offered a passenger seat and better visibility, but the real milestone was the TZ Hydrostable cab of 1987. In development for ten years, this mounted the cab on a system of coil springs, anti-roll bars and shock absorbers to give an unprecedented level of comfort. Take-up was slow at first, due to the substantial extra cost, but by the end of the 1990s, 80 per cent of Renault Ares tractors sold in Britain were specified with the TZ.

Typical of the 1990s range was the 180.94, with 27-speed transmission (forward or reverse shuttle) and nine-speed powershift within each of the three ranges. It was Renault's flagship in the mid-1990s, replaced in 1999 by the 185-hp Ares. In 2001, Renault entered the super-tractor class for the first time, with the still more powerful Atles.

The top-of-the range Ares 800.

There were twin wheels and triple implements for this Ares 800, demonstrating just how much work a modern tractor can do.

RIGHT
In the 1990s Renault built a full line-up of smaller tractors in the range below the big Ceres, including this Pales 240.

OPPOSITE
The Fructus 140 was designed for orchard work. Note the low profile and smooth bodywork.

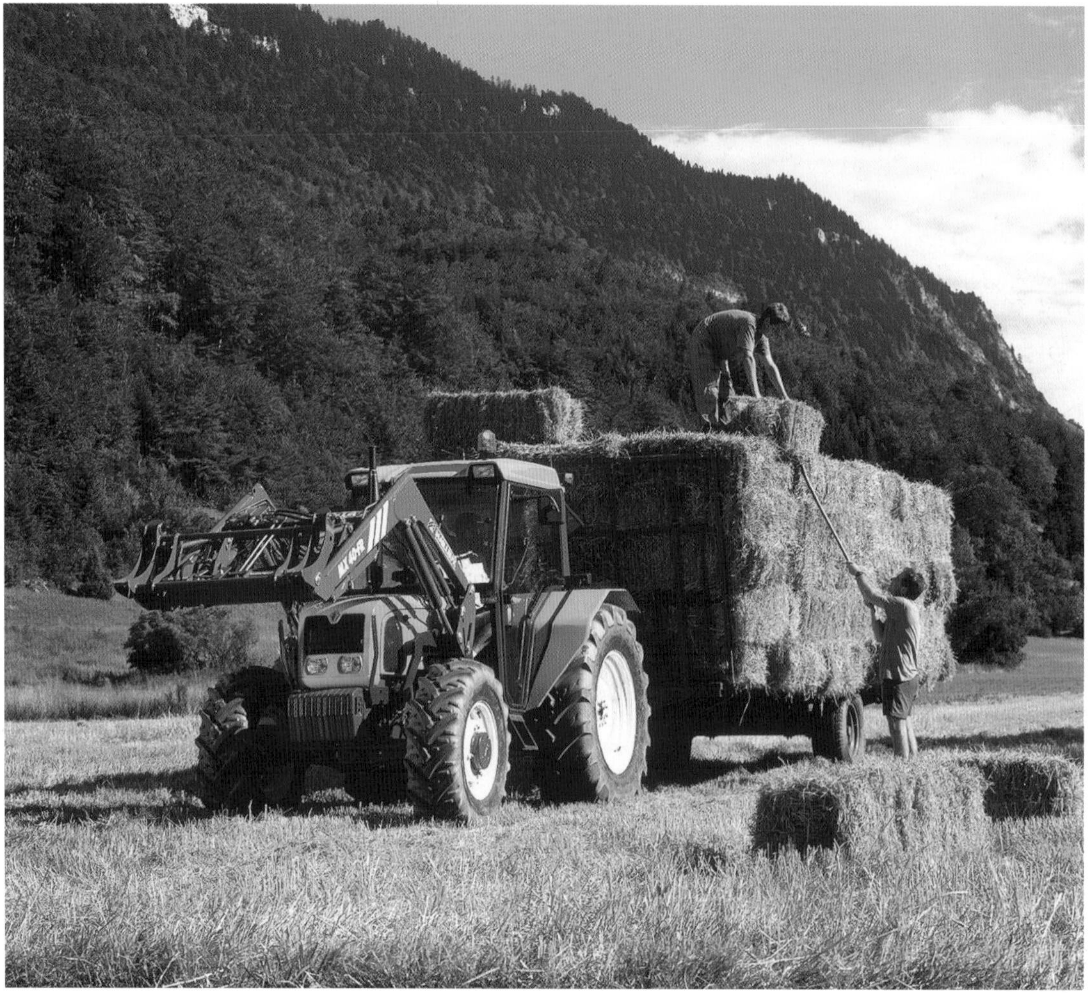

RENAULT
Fructus 140

KUHN
KUHN
RENAULT
340 Cergos

OPPOSITE and LEFT
This mid-sized Renault Cergos 340 was less plush and high-tech than the Ceres, but did its job well nonetheless.

RIGHT and OPPOSITE
For 2001, Renault built its most powerful tractor yet, the Atles. This is the Atles 935 RZ.

RENAULT

RIGHT and OPPOSITE
The mid-sized Temis is Renault's latest offering. The 610 X on ploughing duties, is on the right, and the 650 Z road hauler is shown opposite.

RENAULT
Temis
650 Z

The Rock Island Plow Co. started out making Heider tractors, and built its own up to 1937.

ROCK ISLAND/HEIDER – RUSHTON

The Rock Island Plow Company was a well-established implement manufacturer that by 1912 was offering a full range of ploughs, planters, drills, harrows and cultivators. The opportunity to branch out into tractors came in 1914, when Rock Island arranged to sell the Heider machine. Designed by Henry J. Heider, this was a conventional four-wheel tractor with chain final drive, though the engine was mounted over the rear axle to maximize traction.

Demand for the tractor was so great that the small Heider factory was unable to keep up, so in January 1916 Rock Island bought the whole concern and transferred tractor production to its own plant. However, it continued to use the well-known Heider name until the late 1920s. At first, two tractors were offered under the Rock Island regime. The existing Heider 10/20 was uprated as a 12/20, using a Waukesha four-cylinder engine of 429ci (7 litres). It weighed three tons and cost $1,095 in 1917. Alongside it, Rock Island introduced the smaller 9/16 Model D, which weighed only 4,000lb (1814kg) and cost just $795 (though this soon rose to over $1,000). Like the bigger 15/27 Heider produced from 1924–27, the Model D had a friction drive, which allowed infinitely variable speeds.

A small motor cultivator was offered from 1920, in one-row M or two-row M2 forms, both fitted with mid-mounted implements. Both used the Le Roi 138-ci (2.3-litre) four-cylinder motor, a popular choice for cultivators.

The final tractor from Rock Island (the Heider name had by now been dropped) was the 18/35 introduced in 1927, a conventional four-cylinder tractor powered by a 382-ci (6.2-litre) Buda. A similar 15/25, the G2, was also offered from 1929, this one using a 326-ci (5.3-litre) Buda. All Rock Island tractor production ended in 1937, when the company was taken over by J.I. Case.

RUSHTON

George Rushton was an ambitious man, and even though he was without capital or manufacturing facilities of his own, had

Britain's reply to the Fordson? That was the hope of George Rushton, who built this tractor between 1928 and 1932.

dreams of his company becoming the British Fordson. He approached the London General Omnibus Company, which in 1926 agreed to make Rushton's tractor in its AEC truck and bus factory in London. The company was presumably impressed not only by George Rushton's salesmanship, but also by the growing tractor market in England.

The first prototype, the Tri Tractor, came to nothing, but Rushton decided to buy an American Fordson which he proceeded to copy, piece by piece. Announced in July 1928, the new General tractor was not actually identical to the Fordson, being slightly heavier and more powerful; it was also more expensive to buy. Despite this, Rushton's aim was to sell 10,000 Generals a year, which was ambitious indeed when Fordson production was down to 3–4,000 annually.

London General was by now having second thoughts (and who can blame them), but George Rushton managed to get his tractor into production nevertheless. Fortuitously, AEC production was moving to another factory, so by floating shares Rushton was able to take over the London plant, buy 500 sets of components from AEC, and get the production lines rolling. He soon changed its name to the Rushton tractor, and offered both wheeled and crawler versions.

Sadly, the venture was all over in a couple of years. Why buy a Rushton when a Fordson was cheaper? In fact, why buy a tractor at all, as the Great Depression began to bite? Rushton's tractor business went into receivership in 1932, but even that wasn't the end of the story: the remains were bought by Tractors (London) Ltd., which went on to build the little Trusty horticultural tractor and even produced Rushtons in small numbers.

SAME

Francesco Cassani's name isn't as well known as that of Harry Ferguson or Henry Ford, but he too was a pioneer of tractor technology. The son of a mechanic, the young Cassani soon demonstrated a flair for engineering, and one of his first projects was to build a motor car powered by an aero engine.

But it was the tractor that made Cassani famous. Together with his younger brother, Eugenio, he began to experiment with diesel engines. At the time (the early 1920s) this was new technology, as diesels were well-established in heavy-duty applications such as ships and locomotives, but their use in smaller vehicles was in its infancy. So when Cassani unveiled his first tractor in the early- to mid-1920s it was the first diesel-powered machine to have been produced outside Germany. Cassani's own diesel engine was no miniature, being a 775-ci (12.7-litre) twin-cylinder that produced 40hp at a lumbering 450rpm. It was a full diesel rather than the crude semi-diesel that was said to be 60 per cent cheaper to run than the gasoline equivalent.

Cassani contracted another company to build his tractor, but only small numbers were produced before bankruptcy overtook the sub-contractor. Undaunted, he went on to develop a small 10-hp three-wheeled tractor, this time with a gasoline engine. Later, he founded SAME (Società Anonima Motori Endotermici) to produce tractors himself, rather than having to rely on sub-contractors (until then, his tractors bore Cassani's own name). War intervened, however, and a mere 33 machines were built between 1942 and 1948.

The turning-point really came in 1950 when a new range of 20-hp twin-cylinder tractors was launched. By that time, SAME was already selling a 10-hp three-wheeled tractor with reversible seat, and the following year began to offer four-wheel-drive on nearly all of its tractors. This was a far-sighted move when four-wheel-drive was almost unknown in tractors, though less so in Italy, where smaller machines often had quite advanced features. Another notable feature was SAME's extensive use of modular engineering. As early as 1951, its family of single-, twin-, three- and four-cylinder air-cooled diesels shared many parts in common, thus reducing costs. This modular principle is now well-established, and SAME itself was still making use of it in the 1990s.

The company certainly wasn't afraid of innovation and unveiled a new hydraulic depth control in 1960, which used the lower rather than the top links. The SAMECAR was a load-carrying/hauling tractor in the same mould as the German Unimog, while another 1960s product was the 480 Ariete ('Ram') wheeled tractor, with four-wheel-drive, eight-speed transmission and 80hp from its air-cooled four-cylinder 305-ci (5.0-litre) diesel. By 1972, SAME tractors were the best-selling four-wheel-drives in Italy, outselling even FIAT by three to two.

The company continued to expand, taking over Lamborghini tractors in 1972 and the Swiss Hurlimann concern five years later. Unusually, SAME has retained its independence, and even took over Deutz-Fahr in 1995 to create a giant European enterprise. By this time, SAME was offering a whole range of machines, all of which (apart from the mini-tractor range) used a variation on the company's 1000-series diesel engine. This one basic unit comprised a family of engines on the modular principle, by juggling bore sizes, strokes and the number of cylinders. So every SAME tractor, from the three-cylinder 60-hp Dorado 60 to the six-cylinder near-120-hp Titan 160 was powered by the same basic engine. Unusually, the 1000-series was air-cooled, with oil-cooling for the cylinder block;

SAME
EXPLORER 80 II L.P.
SAME
THE STOCKMANS TRACTOR
• 4 cylinder 80 din. H.P. engine
Greater lugging capacity
• 12×12 synchro-shuttle gear box
• 2 speed P.T.O. with 'Economy' gives 4 speeds
• Front wheel oil-immersed disc brakes
Give true predictable 4 wheel braking
• Low cab height only 2330 mm (7'8")
SAME

Francesco Cassani's pioneering spirit led to the successful SAME tractor.

at the time, Deutz-Fahr was the only other company which was persisting with air-cooled diesels for full-size tractors.

In the mid-range, Explorer II came with or without a turbo, producing up to 90hp, and in the next class up, powered the 80–100-hp Silver range which, incidentally, was styled by Giugiaro, the famous Italian car designer. There was four-wheel-drive, of course (electronically-controlled), and Agroshift, a 15-speed transmission incorporating three ranges. Next up came the Antres, with the 1000-series diesel in six-cylinder turbo form, giving 127hp. This also offered the most elaborate transmission of all the 1990s SAMEs: a six-speed gearbox with four ranges plus a push-button 20 per cent shift up or down on all of those ratios. That made 72 speeds in all, covering 1– 25mph (2–40km/h). The SAME flagship of the 1990s was the Titan range, with the intercooled 1000-series offering 145, 159 or 189hp and a 'mere' 27-speed transmission. Moreover, SAME announced an automatic transmission for tractors – Automatic Power Shift – in 1996. It looked as though Francesco Cassani's flair for innovation was in safe hands.

Later SAMEs were up-to-the-minute four-wheel-drive machines. The company now owns Lamborghini and Hurlimann.

BELOW and OPPOSITE
The Samson M was General Motors' answer to the Fordson, though hardly a success. In fact, General Motors has avoided tractors ever since.

SAMSON
Ford and General Motors were bitter rivals in the automobile business, so when Henry Ford announced his cheap, mass-produced Fordson tractor in 1917, General Motors chairman William Durant decided that his company should not be left out of the running. Unlike Ford, however, General Motors didn't have the luxury of years of experimentation under its belt; it needed a tractor in double-quick time.

So it bought Samson, of Stockton, California, whose three-wheeled Sieve Grip had been announced in 1914. The Sieve Grip (named after its pronounced rear-wheel lugs) was a distinctive low-slung machine which came in single-cylinder 6/12 or four-cylinder 10/25. General Motors added its own 426-ci (7-litre) four-cylinder motor to produce a 12/25 Sieve-Grip, but its relatively high price of $1,750 put paid to any thoughts of toppling the Fordson.

But General Motors already had a better idea. In December 1918 it announced 'a tractor and a price'. The tractor was the Model M, a modern four-cylinder machine which competed directly with the Fordson and had a price of just $650. In fact, it was the only real competition Ford had at the time, especially as the $650 included driver platform, mudguards, governor and belt-pulley, all of which cost extra on Henry's tractor. Power came from a 276-ci (4.5-litre) four-cylinder Northway motor (very close in size to the Fordson). The multi-plate clutch ran in oil while the transmission and rear axle were built as a unit. The Samson M actually turned a modest profit for General Motors, and a bigger three-plough Model A was planned to follow it.

But instead of concentrating on the Model A, General Motors was keen to jump on the cultivator bandwagon. Cultivators were selling very well at the time, though the boom was not to last. It bought the rights to the Jim Dandy cultivator, producing it as the Iron Horse, but this was a substandard machine of doubtful reliability and worse stability. There was also fierce competition from established cultivators. The Iron Horse actually lost General Motors a great deal of money, as did the entire Samson tractor operation (the M's modest profits apart). In 1922, less than four years later, General Motors pulled out of the tractor business. Henry Ford was welcome to it!

RIGHT
The adaptable Saunderson was also used for forestry work.

BELOW
Saunderson G-models awaiting delivery by train. For a time they were Britain's best-selling tractors.

OPPOSITE
An early, fully restored Saunderson twin-cylinder tractor.

SAUNDERSON

H.P. Saunderson was an English tractor pioneer who had spent part of his youth in Canada, and came home to import Massey-Harris machines in 1890 before producing his own from around 1903.

Made in Bedfordshire, England, early Saundersons were as much load carriers as tractors. Notable was the Saunderson Universal, powered by a 30-hp single-cylinder engine which sat directly behind the driver. The Universal was a practical, useful machine, with a load capacity of two tons on its platform, plus another two tons on the trailer. It was awarded a silver medal at the 1906 Royal Show.

In fact, the Universal proved so useful that Saunderson was able to set up a practical

SALLY

SAWYER-MASSEY
SAWYER MASSEY
SAWYER
MASSEY
CO. LIMITED
HAMILTON
CANADA
SAWYER-MASSEY
20-40
Nº 6263

demonstration to the press that same year. In front of the assembled journalists, a Universal pulled two 6-ft (1.8-m) binders to harvest 2 acres (0.8 hectares) of wheat. Then it transported the sheaves to a thresher, which it powered via its belt pulley, doing the same for a grinder, which produced flour. While a baker was busily using this to bake a batch of loaves, the Universal was used to plough the harvested acres, cultivate it, and sow the seed for the next crop. In a single afternoon, one tractor had harvested, transported, threshed, ground, ploughed, cultivated and seeded. As a finale, the journalists were able to munch on freshly baked bread!

Saunderson had successfully shown how useful a modern tractor could be, though his later models were more conventional and did without that rear load platform. Nevertheless, the 25-hp Model G, introduced in the early- to mid-1900s, became Britain's best-selling tractor, and was followed by the streamlined Light Tractor. But Saunderson's company was still too small to compete with the likes of Fordson, and was later assimilated by engine manufacturer Crossley. Tractor production ceased in the late 1920s.

SAWYER-MASSEY

The Canadian Sawyer-Massey concern had its roots in the blacksmith's shop of John Fisher of Hamilton, Ontario, who built a crude grain thresher. When he died, an employee named L.D. Sawyer took over the company with his two brothers, and from then on the renamed L.D. Sawyer & Co. expanded into portable steam engines in the 1860s and horsedrawn machinery from 1887.

The Massey connection came five years later, when the Massey family (of Massey-Harris fame) bought 40 per cent of the company and Sawyer-Massey was born. However, Sawyer-Massey had no other links with the Massey-Harris or Massey-Ferguson companies, though it did co-operate with Massey-Harris in the distribution of threshing machines. By 1910, Sawyer-Massey had become one of the biggest steam engine and thresher manufacturers in Canada. So it decided to double steam production, an odd decision, on reflection, with gasoline power on the horizon. The Massey family evidently thought so too, and pulled out, though the Sawyer-Massey name remained.

But Sawyer-Massey's commitment to steam wasn't quite as total as it might have seemed. The same year it decided to double production and a new gasoline tractor was unveiled. This could pull a six-bottom plough and cooled its engine by means of induced draft from the exhaust, like a steam traction engine. In fact, most Sawyer-Massey gas tractors were heavy-duty machines that owed much to steam traction engine technology.

However, the company was not interested in change for its own sake, and in 1911 settled on a common four-cylinder layout that its tractors would use in the 22/45. By 1918, a whole range was offered: 11/22, 12/25, 18/36, 20/40 and 27/50 (the latter an upgrade on the original 22/45). There was also a smaller Waukesha-powered 10/20 and a bigger 30/60 to rival the Advance-Rumely OilPull. Sawyer-Massey relinquished the tractor market in the early 1920s, transferring its resources to road-building machinery instead.

SCHLUTER

Schluter built its first tractor in 1937, though the family firm had been in existence since 1899. Three generations of Schluters were to pilot the company (all of them named Anton) until a succession of owners came and went in the 1980s and '90s.

That first tractor was a single-cylinder diesel, though during the Second World War Schluter built tractors to run on producer gas. This was a gasoline substitute produced by adding water to hot wood or coal. Thus powered, the 25/28-hp Schluter could tow 15 tons. The company concentrated on simple single- and twin-cylinder diesel tractors for most of its first 20 years in the tractor business, during which time it churned out about 30,000 machines.

In fact, many Schluters of the 1950s were very similar to the pre-war versions. Compare

OPPOSITE
Sawyer-Massey, a well-established producer of steam machinery, also built tractors up to the early 1920s.

BELOW
From modest beginnings, Schluter of Germany went on to produce high-powered super-tractors in the 1970s and '80s.

BELOW and OPPOSITE
Many European countries built their own version of the basic single-cylinder diesel tractor, which in France was the SFV/Vierzon.

the 1939 DZM25 (25-hp twin-cylinder) with the 1953 AS15D (15-hp 98-ci/1.6-litre engine) and one will find two small tractors of a very similar layout. One feature which survived the war was the flat seat on one mudguard for a passenger, a distinctive feature of small German tractors.

But the market was changing, and Schluter could not afford to ignore it. In fact, the company was one of the first European manufacturers to produce high-horsepower machines, which it did from the 1960s. As the decade progressed, its engines became larger and more powerful: Schluter offered four-cylinder diesels, then six- and even seven-cylinder units. The culmination was an eight-cylinder 580-ci (9.5-litre) engine which produced 180hp with the help of a turbo – a lot of power for the time. Nor was that the biggest Schluter. The Super-Trac of 1978 used a 500-hp MAN V12.

From 1980 Schluter offered its own six- and eight-cylinder engines of up to 200hp in a new range of tractors. Four-wheel-steering through equal-sized wheels and hydraulically-tilted cabs (Schluter had been fitting cabs since 1966) were other features. But the company was too small to survive on its own, and was hit especially hard when war in the former Yugoslavia wiped out one of its best export markets. It was later taken over by Schleppertile Egelseer GmbH, and appeared at the 1996 European Agricultural Show in Hanover with the four-wheel-drive Eura Trac.

SFV/VIERZON

At various times during the 1920s to the 1950s, Lanz of Germany, Landini of Italy, Marshall of England, HSCS in Hungary and Vierzon of France all produced their own particular version of the simple European tractor powered by a big single-cylinder diesel engine. Whether a hot-bulb semi-diesel or a full diesel, this layout based around a horizontal cylinder was a standard European design for decades, though of course the various makes differed in many other ways.

The French version was built by the Société Française de Matériel Agricole et Industriel de Vierzon, also known as SFV, Vierzon or simply 'Société'. The company had begun life in the farm machinery business

SOCIÉTÉ FRANÇAISE VIERZON
SOCIÉTÉ FRANÇAISE
VIERZON

RIGHT
Vierzon's tractor production began around 1930 and this poster reflects that era.

BELOW
The later, smaller, Vierzon 204 with modern bodywork.

OPPOSITE
The Silver King was built by Fate-Root-Heath of Plymouth, Ohio.

in 1847, producing steam engines from 1861, but it was another 70 years before its first tractor was announced. This was powered by a 50/55-hp semi-diesel hot-bulb engine, so-called because combustion occurred by means of a hot spot in the cylinder-head (in a full diesel, combustion is caused by compressing, and therefore heating, the intake air to a high degree before fuel is injected). Hot-bulb engines had a cold start ritual in which the hot bulb had first to be heated manually using a blow torch. Once running, the engine's own heat would provide the necessary means of combustion.

After the Second World War, SFV tractors

continued much as before, though there were detail improvements and a squared-off hood which distinguishes pre-war SFVs from post-war models. A smaller tractor, the 19-hp 201, was introduced, powered by a 195-ci (3.2-litre) version of the semi-diesel. It was later uprated to 25hp and also came in special narrow 201E format; at less than 3-ft (1-m) wide, it was ideal for working vineyards, making it an important part of the French tractor market. But SFV didn't neglect its big tractors either, and the 551 employed a huge cylinder measuring 9-in (23-cm) across. With a 10.4-in (264-mm) stroke that produced a 668-ci (10.9-litre) capacity, it was the largest of the post-war SFVs.

But like its rivals at Lanz, Landini and Marshall, the SFV was looking increasingly outmoded when compared with the new breed of lighter-weight multi-cylinder tractors. It was taken over by Case in the late 1950s, and SFVs began to use Peugeot gasoline or Normag diesel engines. None of this could save the company, however, and SFV ceased production in the early 1960s.

SILVER KING

Silver King wasn't so much a make of tractor as a name. The actual manufacturer was the Fate-Root-Heath company of Plymouth, Ohio, which wisely decided to give its products a more evocative name. All were small row-crop or standard-tread tractors of attractive appearance, but despite being early in the field with features such as electric starting and lighting, Silver King tractors failed to see the 1960s.

The company's first tractor wasn't named Silver King at all, but the Plymouth. This little machine, rated at 10/20hp, was powered by a four-cylinder Hercules engine of 113ci (1.8 litres). It was a lightweight at 2,170lb (984kg) but could run up to the relatively high road speed of 25mph (40km/h). Like Minneapolis-Moline, Fate-Root-Heath provided a high top ratio for higher road speeds, though in this case with a four- rather than five-speed transmission. The feature became a trademark of Fate-Root-Heath tractors.

The Plymouth tractor was renamed Silver King in 1935, while the original model became the R38. It acquired a slightly bigger Hercules engine in 1937, with a 3.25-in (83-mm) bore giving 133ci (2.2 litres). By then, a row-crop tricycle version was on offer, which was otherwise similar to the standard-tread.

SILVER KING
SILVER KING

Tested at Nebraska in March/April 1936, this produced 16.4hp at the drawbar, 19.7hp at the belt. Gear speeds gave 2.25mph (3.6km/h), 3.35mph (5.4km/h), 5.5mph (8.8km/h) and 14.5mph (23km/h) at the Hercules' rated 1,400rpm; increased engine speed allowed that impressive 25mph in top gear. The tractor actually suffered from overheating due to an aluminium-painted radiator and with no shroud. Fitting a shroud, and leaving the radiator unpainted, cured the problem.

From 1940, Fate-Root-Heath introduced the bigger 600, 660 and 720, the numbers referring to the tread widths of 60, 66 or 72 inches (152, 168 or 183cm), and there was a standard-tread version as well. The engine, a Continental this time, measured 162ci (2.6 litres), which according to Nebraska put out 31.2hp at the rated 1,800rpm; unlike the previous Silver King tested, this one didn't overheat. It retained a four-speed transmission, allowing up to 19.4mph (31km/h) at rated speed, but as high as 30mph (48km/h) with higher engine speeds, which probably made it, by some margin, the fastest tractor of its time.

But by 1956 Fate-Root-Heath had pulled out of the tractor business, selling the rights to the Silver King to the Mountain State Fabricating Company of Clarksburg, West Virginia. Mountain State failed to persevere, however, and after another two years the Silver King tractor was off the market for good.

SOMECA

La Société de Mécanique de la Seine was the tractor building arm of French car manufacturer SIMCA (another acronym, this time of the Société Industrielle de Mécanique et de Carrosserie Automobile). SIMCA had been founded in 1934, with the express purpose of building FIAT cars under licence.

In an attempt to find a fast route into the booming European tractor market, SIMCA bought an existing French tractor maker – MAP (Manufacture d'Armes de Paris) – in 1952. The MAP tractor used a most unusual engine, a twin-cylinder opposed four-piston supercharged diesel. Two of these engines were later fitted to a Delahaye racing car, which broke several diesel speed records (120mph/193km/h was the maximum). MAP also built 15,000 tractors up to 1955, powered by this and other engines.

SOMECA already supplied some components to MAP, so the link already existed. The first post-takeover SOMECA tractor was the DA50, with 37hp at 1,500rpm, and which used an OM four-cylinder diesel, OM being part of the FIAT empire. A smaller 50 and bigger 55 soon followed, and later the 615/715. All these tractors were based on FIAT/OM designs, which was logical given SIMCA's existing tie-up with FIAT. Whatever their origin, SOMECA tractors were successful in their home market, and over 40,000 were built by 1960. By the mid-1960s, the range had broadened to cover engines from 67ci (1.1 litres) to 250ci (4.1 litres).

For many years Steigers only came in lime green. This is a Puma 1000.

SIMCA was later taken over by Chrysler, but SOMECA ended up as part of the New Holland empire, with FIAT still a majority shareholder.

STEIGER

Modern super-tractors have several features in common: four-wheel-drive through equal-sized wheels, an articulated chassis to retain some manoevrability, and a massive turbo-diesel engine of six or more cylinders.

This format was invented by the Steiger brothers, Maurice and Douglas, and it was so successful that most modern super-tractors still follow the same pattern. The Steigers probably never intended to make it big in the tractor business. They were farmers with 4,000 acres (1600 hectares) at Red Lake Falls, Minnesota in the late 1950s, and found that none of the existing tractors was big or powerful enough for their needs. Four-wheel-drive was still a rarity, and no mainstream manufacturer had breached the 100-hp barrier.

So the Steigers rolled up their sleeves and built their own, making use of existing parts, some from Euclid machines, plus a 238-hp Detroit Diesel. This made it around three times more powerful than the biggest tractors available from John Deere, Case and Ford at that time. It weighed a massive 15,000lb (6804kg) and proved very reliable, amassing 10,000 hours of work on the Steiger dairy farm. With its tiller steering, it was a little crude, but neighbours were so impressed by the Steiger No.1 that they began asking for copies. The first Steigers made for customers were slightly smaller than the prototype. 'It was a powerful beast,' wrote tractor historian Peter Simpson later, 'but a numb lump ...Its tiller steering made it difficult to drive and Steiger's prospective customers wanted something more manageable.'

So the Steiger No.2 used a more modest Detroit Diesel of 100hp, while the 1200 was launched in 1963 with a 118-hp 3.71 Detroit Diesel and a conventional steering wheel replacing the tiller. But it kept four-wheel-drive and the Steigers' patented power splitter, which allowed the chassis to articulate and provide a much tighter turning circle than four-wheel-drive on such a huge machine would normally allow.

Business boomed through the 1960s. The Steigers weren't into mass-production, but were soon building 100 super-tractors a year. Bigger tractors – the 1700, 2200 and 3300 – followed, now with cabs, dual wheels at each corner, and lights. In fact, Steiger was doing so well that a consortium of businessmen decided to invest in the company, moving production away from the farm and into a disused tank factory at Fargo, North Dakota in

The Steiger 1360 Panther demonstrating the basic layout that all Steigers would follow: four-wheel-drive through equal-sized wheels, articulated steering, and a large front-mounted diesel engine.

case
CASE INTERNATIONAL

1969. This was soon outgrown and the company moved into a 420,000-sq ft (39018-m^2) plant five years later, which was now the biggest four-wheel-drive tractor factory in the world; by 1975 it was able to produce 20 super-tractors per shift. Exports began as well, and subsidiaries were formed in Australia and in Central and South America.

But although the Steigers were doing well, none of their tractors were tested by Nebraska until 1971. This simply reflected the nature of their market for, in the 1960s, still only a minority of farmers could afford to buy a giant 4 x 4 tractor, though the 1970s would prove to be a boom time. In the meantime, the Bearcat diesel tested from 9 September to 6 October (most Nebraska tests took around ten to 14 days) provided 159hp at the drawbar; brake horsepower couldn't be measured, as this particular Steiger had no PTO shaft. It was powered by a Caterpillar V8 of 636ci (10.4 litres) rated at a high 2,800rpm. Transmission was ten-speed, covering a range of 2.4–19.3mph (3.9–31km/h), and that maximum drawbar pull was obtained in fourth gear. It was aided by 1,544lb (700kg) of liquid ballast – 212lb (96kg) in each rear wheel, 560lb (254kg) in each front. An inner tube had to be replaced, but otherwise the first Steiger tested at Nebraska gave no trouble in 44 hours of running time.

Meanwhile, Steiger tractors got bigger by the year. Take the Panther ST310 of 1977. It was powered by a six-cylinder Cummins diesel of 855ci (14.0 litres) and later upgraded to 893ci (14.6 litres), giving 270hp at 2,100rpm. Another upgrade made it the 325-hp ST325 in 1976, with 20 forward speeds and four reverse. All the other essentials remained unchanged: articulated chassis, four-wheel-drive, equal-sized wheels. Nor was that the biggest. The Panther 3300 (Detroit Diesel V8-powered) drove 350hp through a 16 x 8 transmission. Working hard, it could cover 38 acres (15 hectares) an hour. Incidentally, the Steigers were very fond of naming their tractors after big cats, the association with power and strength being obvious; as well as Panthers, there were Tigers, Lions, Pumas and Cougars.

The biggest Steiger ever tested by Nebraska, in terms of both weight and engine size, was the 1978 Tiger III ST450. The name suggests 450bhp, though this could not be tested as the tractor had no PTO. However, it did manage 357hp at the drawbar, which equated to a pull of over 20,000lb (9072kg), quite good enough at that time. All this power came courtesy of a giant Cummins turbocharged six whose 6.25-in (159-mm) bore and stroke produced 1,150ci (18.8 litres). This drank diesel at the rate of over 25 gallons (114 litres) per hour under load. But this figure is misleading. Using Nebraska's usual measure of hp/hr per gallon, which takes into account the amount of work the tractor is extracting from each gallon, the biggest Steiger returned 14.18hp/hr per gallon. Of all the tractors tested by Nebraska up to 1984, this put it about halfway up the diesel class, reflecting the extra efficiency of big tractors. To put this in perspective: the most economical tractor Nebraska tested up to 1984 was a John Deere 1650 (1983) with 18.64hp/hr per gallon. And the worst? The gasoline-powered Shaw Du-All model T25 (1927) at 3.30hp/hr per gallon.

To return to the Steigers, who also did good business by selling their machines to the mainstream manufacturers: there was a long-standing association with Ford, while the Allis-Chalmers 440 was no more than a rebadged Steiger Bearcat; about 1,000 of those were sold between 1972 and '76, when Allis-Chalmers was ready to unveil its own big 4 x 4. Steiger also assembled the International Harvester 4366, later replaced by the 4368 powered by International's own V8 diesel. International already had a stake in Steiger, buying up shares in 1972. Although the Steigers had started out with Detroit Diesel engines, and later went over to Cummins, it did use Caterpillar units for some of its bigger machines in the 1970s. The Cougar II, for example, used a six-cylinder turbo-diesel Caterpillar, and the Bearcat II a 638-ci (10.4-litre) V8.

But the tractor slump of the 1980s proved too much for a small independent such as Steiger, with expensive 4 x 4 machines the worst hit. A saviour came in 1986, when the company was taken over by Case-International. With hindsight, it was inevitable that someone would save the well-respected Steiger name, not that this was Case-International Harvester's primary intention. The Case-IH 9250 of the late 1980s was built by Steiger, but was badged a Case, pure and simple. It was the new 9300-series that brought a change of heart in the 1990s. The Steiger name returned (though still in Case-International Harvester corporate colours of red-and-black) on a whole range of machines ranging from the 240-hp 9330 to the 425-hp

OPPOSITE
It may be wearing Case-IH badges, but the 9250 was a Steiger through and through.

Steyr retained its independence until 1996, when it was taken over by Case.

9390. Engines were built by Case or Cummins, depending on the model, and the basic 12-speed transmission could be replaced with a 12-speed powershift or 24-speed Syncroshift. But the ultimate 9300 for the 21st century was the new Quadtrac, still with articulation, but with four rubber tracks replacing the wheels. And the name on the grille? Steiger.

STEYR

Steyr, Austria's foremost tractor manufacturer, came to the business by degrees, starting out by making guns (hence the circular Steyr logo which represents a shooting target) before progressing to bicycles. The company's first powered vehicles came in 1920, both cars and Excelsior motor ploughs, which were built under licence from Laurin & Klement of Czechoslovakia. Trucks followed, and in 1928 the first Steyr tractor.

Production was on a limited scale until 1947, when true mass-production began (the company would build 160,000 tractors by 1965). They were quite different from the machines offered before the Second World War, which were largely based on the Fordson. Instead, the new generation of Steyrs were in the more basic European mould of the 1950s, with single- or twin-cylinder engines. Typical was the 30-hp 180a of 1955, though Steyr continued to offer small tractors into the 1960s, such as the twin-cylinder 28-hp 188 of 1964.

Horsepower and sophistication gradually increased through the 1960s, when multi-cylinder diesel engines from Perkins and MWM were utilized, and by the 1970s Steyr

LEFT
The Steyr 8080 bio-diesel: the fuel derived from rapeseed oil is widely used in Austria.

had progressed from its beginnings in small tractors to offer full-sized machines as well. The 760a of 1974 was a 66-hp four-cylinder machine with modern squared-off styling. Steyr weathered the 1980s slump independently, and in 1996 announced the new 9000-series, a fully modern droop-snoop tractor in the 100–150-hp class. All four models were powered by turbo-diesel engines designed by Steyr but built for them by Valmet of Finland and which included the four-cylinder 105-hp 9105, and the 9115, 9125 and 9145, all of which used a six-cylinder engine. There was a 24-speed powershift transmission with push-button-operated shuttle for forward/reverse pre-selection. The tractor's turning circle was tighter than its predecessor's (at 50 degrees) while the hydraulic pump had a bigger capacity, giving maximum lift of 19,841lb (9,000kg).

The same year that the 9000-series was announced, Steyr was taken over by Case-International Harvester (or to be more accurate, the parent company Tenneco). It is likely that Steyr and Case were already co-operating before the takeover, for in April the same year it was revealed that Steyr would build the new Case C-series range (from 42ps C42 to 70ps C70), with an identical Steyr-badged range alongside it. It was also to work with Case on development of the 3200/3400 compacts. This was an eventful year for Steyr, for in October there were press reports that Korean engineering giant Daewoo was to buy 65 per cent of the shares in the Austrian tractor and gun business, though its bus and truck arm would not be included. However, in 2002, Steyr tractors were still part of the CNH Global empire, alongside Case.

BELOW LEFT
All-new for 1996 was the Steyr 9000-series, which featured Valmet-built engines. The Austrians would soon be co-operating with Case to expand its range.

RIGHT
Tractor or truck? The Terra Gator 1664T.

OPPOSITE
The Turner Yeoman was a brave attempt to produce an all-British V4 diesel tractor.

TERRA GATOR

In the early 20th century, Henry Ford popularized the tractor with his cheap, simple Fordson, even though he wasn't the only one to do so; but he was easily the most successful. Half a decade later, International unveiled the adaptable Farmall, a tractor that could do just about any job on a farm that needed doing. Together, they transformed the role of the tractor as a large, expensive, specialized piece of machinery to a do-it-all workhorse that thousands of farmers could afford.

Now the wheel has come full circle. Farms in the Western world get larger by the year, so big, expensive, specialized machinery is viable once again. It is now worthwhile for larger farms to have their own combine harvester, a specialist yard loader, a couple of high-horsepower tractors, a spreader, and a high-speed machine for road-hauling. The Terra Gator is one such specialist in that it is a high-capacity spreader or sprayer that is half-tractor, half-truck. Over 10,000 of these have been built, with their huge, low-pressure tyres designed for minimal soil impaction and single-wheel or twin-wheel front-ends. Ag-Chem of Holland, which builds the Terra Gator, also makes narrow-wheeled, wide-tread specialist sprayers. The company is also the most recent addition to the AGCO group.

The 8103 Terra Gator was unveiled in 1998, powered by a John Deere six-cylinder turbo-diesel engine of 519ci (8.5 litres) of which 320hp is claimed. The transmission was built by Ag-Chem itself. This Terrashift was a powershift set-up, with clutchless changing between very closely-spaced ratios. The rear axle, though, came from John Deere, allegedly to increase reliability. A new rectangular tube frame was said to provide more strength and flexibility. Variations on the theme soon appeared, such as the 400-hp 9103, powered by a Caterpillar diesel, and the four-wheel-drive 8144. These days, specialization seems to be the key to successful farming – as long as one can afford it.

TURNER

In the 1950s the Yeoman of England was a brave attempt to produce a modern diesel tractor by Turner Manufacturing, with an unusual V4-powered unit. It was brave and original but, as it turned out, unreliable, too expensive and not powerful enough.

The company that built it had its roots in the mid-19th century, and was a well-established maker of winches, machine tools and stationary engines. After the Second World War, Turner decided to diversify into diesel engines, developing a family of single-cylinder V-twin and V4s, all with the same 3.75 x 4.5-in (95 x 114-mm) bore x stroke. Both twin- and four-cylinder versions had a 68-degree engine, and it was the biggest (of 198ci/3.2 litres) that formed the basis of Turner's first tractor.

The omens looked good. There was an overwhelming demand for tractors in post-war Britain, and the Government was encouraging exports to clear the nation of its wartime debt; moreover, tractors were highly exportable, and the giant Nuffield concern had successfully made its mark with its own first tractor.

Alas, although the Turner Yeoman of England looked and sounded impressive (the

The Universal 600: made in Romania, finished in the United States of America.

V4 had its own distinctive exhaust note), at £798 it was just too expensive to compete with mass-produced opposition from Fordson, Ferguson and Nuffield. It had a four-speed transmission and electric starter, but hydraulic lift, power take-off, lights and differential lock all cost extra. But the Turners that were sold soon began to give trouble; despite improvements at the prototype stage, the cooling system was still inadequate and overheating could occur. The Marles steering box was unreliable as well, being intended for automotive rather than field use, and the transmission was subject to failure in both third gear and at the crown wheel. A Mark 3 Yeoman addressed some of these defects, and the price was cut substantially; but it still cost £200 more than a Fordson Major. In 1955, Turner abandoned its tractor after a mere 2,131 had been sold; one theory is that the company agreed to cease production in exchange for a contract to supply timing gears and oil pump drives to Fordson. In fact, transmissions became Turner's main business. Now part of Caterpillar, it supplies transmissions to Manitou and New Holland as well as to its parent company.

UNIVERSAL

Universal tractors were a product of the Long Manufacturing Company of Tarboro, North Carolina. But they weren't American-made. Universals were actually built by Uzina Tractorul Brasov (UTB) of Brasov, Romania. Almost complete, they were then shipped to the United States and finished off by Long, which added some American components. The idea was to market low-cost tractors with an American sheen; this was fairly successful, with Long/Universals on sale in North America throughout the 1960s, '70s and '80s and right into the '90s.

Long Manufacturing had entered the tractor business in 1949, building its own small Model A, powered by a 111-ci (1.8-litre) Continental engine. It looked neat and up to date, with 20.6-drawbar-hp and 30.3hp at the belt when tested at Nebraska. However, Long later turned to importing the cheaper Romanian machines. It also imported at least one Landini from Italy (sold as the Long R9500 in 1972), but most Universals orginated in Romania.

In turn, UTB tractors owed something to

The three-cylinder 533 DT was Universal's mid-range tractor for the 1980s, derived from the 530 turbo of 1981. There was also a non-turbo 510 and four-cylinder 610.

FIAT designs, and in 1972 Long was offering the U350, U445 and U550. The bigger two were powered by UTB's own four-cylinder diesel, in the case of the 550 a 191-ci (3.1-litre) rated at 2,400rpm. It produced 46.7hp at the drawbar, according to Nebraska, and 53.6hp at the PTO. Transmission was eight-speed and the U550 weighed 4,570lb (2073kg) before the addition of test weights.

By 1981 there were three tractors in the range, again all powered by UTB's own diesel engines: the three-cylinder 510 (non-turbo) and 530 (turbo), plus the four-cylinder 219-ci (3.6-litre) 610. Sadly, Long was unable to survive the troubled 1980s unscathed, and filed for Chapter 11 bankruptcy in June 1985. Two years later, it bounced back, revitalized by a fresh injection of capital, though with all its sales branches closed.

For 1990, four restyled tractors were introduced. The 360, 460, 510 and 610 were all replaced by the 2360 (35-PTO-hp), 2460 (42-hp), 2510 (49-hp) and 2610 (64-hp). All were powered by three-cylinder diesels, apart from the 2610, which retained the 219-ci four; all had eight-speed tranmissions and the option of front-wheel-assist. A smaller 2260 was added in 1994, with a twin-cylinder engine giving 24hp at the PTO. This had a six-speed transmission and a fold-down roll bar. Long-badged tractors are still available in 2002.

URSUS

Zakladow Mechanicznych (Ursus) has long been Poland's foremost tractor manufacturer.

Ursus tractors owed much to Zetor until it came to an agreement with Massey-Ferguson in the 1970s.

The Ursus C-385 was a product of the company's Zetor period. Eastern Bloc tractors found a sales niche in the West, due to simple specifications and low prices.

But the company is far older than its tractors, having been inaugurated in 1893 to build equipment for the food industry. From its Warsaw base, Ursus quickly branched out into internal combustion engines, and by 1913 was producing nothing else. Some were powerful beasts of up to 450hp, and the company had built an impressive 6,000 motors before the outbreak of the First World War.

It wasn't until 1922 that Ursus built its first tractor, though a prototype engine to power it had been run four years earlier. But there was no question of going into mass-production, and only 100 or so Ursus tractors were produced over the following five years; in any case, the company was now concentrating on trucks and buses. But it collapsed in 1930, only to be saved by the Polish Government, and went on to produce all sorts of vehicles during the Second World War, including 700 military tractors.

Once peace had been restored, Ursus finally found its way into serious tractor production, churning out a copy of the German Lanz Bulldog from 1947. In the late 1940s and early '50s the single-cylinder diesel Lanz was fast becoming the standard

European tractor, and the Ursus wasn't the only Lanz-inspired machine. Sixty thousand of them were built by Lanz alone before production ended in 1959. From Lanz, Ursus then looked to Zetor of Czechoslovakia for inspiration. This fellow Eastern Bloc tractor manufacturer was well-established, and over the next decade or so, the two concerns would share many components.

Although some of these were built by Ursus for Zetor, including at various times front axles and hydraulics, it has to be said that for most components the reverse was true. Zetor was technically ahead of Ursus, and by the early 1970s about half of all Ursus components came directly from Czechoslovakia. The new generation of post-Lanz Ursus tractors began with the twin-cylinder C325, which was tested by Nebraska in July 1961. Powered by a 111-ci (1.8-litre) diesel, it produced 21.7hp at the drawbar and 24.6 PTO-hp at the rated 2,000rpm. This was later updated as the 120-ci (2.0-litre) C335, tested in 1968. Also at Nebraska that year was the four-cylinder C350, a 43-PTO-hp machine, while the bigger Ursus 4011, which had been introduced three years earlier, was basically the same as the Zetor 4011.

A new era began for Ursus in the 1970s when it brokered a deal with Massey-Ferguson in which the Poles would build a range of MF-based machines of 38–72hp. This was the third such partner for Ursus and appears to have been a success, for in 2002 the company was still offering a range of machines with Massey-Ferguson overtones. In North America, these kicked off with the 2812, a 38-hp three-cylinder tractor at $10,495 (the low price of East European tractors has always been a key selling point) to the top-range 4824 (65-hp Perkins diesel, optional four-wheel-drive). But the world was changing, and following the collapse of the Eastern Bloc, Ursus was privatized in 1998. There was a suggestion that AGCO might take the company over, but at the time of writing Ursus remains independent.

VALMET

It is difficult to find a better example of the concept of turning swords into ploughshares than Valmet. Finland's own tractor manufacturer built military materiel during the Second World War, but its precision engineering skills translated well into tractors as well as other products. (The early prototype Valmets had the clutch and gearbox connected by a cannon bore!) The first 12-hp prototype was complete in 1949, but it was three years before the Valmet 15 finally went into production.

It was the perfect time to sell a small tractor in Finland, where tens of thousands of small farms had been set up by evacuees and former soldiers. Unlike the single-cylinder diesels popular elsewhere in Europe (and indeed Valmet's own prototype) the 15 used a 92-ci (1.5-litre) four-cylinder kerosene engine which started on gasoline. This simple one-plough machine was lightweight, nimble, and sipped kerosene at the rate of 0.66 gallons (3 litres) per hour – just the thing for post-war Finland. Although it proved adept at all the usual farming tasks, one uniquely Finnish attachment was an ice saw driven off the belt pulley, used for

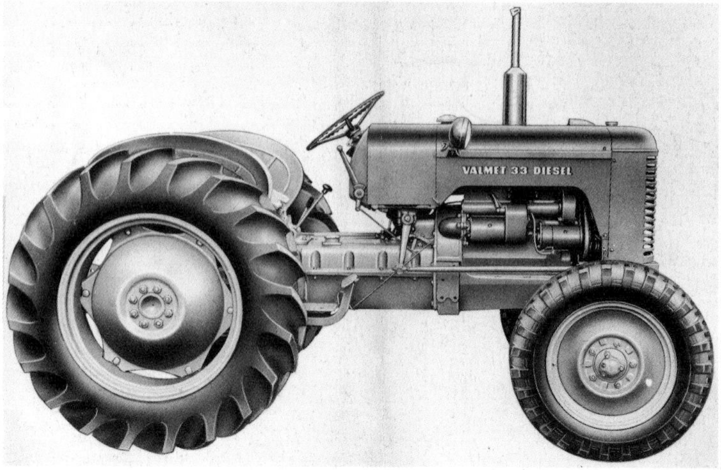

The 33 was Valmet's first diesel tractor, using a home-grown direct-injection three-cylinder engine.

Another early Valmet, this one a kerosene- (paraffin-) powered 53. For its first tractors the company placed economy and reliability above advanced specifications.

ABOVE
The 361 from 1961 marked the start of a new era for Valmet. It was a great success, and more new models soon followed on.

RIGHT
The Valmet Synchro had twin clutches – one for the drivetrain, one for the PTO – and allowed independent operation of the PTO. Another innovation was hydrostatic crawler gear that allowed speeds below 1.8mph (3km/h).

carving blocks of ice out of frozen lakes.

But as time went on the little Valmet began to look rather meagre compared with the bigger Fergusons and Fordsons, its natural rivals. So in 1955 a 19.5-hp version was launched (it actually gave 22hp on gasoline), complete with hydraulic lift. But even this wasn't enough, and Valmet quickly got to work on its own three-cylinder diesel engine. With direct-injection and a capacity of 165ci (2.7 litres), the new Valmet 33 produced 37hp at a relatively high 2,000rpm and was in fact the first high-speed diesel of this type. Cold starting was a particular concern in its home market, so the new motor was tested in Lapland in the depths of winter. It was also water-cooled, though many argued that air-cooling was needed to prevent freezing up in Finland's cold winters. But the country also has hot, dusty summers, so water-cooled it had to be. To match the modern engine, the 1957 Valmet had a six-speed transmission, a 2976-lb (1350-kg) hydraulic lift (though no three-point-hitch as yet) and could attain a useful 18mph (29km/h) on the road.

By world standards Valmet was still a small producer: only 1,537 33D tractors were built over two years – but it was thriving. A new 361D with modern squared-off styling was launched in 1961. It retained the 33D's excellent cold starting (from -13F or -25C on standard equipment, it was claimed) with more power, i.e. 42hp at 2,000rpm. Production was rising too, and nearly 15,000 361Ds were built by the mid-1960s. Valmet now had a factory established in Brazil, while a Portuguese company was making the 361D under licence.

One interesting variation on the 361D was the 363D all-terrain tractor. This had four-wheel-drive and an articulated chassis and was virtually a Steiger in miniature. With its high ground clearance and good traction, it was a natural for forestry work, which in Finland was plentiful. Alongside it, Valmet

The six-wheeled 1502, aimed at reducing compaction while allowing high speeds. Its weight and cost, however, was rather daunting, but it did find a niche in the peat industry.

In the 1980s, Valmet collaborated with Volvo to produce the so-called Nordic tractor, while in the '90s it teamed with Massey-Ferguson to build the Mega 8000-series. This was a natural progression as Valmet was already supplying engines to Massey-Ferguson. By this time the Valtra brand name was in evidence following Valmet's incorporation with Sisu and eventually with Partek.

launched its biggest tractor yet, the 864, with a new four-cylinder diesel producing 77hp through an 8-speed transmission. There was little demand for such a large tractor on small Finnish farms, but it found a market in contract work and in the forests. Meanwhile, the 361D now enjoyed 52hp as the Valmet 565 and benefited from a syncromesh gearbox: 'Drive your tractor like your car', went the advertisements.

The Scandinavians seem to have a natural affinity for ergonomics or designing for people, and the new Valmet 900 of 1967 was one of the first tractors with an integrated cab, rubber-mounted to reduce vibration and noise, and with great attention paid to the design inside. At the time, most tractor cabs were noisy, drafty things, seemingly bolted on as a mere afterthought. The new Valmet cab was relatively quiet, with its own heating and ventilation system. The instrument panel and controls were all designed with convenience in mind and steering was hydrostatic to save strain on the biceps. Mechanically, the 900 was a straight update of the 864, with 89hp from a bigger 256-ci (4.2-litre) diesel, an eight-speed transmission, and three-speed PTO, plus high-capacity hydraulics. So successful was the 900 with cab concept that a smaller 54-hp 500 was soon launched on the same lines to replace the 565. The gap between them was filled by the 75-hp 700 in 1968.

Like may others, Finnish farmers and contractors were now demanding more power, and Valmet responded by turbocharging the 900's four-cylinder engine. This gave 102hp from the same 256ci, and the same year four-

wheel-drive was made an option on both the 900 and the new turbocharged 1100. In 1971, a new 502 continued the 900's tradition with another all-new cab, this being one of the quietest on the market. The cab's flat floor, with all the major controls on the right-hand side, was a further development in ergonomics. Valmet's bigger tractors soon followed suit, and by 1973 the company was the market leader in Finland, outselling Massey-Ferguson, Ford and International.

One innovation at this time was the six-wheeled 1502. This radical new tractor used four small wheels at the back, rather than two large ones, the idea being to minimize ground pressure while maintaining speed. For sticky conditions, the four-wheel bogie could be lifted on hydraulic struts for the fitting of rubber tracks. The 1502's radical chassis was matched by a similarly radical, glassed-in cab, and Valmet's biggest engine yet, a 405-ci (6.6-litre) six-cylinder turbo of 136hp. But the oil crisis was starting to bite, and farmers fought shy of such a large, expensive machine. In any case, it was really too heavy compared with conventional tractors. Instead, the 1502 was adopted by the peat industry, which appreciated its low ground pressure.

The 1502's engine had other uses as well. Halved in size as a three-cylinder 203-ci (3.3-litre) engine of 58hp, it neatly filled the gap between 502 and 702 (the new 602 was introduced in 1978). The following year, Valmet's old four-cylinder motor was replaced by a four-cylinder version of the same family for the 72-hp 702. A turbocharged three in the 602 Turbo gave 66hp and filled another gap, while the 702 was lightly turbocharged (as

LEFT and BELOW LEFT
In the 1990s Valtra gradually replaced Valmet as the brand name. This is the big S-series.

RIGHT, BELOW and OPPOSITE
The distinctive Valtra T-series, was one step down from the S. Now owned by Partek of Finland, Valtra's future seemed secure.

much to reduce emissions as to increase power) for the 82-hp 802. More radical was the supercharged 1203, which used a Comprex pressure-wave supercharger in place of a turbo. This allowed 110hpDIN and 424Nm, all Valmet's power figures being taken from the crankshaft rather than the PTO.

There was exciting news in 1979, when Valmet joined forces with Volvo BM to jointly develop a tractor. Announced three years later, the so-called Nordic tractor was thoroughly modern, with its sloping nose and spacious cab. All four models were turbocharged with

four-wheel-drive, and all were powered by Valmet engines, from the 65-hp 505 to the 95-hp 805. The transmission was fully synchronized, with powershift Trac-Trol giving an under or overdrive and up to 25mph (40km/h) on the road. A six-cylinder 905 soon joined the range, powered by a 105-hp non-turbo six-cylinder diesel, and a new 04-series range replaced the smaller Valmets. All these tractors were badged 'Volvo BM Valmet', though the company's factories in Brazil and Tanzania continued to produce pure Valmet machines.

However, this confusion of names didn't last long for in 1985 Valmet bought out its partner. The Finns had come out of the short-lived partnership well, with a completely new tractor range and increased sales; by 1987, one in four new tractors was a Valmet in both Finland and Sweden. Meanwhile, the Power Plus range launched that year increased power for the larger tractors from 72hp for the 505 to 110hp for the 905. The smaller 305 and 405 continued.

As for the other end of the range, the Volvo BM link had brought the big 2005 and 2105 into the Valmet fold. But by the late 1980s these tractors were in basic design 20 years old. Rather than design their own big tractor from scratch, Valmet agreed to have it built for them by Massey-Ferguson at its Beauvais plant in France. There was already a link here, as Valmet was supplying engines for the 180-hp MF 3680. Introduced in 1989, the new Beauvais-built Mega 8300 and 8600 were quite a mixture of components: Valmet

VALTRA
VALTRA

engines, Massey-Ferguson transaxle and hydraulics, while the cab and driven front axle came from Italy, with final assembly at Beauvais. With 140hp (non-turbo) and 170hp (turbo) from its six-cylinder diesel, this was the most powerful Finnish tractor yet.

But Valmet, having seemingly accepted that it was too small to produce tractors entirely alone, joined forces with Steyr to built a completely new range covering 90–140hp. As it happened, the co-operation was ended even before a tractor reached the market: Steyr's bank forbade it. But all was not lost, as much work had been accomplished and Valmet was able to launch the new 20-series engine in 1990. This powered the Mega 8100, which combined its 120-hp engine with a new transmission and fresh '90s styling. The following year, the all-new Mezzo range of tractors, covering 79–105hp, amply demonstrated that the years working with Steyr had not been wasted.

Despite the fanfare of the launch, however, things were going badly. The tractor market in both Brazil and Scandinavia was collapsing, leaving Valmet with stocks of unsold machines. Hundreds of people lost their jobs, and those that survived had their salaries pegged. The company was reorganized and stocks of unsold tractors were discounted direct from the factory. This led to the company building tractors to customer order only, which incidentally allowed them to offer a range of colours, a first for any tractor manufacturer.

Matters gradually improved in the 1990s, and new tractors launched in 1993 were the Mega 8400 (140hp and three-range powershift) and the 6600 and 8100 (also with this Delta powershift). All this time, Valmet had been state-owned, but in 1994 it was incorporated with Sisu, another state-owned Finnish company, which made trucks and armoured vehicles.

More new tractors were to come, despite the reorganizations. In 1995, the new Mega 50 (110-hp 8050 and 125-hp 8150) replaced the 8100. They were launched in Paris by floating them down the Seine on a barge, while 'Vikings' drove the tractors later that evening: this was apparently in memory of a Viking invasion of the French capital over 1,000 years earlier. The French reaction to this re-enactment is not recorded! Also new was the 8450 (same power as the 8400 but more torque) and 160-hp 8550. There was also an 8750 Sigma Power, which was identical to the 8550 apart from a more sophisticated PTO which allowed the engine to produce up to 190hp, or 172hp at the PTO. Sigma made a great impact, offering very high PTO power in a lighter-weight tractor.

In 1997, Valmet was taken into private hands for the first time when Sisu was sold to Finnish company Partek. Part of the original agreement with Sisu was that the Valmet name would only be used on tractors up to May 2001, though the brand name Valtra had gradually became more prominent through the 1990s. The first tractors to bear this name were the articulated City and Forest machines, based on the existing Mezzo tractor and which came in 95-, 105- or 115-hp forms and with hydrostatic or gear transmission. More conventional was the new 100 of late 1997, covering the 60–90-hp range, logically named 600 (60hp) to 900 (90hp). Smaller and simpler was the Italian-built 3000-range, covering 52–76hp and which used a Deutz air-cooled engine. In 1998, the HiTech range of 90–200hp replaced the faithful Megas, with electronically-controlled transmission and pneumatic front suspension.

So Valtra, as it now was, faces the 21st century with confidence, having built nearly 750,000 tractors – which is not bad for a maker of cannons!

VERSATILE

Versatile was the Canadian Steiger, a maker of giant four-wheel super-tractors, with equal-sized wheels and articulated chassis. Its roots lay in the Hydraulic Engineering Company of Toronto, which set up shop in 1947 making small agricultural implements. Three years later, it moved to a new factory in Winnipeg, where Versatiles would be made for half a century.

Gradually, the company branched out into larger implements, such as a self-propelled swather in 1954, though it wasn't until 1963 that the Hydraulic Engineering Company placed its shares on the open market. With the new capital came a new name: Versatile. Three years on, and Versatile was ready to launch its first super-tractor, though the D100 was small by Steiger standards. It was powered by a British Ford six-cylinder diesel of 125hp, and only around 100 of these early Versatiles were built before it was replaced by the D145.

Versatile's four-wheel-drive tractors gradually got bigger, and by 1976 it was offering four: the 700, 800, 850 and 900, all

now with a 'Series 2' tag. A 750 was added to the range that year, powered by an 855-ci (14-litre) Cummins six-cylinder engine, which produced 220hp and drove through a 12-speed transmission.

The year before, Versatile had sought a fresh injection of capital in negotiations with Hesston, the U.S. implement manufacturer that also imported FIAT tractors to the States and sold them under its own name. However, the difficult economic situation of the mid-1970s precluded this, though in 1977 a controlling interest in Versatile was acquired by Cornat Industries, which solved its financial problems for a while.

In fact, 1977 was an important year for the Canadians. There were several revisions to the big tractor range, which now included the 500, a four-wheel-drive machine with adjustable wheel-tread and live PTO. It was powered by a Cummins V8 with 160-PTO-hp (192 at the crankshaft). Further up the scale was the 250-hp 825 and the new 950, another Cummins V8 tractor, though this one boasted 903ci (14.8 litres) for 348hp at the crank.

But the big news was a much smaller tractor than any of these, the little 150 with just 60hp at the PTO. Its secret lay in its full name: the 150 Push-Pull. This was one of the first bi-directional tractors, with a 180-degree swivelling driver's position so that it could work equally well in either direction. In 'pull' mode it operated like a conventional tractor, but in 'push' the driver turned around, engine behind him, and had a perfect view of implements such as swathers or loaders. Naturally, the 150 had an articulated chassis, like the big Versatiles, which made it

A sleeping dinosaur? A faded, well-worn Versatile rusts quietly away under a bright blue sky. It would be interesting to know how many acres it has worked in the past 20-odd years.

VERSATILE
875

extremely manoevrable for yard work, where the bi-directional facility was most useful. Given the need to rapidly swap between forward and reverse, the 150 had a hydrostatic transmission, with three ranges in either direction.

Clever though the 150 was, Versatile wasn't about to abandon its bread-and-butter big tractors. The following year saw four new super-tractors announced, all with Cummins Constant Power engines, so-called because they promised to provide the same power even at 400rpm below rated speed. There was an 835 (230-engine-hp, 39 per cent torque rise), an 855 (250-engine-hp, 36 per cent torque rise), 875 (280-engine-hp, 31 per cent torque rise) and 935 (330-engine-hp, 27 per cent torque rise). These four replaced the Series 2 machines which had been unveiled in 1976.

It is doubtful, however, that any of these attracted as much attention as Big Roy. Roy was a prototype super-tractor, the biggest Versatile had ever made, and was shown to the public in late 1977. Everything about Big Roy was exactly as the name implied: eight-wheel-drive, four powered axles; 600hp from a 1,150-ci (18.8-litre) Cummins; shipping weight 54,450lb (24699kg). But it never made it to production.

The little bi-directional 150, on the other hand, was doing well, and in 1980 a Series 2 was introduced with a revised cab. The same year, the 500 was powered up as the 555, now with a 220-engine-hp Cummins and 15-speed transmission, and there was a new 895 top-of-the-range at 330-engine-hp. A still bigger Versatile arrived in 1982, using the 1,150-ci intended for Big Roy; turboed and intercooled, it gave 470-engine-hp, while the 150 was given more power as the 70-PTO-hp 160.

The following year, all the big Versatiles were updated as the Series 3: the 835, 875 and 895 all received the latest Cummins Big Cam III motors (more fuel-efficient than before), and there was a new, more ergonomic cab with seven-way adjustment for the seat and a seven-position steering wheel. Three new tractors – the 945 (335-engine-hp), 955 (350hp) and 975 (360hp) – replaced the old 855, 935 and 950. The 160 received a major update in 1984, with a bigger CDC four-cylinder diesel giving 84hp at the PTO; otherwise, all the essentials were unchanged, including the four-wheel-drive, articulation, and swivelling driver's platform on what was now named the 256. A turbocharged and intercooled 276 came along the following year, with 100hp at the PTO.

No one could accuse Versatile of complacency: updates were unveiled almost every year, at a time (the 1980s) when tractor sales in North America had slumped, with big 4 x 4 machines affected worse than most. But it was undaunted: for the 1985 model year the company launched its Designation 6-range, which included the 836 (210-engine-hp) and the 976 (335-engine-hp). All had the option of a 12-speed manual or 12-speed full powershift transmission, plus a 15-speed manual with PTO for the three 'smaller' models, or one should probably say 'less large'.

But Versatile was facing increasing competition from large conventional tractors from the mainstream manufacturers; with front-wheel-assist, these allowed better traction than two-wheel-drive machines, but were still cheaper than a full 4 x 4. To meet them, Versatile introduced the 756, still with the articulated chassis and a 168-PTO-hp Cummins. To keep the cost down (essential when competing with the likes of Ford and John Deere), it was only built to order.

None of this was enough, however. Not only was Versatile struggling in a depressed market, its parent company also had financial problems of its own. In 1986, the Winnipeg factory was temporarily closed while a solution was sought. Early the following year, the answer came when Ford-New Holland took over Versatile, providing it with a ready-made range of super-tractors. That was in February, and by July the Winnipeg plant was up and running again. It really was business as usual, with a new 846 replacing the 756, 836 and 856 in 1988. With a 611-ci (10.0-litre) Cummins, the 846 came with outboard or inboard planetary axles, the latter to allow adjustable tread for row-crop work. Transmission was 12-speed constant-mesh. A 946 came along the year after, displacing the 936, with 325-engine-hp from the familiar 855-ci (14-litre) Cummins. It also came in Ford-New Holland blue, instead of the old red-and-gold of Versatile, though the Versatile badge lived on, albeit in small print. The familiar bi-directional tractor was also part of the new regime, now named the Ford Versatile 9030, in Ford colours with Ford four-cylinder turbo-diesel, strong frames, and higher three-point-lift capacity at both ends.

There was a radical redesign in 1994 as well, when the 846, 876, 946 and 976 were

OPPOSITE
The Versatile 875, one of a long line of giant super-tractors from the Canadian experts. All had four-wheel-drive, articulated chassis and massive dimensions. This one was powered by a 280-hp (31 per cent torque rise) Cummins, but even so was dwarfed by the 600-hp prototype Big Roy.

Ford
FORD
NEW HOLLAND
846
DESIGNATION 6
VERSATILE

replaced by a new range: 9280, 9480, 9680 and 9880 with 250-, 300-, 350- and 400-engine-hp respectively. The smallest continued to use the 611-ci (10.0-litre) Cummins, while the others had its 855-ci (14-litre) big brother. A new Quad-Sync transmission gave four synchronized shifts in each of the three ranges, providing 12 speeds in all, while 12-speed powershift was an option on the two largest tractors.

That same year it was announced that the Ford name would be phased out, leaving the company name as New Holland, pure and simple. And Versatile? Well, the name was sufficiently well-regarded for New Holland to continue using it. When an all-new bi-directional tractor was launched in 1998, it still carried the Versatile badge, albeit in very small print below a very large 'New Holland' badge. This was the TV140, an up-to-date continuation of the original concept which Versatile had pioneered nearly 20 years earlier. Power now came from a 135-hp six-cylinder diesel, but the idea was unchanged.

Not that it was built at Winnipeg. In 1999, New Holland merged with Case to form the giant CNH Global corporation – so huge, in fact, that the competition authorities insisted that it close or sell a couple of plants. One of these was Winnipeg, which was sold in 2000 to Buhler Industries. The last concrete link with Versatile of Canada had ended.

VOLVO

Volvo's history as a tractor maker has always been firmly entwined with that of Bolinder-Munktell. Founded in 1927, Volvo decided to start building tractors during the Second World War when cars and trucks were becoming more difficult to produce. The simplest and quickest way to do this was to link up with an existing specialist, and fellow Swedish concern Bolinder-Munktell was the obvious choice. An agreement was signed in 1943 by which Volvo would purchase all its transmissions from Bolinder-Munktell, and that the two companies would build similar tractors that differed only in engine, colour and brand name.

As a result, the new Volvo T41 of the following year was really the same as the Bolinder-Munktell GBMV-1, also new that year. The Volvo version was powered by an Otto four-cylinder engine of 275ci (4.5 litres), though its successor T43 was Hesselman-powered. Both these and the Bolinder-Munktell equivalent used a five-speed Bolinder-Munktell transmission which permitted up to 10mph (16km/h) on rubber tyres; the top ratio was blanked out on steel wheels.

After the war, the demand from small Scandinavian farms was for a smaller tractor, so the Volvo T21 of 1947 used the company's own little four-cylinder gasoline engine of 121ci (2.0 litres), quite different from the twin-cylinder two-stroke diesel powering the equivalent Bolinder-Munktell 10. Both tractors, however, shared a five-speed Bolinder-Munktell transmission.

Volvo, of course, was a much bigger concern than Bolinder-Munktell, and took the logical step of taking it over in 1950. All tractor production was transferred to the Bolinder-Munktell factory in Eskiltuna, though the well-respected Bolinder-Munktell brand name continued to live on.

By 1949 Volvo had launched a third gasoline tractor, the T31, but within a few years had transferred to diesel with Bolinder-Munktell's new family engines, based on a cylinder of 69ci (1200cc). This, incidentally, shared the same cylinder dimensions as a Volvo truck engine, though whether this was by design or coincidence is not known.

The first Volvo tractor to make use of this engine was the T55 of 1953, using a 53-hp four-cylinder version. The following year it was joined by a three-cylinder T35/36 with 42.5hp. This was ideal for export, but Volvo still lacked a small diesel tractor for the home market. This was the T230 Victor, this time with a twin-cylinder engine from the Bolinder-Munktell family, giving 30hp. At 3,638lb (1650kg), the Victor was heavy when compared with the rival Ferguson. It was later replaced by the T320 Buster, powered by a 40-hp Perkins three-cylinder diesel, which proved smoother than the Bolinder-Munktell twin.

Until now, the almost identical lines of tractors had been finished in Bolinder-Munktell green or Volvo red, according to the dealer network to which they were bound. But in 1957 Bolinder-Munktell took over the distribution operation as well; now all its tractors were Bolinder-Munktell-Volvos painted red. The Volvo connection was especially useful in export markets, where it was better known than Bolinder-Munktell.

A couple of years later, the new Bolinder-Munktell Volvo T350 Boxer retained the Bolinder-Munktell diesel (though now upsized to 232ci/3.8 litres in three-cylinder form) but had an updated transmission, which

OPPOSITE
Look closely, and you'll see a Ford badge on this 846. Ford saved the company from probable closure in 1986, and the Versatile name is now absorbed into CNH Global.

One of the Nordic tractors, a joint venture between Volvo and Valmet to replace two ranges with one. The first 05-series covered the 65–95-hp range in 1983. They were later joined by the six-cylinder 905 and later still by this 2105.

was badly needed. This was now ten-speed, joined by a live PTO, multi-disc clutch, and differential lock. An advanced hydraulic system – Terra-Trol – was added later. At the same time, the T55 was uprated as the 73-hp T470 Bison. (All these power figures, incidentally, are taken from the engine, not the PTO.)

In the 1960s not only was the horsepower race being waged in North America, it was also happening elsewhere, and Volvo launched its first 100-hp tractor in 1966. The T800 used Volvo's own D50 diesel, a six-cylinder motor of 315ci (5.2 litres), married to an eight-speed transmission plus new squared-off styling. Turbocharged models soon followed, which included the 113-hp T810/814 (later increased to 136hp). The following year the T350 Boxer became the 62-hp T600, while in 1969 the little T430 Buster received a new two-speed powershift called Trac-Trol.

At this time Scandinavian manufacturers led the world in safety and cab design; the Swedish Government had made roll-over protection mandatory from 1959 and the Bolinder-Munktell-Volvo T650 came with an

Prior to the Valmet connection, Volvo-Bolinder-Munktell made conventional tractors such as this 1970 T650 Turbo.

White mixed and matched existing components to produce its own tractors: this Field Boss 4-150 used a Cummins power unit and Oliver transmission.

all-new cab in 1970. Volvo's car and truck experience was exploited to produce a quiet and comfortable environment for the driver (though the rival Valmet 502 proved to be quieter still). With a new four-cylinder diesel and eight-speed transmission (16-speed with Trac-Trol), the T650 saw its maker well into the 1970s.

Reflecting outside perceptions, the tractors were rebadged Volvo-Bolinder-Munktell in 1973 because the Volvo name was far better known outside of Sweden. The first new model to bear this name was the T500 of 1974, with Perkins 4.236 diesel engine, hydraulics, front axle from International, and an improved version of the T650 cab. A turbocharged T650 and the 90-hp T700 had the two-range Trac-Trol transmission as standard.

At around this time, Volvo decided to restrict its own designs to 80-hp-plus tractors, its smaller machines using Perkins and International components. So the T500 multiplied into the 56-hp 2200 and 68-hp 2250, with a four-wheel-drive option using Japanese Kimco axles. The 800-range, still Volvo-powered, was replaced by the 2650 and 2654, still with 140hp and Trac-Trol transmission but a redesigned cab.

Volvo-Bolinder-Munktell's tractor history changed course in 1978 when it signed a joint agreement with Valmet of Finland to develop a new tractor to replace the T650 and T700. This was realized, but within a few years Volvo decided to pull out of the tractor market altogether (see Valmet). It sold all its tractor interests in the Scantrac joint venture to Valmet in 1985.

WHITE

White Motors, which made trucks, entered the tractor market by acquisition. In the early 1960s there was no lack of small/medium manufacturers finding survival increasingly difficult, and White had no trouble finding suitable candidates for its new venture. It bought Oliver in 1960, Cockshutt in '62, and Minneapolis-Moline the year after.

The White American 60, a brave attempt to build a mid-sized tractor in the United States. It lasted three years.

PLAINSMAN
A4T-1600

These and others were merged into the White Farm Equipment Company, which increasingly mixed and matched components between the different lines. This was to be a source of aggravation to tractor enthusiasts in years to come, but probably made economic sense at the time.

In 1974, White dropped the respected old names altogether. From now on, all its tractors were badged as Whites, though of course many were still made in the old factories and continued to use existing components. Thus the new White 4-150 Field Boss was not as new as it seemed, with a Cummins V8 diesel and two Oliver two-wheel-drive power trains, one at each end of this four-wheel-drive articulated tractor. The 2-150, which followed, was based on the old Minneapolis-Moline 1355, while Oliver's 18-speed transmission was also used in the 2-135 and 2-155 of 1976. The row-crop 2-70 was also unveiled that year, really an updated Oliver 1655, with a 47-hp 2-50 and 63-hp 2-60 slotting in beneath. The latter two were FIAT tractors, imported from Italy and painted in White silver. In fact, the entire history of White tractors proceeded thus, mixing and matching existing components and importing tractors until it was hard to say whether any could be classed as true White tractors, born and bred.

The FIAT connection didn't last long, however, as the 2-50/2-60 were dropped in 1977, replaced by a range of machines from Iseki of Japan and covering 28–61hp. After 20 years in the tractor business, White appeared to have lost interest, and decided to sell the concern (White Farm Equipment) to an investment company: but the name continued, selling White-badged Isekis to cover the lower end of the range, and launching two big 4 x 4 machines in 1984, the 225-hp 4-225 and 270-hp 4-270.

Unfortunately, White Farm Equipment's new owners had no stomach for the tractor business, and filed for bankruptcy the following year, though there were still people out there with the will to save it. Another new owner stepped in, renamed the company White-New Idea, and made big changes to the range of U.S.-built tractors. Five tractors, covering 94–188hp, were launched, all powered by CDC diesels, CDC being the joint engine venture of Case and Cummins. The 2-180, the last two-wheel-drive tractor with a V8 engine, was replaced in 1987 by the Field Boss 185, now with a CDC 505-ci (8.3-litre) six-cylinder engine: transmission was six-speed with three ranges.

OPPOSITE
The four-wheel-drive articulated Plainsman was sold as a White in Canada and as a Minneapolis-Moline or Oliver in the United States.

BELOW
White abandoned the American-made 60 and 80 in favour of imports from Lamborghini, such as this 6065.

The White 6105 was the highest-powered of the new Lamborghini-sourced range; however, the bigger tractors were still made in the United States.

The name Field Boss was set to go in 1988, while a new quieter cab came in, along with a Field Facts computer system. Four new tractors were introduced, all built at a new $2-million factory at Coldwater, Ohio (the old Charles City plant, inherited from Oliver, and before that, Hart-Parr, was now a foundry and machine shop only). These kicked off with the 94-PTO-hp 100, then the 118-hp 120, 137-hp 140 and 160-hp 160, with 359-ci (5.9-litre) or 505-ci (8.3-litre) CDC motors.

In fact, White-New Idea seemed determined to turn itself into an all-American company. The Isekis were dropped in 1989, replaced by the White 'American' tractors. The 60-hp 60 and 80-hp 80 were the smallest tractors then actually built in the United States, both powered by a CDC four-cylinder diesel, with or without turbo. They had a six-speed transmission, though 18-speed was optional, and in a bid to appeal to nostalgic farmers, were available in Oliver green, Cockshutt red, Minneapolis-Moline gold or White silver.

It was a brave move, but it failed. Within three years the American-range had been replaced by Lamborghini tractors from Italy – the 6065, 6085 and 6105, the last digits referring to their power outputs. Meanwhile, the big home-built tractors all acquired more

After the AGCO takeover, White gradually updated its big tractors, such as this 192-hp 6195, with a full powershift and 18-speed transmission, and began to share AGCO components as well as complete machines.

power in 1991, with up to 195hp at the PTO, and the Workhorse name, and though described as new tractors, they were really only updates of what had gone before. White also had a contract to build big tractors on behalf of Deutz-Allis, using Deutz air-cooled engines.

But it wasn't enough. The year that the Workhorse appeared, the White tractor business succumbed to a takeover by the rapidly growing AGCO concern and White-New Idea, the implement business, followed two years later. This at last gave it the stability to survive, assisted by a recovering market in North America. Although the compact Iseki tractors had been dropped, the Lamborghini link was maintained and the U.S.-built AGCO-Whites were now restricted to the 120-hp-plus range. The latter were updated as the 6125 (121-PTO-hp), 6145, 6175 and 6195 (192-PTO-hp). As ever, they were CDC-powered, but did feature a new 18-speed full powershift transmission. The cab was moved 15-in (38-cm) forward and 2-in (5-cm) higher to improve comfort and visibility.

From now on, the AGCO-White story was one of increasingly shared components and sister lines. In 1997, for example, six Whites in the 70–145-hp range came from Massey-Ferguson factories in Europe, Massey-Ferguson, of course, by now being also part of the AGCO empire. But the four biggest Whites were still built in North America: the 160-hp 8510, 180-hp 8610, 200-hp 8710 and 225-hp 8810, all with the 18-speed powershift.

In 2002, even though White was one of 17 well-known brand names owned by AGCO, its future seemed secure. It offered a range from 23–225hp, AGCO's latest line-up of ST, LT, RT and DT tractors, all available with the White badge among others. A full circle had been turned.

ZETOR

For years, the Czech Skoda cars have been the butt of innumerable jokes. But they deserve better, being surprisingly well-engineered for such low-cost automobiles, which is a reflection on the country that built them. Czechoslovakia had accumulated plenty of engineering know-how before the Second World War, and retained it afterwards as part of the Eastern Bloc. The same is true of Zetor tractors, which are simple, well-engineered and good value for money – certainly technically superior to other comparable tractors such as the Ursus. Zetors therefore have a good reputation in Western Europe, which contrasts strikingly with that of the hapless Skoda; perhaps farmers are shrewder than motorists!

Like Valmet of Finland, the Zetor had its beginnings in military equipment. The factory in which it was built had once been owned by the Brno Arms company, which had churned out tons of munitions until 1944, when British and American bombing raids finally put it out of action. A far-sighted factory management realized that the war was nearing its end, and began work on a prototype tractor which the plant could build as soon as peace was eventually restored.

So within months of the end of the Second World War, the prototype was complete, and production began in earnest in

Zetor tractors acquired a reputation for simplicity and toughness, and deserved it. This is a 1960s 3545.

RIGHT
The Zetor 7540, working on a farm in Cornwall, south-west England.

OPPOSITE
LEFT: Zetor was an early manufacturer of quiet, comfortable cabs, therefore there were big, spacious ones for the 3320 and 3340.

RIGHT: There was nothing out of date about this Zetor 43-41.

1946. The Zetor 25A was quite an advanced little tractor for its time. It had a six-speed transmission when four was the norm, and a twin-cylinder diesel engine. Diesel power would not really enter the tractor mainstream for a few years in Europe, and for a decade in North America, but some of the Zetor engineers had been working on diesel aircraft engines and could visualize similar engines being suitable for tractors.

It was such a success that the second Zetor, a 30-hp machine, used a four-cylinder diesel, designed in-house, like the 25-hp twin. In fact, that new engine provided even more evidence of Zetor's advanced thinking, with a swirl combustion chamber in the piston to promote fuel/air mixing and therefore more efficient combustion.

A new unified range was unveiled in the early 1960s, with two- three- and four-cylinder diesels sharing components. There were Zetormatic hydraulic lifts and ten-speed transmissions. The Czechs were also early producers of quiet, effective, factory-built safety cabs. Their tractors may have been cheaper than Western rivals, but they were in no way antiquated. A six-cylinder turbocharged Zetor, the 12011, was to follow.

A reputation for up-to-date engineering at a low price enabled Zetor to export many tractors to both Western Europe and the United States. A 5511 Zetormatic, for example, was tested by the University of Nebraska in May 1967. From its 191-ci (3.1-litre) four-cylinder diesel, it produced 44hp at the drawbar, 51 at the PTO, and the ten-speed transmission covered a range of 0.74 to 16.8mph (1.2 to 27km/h). Apart from a failed fuel return line, Nebraska found no faults in over 54 hours of running time. Licensing agreements were signed through the 1950s and '60s to build Zetors outside Czechoslovakia, notably in India and Iraq.

Zetor continued to thrive throughout the 1970s, but faced a less certain future after the collapse of the Eastern Bloc in 1990. However, it did reach an agreement with John Deere to build some lower-specification tractors for the company for export to Asian and African markets. By 2002, it could claim to have built over a million tractors in its 50 years in the business, and to have offered a full range of tractors from 43–110hp, with three- or four-cylinder diesels, plus 30–48-hp compacts sold under the Century brand.

BIBLIOGRAPHY

*Condie, Allan T, *Massey-Ferguson 1958–82*, Condie, 1995

*Earnshaw, Alan, *David Brown Tractors 1936–1964*, Trans-Pennine, 2000

*Ertel, P.W., *The American Tractor*, Salamander, 2001

*Farnworth, John, *A World-Wide Guide to Massey-Harris, Ferguson & Early Massey-Ferguson Tractors*, Japonica Press, 2000

*Fay, Guy, *International Harvester Tractor Data Book*, MBI, 1997

*Fraser, Colin, *Harry Ferguson – Inventor & Pioneer*, Old Pond, 2000

*Fredricksen, Erik, *The Legendary LTX Tractor*, Fredriksen, 2000

*Gay, Larry, *Farm Tractors 1975–1995*, ASAE, 1995

*Gibbard, Stuart, *The DOE Tractor Story*, Old Pond, 2001

*Heath, Anthony J, *David Brown Tractors 1965–1988*, Trans-Pennine, 2000

*Larsen, Lester, *Farm Tractors 1950–1975*, ASAE, 1975

*Letourneau, Peter, *Case Tractors*, MBI, 1999

*Macmillan, Don & Roy Harrington, *John Deere Tractors & Equipment: Volume Two 1960–1990*, ASAE, 1991

*Morland, Andrew & Nick Baldwin, *Classic American Farm Tractors*, Osprey, 1988

*Morland, Andrew & Peter Henshaw, *Modern Farm Tractors*, Motorbooks, 1997

*Morland, Andrew & Peter Henshaw, *Allis-Chalmers Tractors*, Motorbooks, 1997

*Niskanen, Hannu, *From Munktell to Valtra*, Valtra Inc, 1999

*Pripps, Robert, *Big Green – John Deere GP Tractors*, Motorbooks, 1994

*Pripps, Robert, *The Big Book of Caterpillar*, Voyageur Press, 2000

*Pripps, Robert, *Case Tractors*, Motorbooks

*Ramussen, Henry, *International McCormick Tractors*, Motorbooks, 1989

*Updike, Ken, *International Harvester Tractors 1955–1985*, MBI, 2000

*Wendel, Charles, *Encyclopedia of American Farm Tractors*, Crestline, 1979

*Wendel, Charles, *Minneapolis-Moline Tractors*, Motorbooks, 1980

*Wendel, Charles, *Nebraska Tractor Tests Since 1920*, Crestline, 1993

*Wendel, Charles, *The Allis-Chalmers Story*, Crestline, 1993

* Wendel, Charles, *Minneapolis-Moline Tractors 1870–1969*, Motorbooks, 1990

*Williams, Michael, *Farm Tractors*, Silverdale, 2002

Periodicals

**Tractor & Machinery* magazine, Kelsey Publishing

**Classic Tractor* magazine, Kelsey Publishing

**Profi* magazine, Agri Publishing International

D

E

F

G

H

I

J

K

L

M

N